"*Becoming a Man* is one of the best books I have seen on male sexuality, and I recommend it highly. It is factual, readable, and full of common sense."

Wesley J. Brush
The Catholic Sun

"William Bausch's book on sex for boys can help men and boys, girls and women as well, to think through (maybe for the first time) the mystery of sexual development in males. It covers the physical and psychological aspects and offers a moral perspective rooted in the Catholic tradition."

Covenant House

"This is the book that parents, teachers, and youth ministers should give to their teenagers. It is informative, challenging, and helpful, written in a style that can reach the young—maybe even some who have already tuned out....It is by far the best book I have read on the subject....*Becoming a Man* will assist many a young man or woman to be sexually responsible. It deserves the widest possible circulation."

Rev. James DiGiacomo, S.J.

"Finally, a book written by a mature male who has obviously worked through the pain and joy of being a sexual human being. The author treats promiscuity with good-sense teaching and a needed call to 'disciplined delay' for the teenage male....*Becoming a Man* will be a must in the area of teaching sexuality courses, as well as required reading for fathers and sons."

Patti Hoffman
Coordinator of Education in Human Sexuality
Diocese of Davenport

"This is the book for which you have been looking, the book at which boys ought to be looking. Buy lots of copies."

National Catholic Reporter

"This is as good a volume on this topic as you are likely to find."
Catholic New York

"Bausch takes a clear position on chastity without being preachy or negative. In fact, he makes the best and most positive case for pre-marital chastity that I have read....He tackles the tough issues head-on. Masturbation, sexually transmitted diseases, contraception, and abortion are all treated thoroughly, openly, with sensitivity."
James A. Kenny
Clinical Psychologist
and NC Family Columnist

"...the book can very well be used as a guide for girls on their way to becoming women."
Gilbert J. Caneul, Jr.

"Father Bausch gives us a beautiful understanding of the sacredness and holiness of our gift of sexuality that is an excellent guide for adolescents and for married couples...."
Ogdensburg (N.Y.) Pastoral and Matrimonial Center

"...the author provides teens, parents, teachers, and counselors with a superb combination of morally based biological information, proper vocabulary suggestions, intimate insights, and a delightful lace of humor."
Marriage and Family Living

BECOMING A MAN

Basic Information, Guidance,
and Attitudes on Sex for Boys

WILLIAM J. BAUSCH

TWENTY-THIRD PUBLICATIONS
Mystic, Connecticut

Fourth printing 1993

Twenty-Third Publications
P.O. Box 180
185 Willow Street
Mystic, CT 06355
(203) 536-2611
800-321-0411

ISBN 0-89622-357-4
Library of Congress Catalog Number 87-51569

Cover design and symbol design execution by Kathy Michalove
Symbol conceptualization by Richard Haffey
Cover photos—top: John Zierten; bottom: James Shaffer

Acknowledgment

Concerning certain technical matters, two people deserve special gratitude.

DR. CHARLES HAYNE, D.L.

practiced family medicine for four years in the Navy. He now has a private practice in the same field. He has published in medical journals and is on the staff of Freehold General Hospital in Freehold, N.J. His expert knowledge on medical and physical matters was helpful and insightful.

VALERIE VANCE DILLON

with whom I worked for years in a diocesan Family Life Bureau, has continued her professional interest in the family. She is currently Family Life Coordinator for the Archdiocese of Indianapolis. She is the mother of four girls and has written for years on family matters, including a regular column in *Columbia*. Her experience in sex education, her journalistic eye, and her sensitive moral acumen were valuable and welcomed in the preparation of this book.

To Dot Boese
Who Loved Me and My Dogs
In Memoriam

PREFACE

About twenty years ago I wrote a book for boys on sex called *A Boy's Sex Life*. It did well, and for years it ran the usual course of a useful book. Then it went out of print and no more was to be heard about it, especially since other general books were coming on the market. And it would have remained that way except that in 1981 the dreadful AIDS began to make its appearance and by 1987 it was being considered a full-blown epidemic. This disease along with the devastatingly growing figures of teen pregnancies, abortions, and out-of-wedlock births—the largest in the world—prompted a cry for more, for better, sex education. The public sector responded the only way it seems to know how: massive condom advertising and sales. It could not, perhaps cannot, address the basic underlying moral issues. In any case, I began to get a considerable number of calls for the old book which presented both the information and the morality and, if it were out of print, would we reprint it? One look at the twenty-year-old book told me that it was not possible. In those twenty years, as you can readily imagine, so much has changed and so much innocence has been lost. Those figures along with the legalization of abortion, the breakdown of family life (again a world record for divorces), and the so-called sexual revolution created a radically different world. This called for a radically new book. And this is what *Becoming a Man* is: a totally new book.

I want to thank John van Bemmel, my editor, for his careful eye and questioning mind.

The "Bio-Chi-Rho" image (above) combines two venerated ancient symbols to form a new icon with contemporary meaning. The first, and predominate, symbol from antiquity is that of the Chi-Rho ☧ a symbol of Jesus, the Christ. The second, and auxiliary, sign is the biological representation of the male ♂. Merged with one another these two symbols take on a new meaning for our times. This new symbol, the Bio-Chi-Rho, expresses the conviction that each person's quest for sexual maturity involves the integration of physical and spiritual growth toward Christ.

CONTENTS

xii

INTRODUCTION

Becoming a Man, you should realize, is not sexist, just gender, since I'm addressing boys. Actually, this title is a take-off on a twenty-year-old book by a theologian, Gregory Baum. In his book, *Man Becoming,* the idea was that God can be found in our lives as we grow. The same is true here. Sex is not a function as much as it is a revelation of oneself, a powerful sign of our deepest longings to love and be loved. And the boys need to know this so that they can be rescued from the bankrupt cultural view of sex as an appetite to be satisfied, as long as proper precautions are taken. This is euphemistically called "safe" sex—as if sex were ever safe, no matter how antiseptic and sterile it is made.

But why write a special book for teenage boys and not for the general public? The answer is twofold. One answer underscores the word "boy" in that this book represents my small contribution to leveling the Double Standard. Not that I have any illusions as to being successful, but at least I want to make a public nod that it is alive and flourishing and ought to be addressed. For the Double Standard prevails mightily even in our so-called enlightened age.

Columnist William Raspberry is right on target when he writes:

> We (both as a society and, too often, as individuals) want our daughters to be virgins, but we are less than sure about what we want for our sons. We make clear that we prefer our daughters practice sexual abstinence, but we talk to our sons about sexual responsibility. We tell our daughters that the boys will try and that it is their responsibility to resist. We only caution our sons against getting a girl pregnant.
>
> The ambivalence is not lost on our sons. They see

1

through our words to our unspoken attitude: For girls, sex is supposed to wait until adulthood; for boys, it's a part of becoming an adult.

If grown-ups suggest that lesson in subtle, ambiguous ways, our sons' peers drive it home quite directly. The boy who talks of saving himself is thought by his peers to be something less than a full-fledged male.

I want to drive home to the boys that there are really excellent reasons for "saving themselves," even though they are under enormous pressure not to do so. I want to give them a vision, a perspective, and plain good reasons, both commonsensical and religious, for being chaste. And I want to underscore again and again *their* responsibility. Sex and babies are not female problems. The male predator, the unwed father, the pressure-bearing boy must look at himself and be held morally accountable. He must get his values straight and his sense of justice renewed. And I want to do this as plainly and forthrightly as I can, not only because chastity is right for him, but because I found that many boys—more than you think—really want it to be right; they want some support, some sound reasons for being chaste and resisting pressures. We owe it to them to respond.

For if we don't, others will. We live in a sexually promiscuous society, even with the scare of AIDS. The media show no signs of letting up a constant barrage of sexual stimulation, showing only an interest in "safe" sex. Video producers and jeans manufacturers and movie makers spend in the millions to entice your son (and daughter) with sexually stimulating ads that no one, short of being dead, could resist. The media does not, however, pick up the pieces, pay for the unwanted children, hold the girls' hands at the abortion clinics, or sit at the bedside of those suffering or dying from sexually transmitted diseases.

As for the public sector, it can only respond with more "education"; that is, put a health clinic in every school and teach the children how to use contraceptives effectively or where they may obtain an abortion. At the end of 1987 the National Association of State Boards of Education noted that the public schools mandating education about AIDS has tripled within the last six months. The association's executive director, Ms. Blaunstein, reported, "Most state mandates call for instruction for 7th to 12th graders" but her project directors recommend that such instruction start sooner "in grades four to six before the pupils start engaging in risky sex practices or drug-taking." One director noted that although the curriculum tells students about condoms and spermicide, "we don't explain how to use them, where to buy them or how to tell a new sex partner that you want him to use a condom."[1]

All of a sudden, in the space of a few years we have gone from giving high school seniors a course in Family Life to showing fourth and fifth graders how to protect themselves with condoms and spermicides. We must reach our children first to speak of the larger issues of relationship, love, and virtue. And as trusted adults, as parents, we are in a privileged position to do so.

The second answer why I wrote this book for teenage boys underscores the word "teenage." My conviction (along with many others on all sides of the sex education spectrum) is that, whatever the ambiguities and challenges for the young or older single adult, teenagers are simply not morally or psychologically ready to make decisions about sexual intercourse. Even the aging sexual activists of the "anything-goes" Sexual Revolution of the Sixties, who are now parents themselves, are having second thoughts:

> But now as we watch our kids sexually maturing, we find ourselves thinking about the "shoulds" and "shouldn'ts" all over again. What about our kids and "pre-adulthood" sex? Ellen Goodman, a syndicated columnist for the Boston Globe, pinpoints the dilemma: "Our agenda is a complicated one, because we do not want to be the new guardians of sexual repression. Nor are we willing to define sexual freedom as the children's right to 'do it.' We are equally uncomfortable with notions that Sex is Evil and Sex is Groovey." ...Our timidity leaves us floundering about defining sexual propriety in the murky "depending upon"

context of situational ethics.... There are sex educators who say the essential message should be "no teenage sex," but there is a growing consensus among educators and counselors that dictating "no teenage sex" is mostly wishful thinking. For example, Carol Gilligan, associate professor of education at Harvard, says, "We have to say that it may be fine to have sex at 18 but 14 is too young." Elizabeth Roberts, author of *Childhood Sexual Learning*, also opts for making age distinctions for teenage sexual standards: "I just think we have to make some rules again, like 13 is too young. Period." Personally I believe teens under 16 are simply too young to handle the emotional and physical consequences of sex, and need to hear that message loud and clear.[2]

So it is interesting to observe even among liberated parents some common-sense need to set limits, but also to observe for these same parents any lack of a solid philosophy on which to base such limits. Any age cut-off suggestion is therefore arbitrary and leaves unanswered why teen intercourse is OK for, say, 16 on up, but not for 15 on down. Still, their very questioning is at least a sign that they readily understand that sex has to have *some* guidelines and limits and that teenagers, though sexual and physically mature, are not necessarily emotionally and spiritually mature. This book takes the position mentioned above that the "essential message should be no teenage sex" and accordingly Dr. Allen Moore, acting dean at the School of Theology at Claremont, California, speaks its conviction when he writes:

They generally are not emotionally ready to make judgments about the quality of intimate relationships, and they have not reached a level of maturity to take responsibility for their actions. The sociological evidence on abandonment, furthermore, makes it clear that teenagers are not prepared to take social and economic responsibility for the birth of a baby.

Our society's images of being male and female demean the larger moral significance of sexuality. A teenage boy faces the social pressure to "score" and, in so doing, he reduces his partner to a sexual object. And a teen-age girl absorbs the idea that a woman is someone who is sexually desirable to a man; her worth lies in her value as a sexual commodity and her ability to control the male with the sexual favors she provides.

...Youth need to know that sex does not need to be the determinant force in human life. The church's particular challenge in this context is to articulate the view that sexual intercourse is not a casual venture but a special form of intimacy that calls for an ongoing relationship and concern for one another as well as for the new life that might emerge.[3]

Here is another consideration for parents. There is no doubt that peer pressure on your son (and daughter) is enormous and always ranks as an important influence on his sexual actions. Still, there is another truth worth mentioning: Youth generally act out what they perceive to be adult values.[4] Studies continue to show that youth's values are very consistent and continuous with those held by the important adults in their lives. That's you, of course, and the other meaningful adults in your son's life. So your example, the kind of adult people you are and expose your son to, and your willingness to be open to his questions and conversations are a critical context in any kind of sex education.[5] And your sense of religion. As one adolescent psychologist writes:

Adolescent sexual behavior is inextricably linked to the dynamics of the family and the youth's perception of how the parents treat them. Chilman (1983) identified a number of factors in the life of the adolescent which break down the good resolves, making sexual activity not only desired but inevitable. He noted that in addition to such factors as peer pressure, permissive social norms and friends who are sexually active, low levels of religiousness, strained parent-child relationships and minimal parent-child communications are chief among the factors associated with extra-marital intercourse. Similarly

Strommen and Strommen (1985) noted that responsible attitudes were associated with families who were characterized as nurturant, warm and cohesive and in which religion was manifested as an important aspect of personal and family life.[6]

So maybe the message ultimately is to make your own family life better. Deepen your own sense of God. Pray privately and in the community you know as your parish. And be upbeat. There is reason to be hopeful about this whole issue. The kids are really much more honest and virtuous than we may recognize. It's just that they need guidance in a world that hawks some doubtful values. Yes, everyone tells you to talk to your son about sex—and I do encourage it—but the fact is that it really is very difficult to do.[7] Sex is so private and teenagers are quite sensitive about their privacy. So maybe this book will at least help you with the proper information and also perhaps encourage you to speak to your parish or school to come up with some enlightened sex education in a context that celebrates and promotes your values.

A fond hope of mine is that this book, in addition to direct use by teenager and parent, would also be used as a classroom text or at least be required reading in a parochial school or CCD classes, say, in the third or fourth year of high school or freshmen college. The subject of sex needs a great deal of discussion and guidance in today's world. I hope that the subjects raised will give parents or teachers an outline to follow whether they agree with everything I've written or not. Particularly helpful, I hope, are the footnotes: a minor annoyance to the student, but for adults a source for further reading and study. Formerly, I would have written a small handbook to be handed out, period.

But today, there are four factors that prompt a book like this that tries to give a more in-depth look at teenage (and adult) sexuality.

The first is that the social fabric has become unwound somewhat (get a hold of George Gallup's December 2, 1987 address to the National Conference of Christians and Jews, Princeton Religion Research Center, P.O. Box 310, Princeton, NJ 08542) and the statistics on teenage pregnancy and abortions are well known. And too, frightfully, the teenage population, some say, is the next vulnerable segment for the deadly AIDS plague.

Second, there are more nuances regarding sex now, as society and the church as well move away from a mere biological and physical foundation for sexual morality (see, for example, Charles Curran's article in *The Christian Century* [Dec. 16, 1987], "Roman Catholic Sexual Ethics: A Dissenting View" or John Mahoney's excellent book, *The Making of Moral Theology*. [Clarendon Press, Oxford, 1987]) to a more personalist one in such sensitive issues, say, as birth control or homosexuality.

Third, there is the impact of the media plus the propaganda of well organized groups that subvert the Judeo-Christian heritage. For example, hardly any of the popular books I've consulted written for young people move beyond the Planned Parenthood philosophy on abortion. And hardly ever is there even the hint that there are other sides to the question. The extraordinary impact of the media needs a larger look too. So for adults there's the full book plus the footnotes, glossary, index, and bibliography.

Fourth, there seems to be a reaction setting in, a search for more durable and religious values, a statistical trend to a deeper spirituality to live by. Although the book does not explicitly treat this as such, it gives many openings for the sensitive teacher or parent to pursue this area, especially in the lives of the saints.

So, here is the book's targeted audience if you will: the teenage (or soon to be) boy himself; concerned adults, from parents to counsellors; and teachers. Wherever among the three categories it falls, I hope the book is both helpful and hopeful.

My recommendation for this book, after you read it yourself, is to give it to your son (for his birthday, graduation—any excuse) with the advice, "Here, read this and if you have any questions, come and ask me." Chances are, of course, that we'll be on Mars before he does. But the gesture is important. He must know that you know that he knows. This may open doors of communication. I would not hesitate, even further, to suggest that it's a book that you can give to your daughters. Girls may get a new knowledge and, more importantly, a new appreciation for what is at stake for both males and females. Lastly, there is no reason why this book, though written from a Christian perspective, may not find an audience among all believers of good will.

A final word. As you page through this book you'll notice that I've broken up the four Parts with some "Time Out" reflections and among these are some limericks. They're here because I stumbled upon my old tattered volume of them, a slim collection gathered by Bennett Cerf, that old humorist of TV's long-ago "What's My Line?" I thought I would share things that made me chuckle way back them. They're good comic relief, something to remind us that we should never take ourselves too seriously, even when we talk about sex. So, with that being said, I leave you with my defense:

> No matter how grouchy you're feeling,
> You'll find that a limerick is healing.
> It grows in a wreath
> All around the front teeth,
> Thus preserving the face from congealing.

And if you do find some of them mildly risqué, remember:

> The limerick packs laughs anatomical
> Into space that is quite economical.
> But the good ones I've seen
> So seldom are clean,
> And the clean ones so seldom are comical!

QUESTIONS FOR REFLECTION AND DISCUSSION

1. How would you describe the Double Standard? Do you agree with it? Why? Why Not?

2. "The male predator...must get his values straight and his sense of justice renewed." Discuss what is intended by this statement.

3. Should there be sexual standards for teenagers? If so, what do you think they should be?

4. "...responsible attitudes [about sexuality are] associated with families...in which religion was manifested as an important aspect of personal and family life." Discuss this connection between responsibility and the importance of religion.

PART ONE
THE MYSTERY

The Lord God said, "It is not good for the man to be alone. I will make a helper suitable for him."

Genesis 2:18

1
THE MYSTERY

A Native American Tale

Old Man had made the world and everything on it. He had done everything well, except that he had put the men in one place and the women in another, quite a distance away. So they lived separately for a while.

Men and women did everything in exactly the same way. Both had buffalo jumps—steep cliffs over which they chased buffalo herds so that the animals fell to their death at the foot of the cliff. Then both the men and the women butchered the dead animals. This meat was their only food; they had not yet discovered other things that were good to eat.

After a while the men learned how to make bows and arrows. The women learned how to tan buffalo hides and make teepees and beautiful robes decorated with porcupine quills.

One day Old Man said to himself, "I think I did everything well, but I made one bad mistake, putting women and men in different places. There's no joy or pleasure in that. Men and women are different from each other, and these different things must be made to unite so that there will be more people. I must make men mate with women. I will put some pleasure, some good feeling into it; otherwise the men won't be keen to do what is necessary. I myself must set an example."

Old Man went over to where the women were living. He traveled for four days and four nights before he saw the women

---

in their camp. He was hiding behind some trees, watching. He said to himself, "Ho, what a good life they're having! They have these fine teepees made of tanned buffalo hide, while we men have only brush shelters or raw, stinking, green hides to cover us. And look what fine clothes they wear, while we have to go around with a few pelts around our loins! Really, I made a mistake putting the women so far away from us. They must live with us and make fine tents and beautiful clothes for us also. I'll go back and ask the other men how they feel about this."

So Old Man went back to his camp and told the men what he had seen. When they heard about all the useful and beautiful things the women had, the men said, "Let's go over there and get together with these different human beings."

"It's not only those things that are worth having," said Old Man. "There's something else—a very pleasurable thing I plan on creating."

Now, while this was going on in the men's camp, the chief of the women's village had discovered the track Old Man had made while prowling around. She sent a young woman to follow them and report back. The young woman arrived near the men's camp, hid herself, and watched for a short while. Then she hurried back to the women as fast as she could and told everybody, "There's a camp over there with human beings living in it. They seem different from us, taller and stronger. Oh, sisters, these beings live very well, better than us. They have a thing shooting sharp sticks, and with these they kill many kinds of game—food that we don't have. They are never hungry."

The Encounter

When they heard this, all the women said, "How we wish that these strange human beings would come here and kill all kinds of food for us!" When the women were finishing their meeting, the men were already over the hill toward them. The women looked at the men and saw how shabbily dressed they were, with just a little bit of rawhide around their loins. They looked at the men's matted hair, smelled the strong smell coming from their unwashed bodies. They looked at their dirty skin. They said to each other, "These beings called men don't know how to live. They have no proper clothes. They're dirty; they smell. We don't want people like these." The woman chief hurled a rock at Old Man, shouting, "Go away!" Then all the women threw rocks and shouted "Go away!"

Old Man said, "It was no mistake putting these creatures far away from us. Women are dangerous. I shouldn't have created them." Then Old Man and all the men went back to their own place.

After the men left, the woman chief had second thoughts. "These poor men," she said, "they don't know any better, but we could teach them. We could make clothes for them. Instead of shaming them, maybe we could get them to come back if we dress as poorly as they do, just with a piece of hide or fur around our waist."

And in the men's camp, Old Man said, "Maybe we should try to meet these women creatures once more. Yes, we should give it another chance. See what I did on the sly." He opened his traveling bundle in which he kept his jerk meat and other supplies, and out of it took a resplendent white buckskin outfit. "I managed to steal this when those women weren't looking. It's too small for me, but I'll add on a little buffalo hide here and a little bear fur there, and put a shield over here, where it doesn't come together over my belly. And I'll make myself a feather headdress and paint my face. Then maybe this woman chief will look at me with new eyes. Let me go alone to speak with the women creatures first. You stay back a little and hide until I have straightened things out."

So Old Man dressed up as best he could. He even purified himself in a sweat bath which he thought up for this purpose. He looked at his reflection in the lake waters and exclaimed, "Oh, how beautiful I am! I never knew I was that good-looking! Now that woman chief will surely like me."

Then Old Man led the way back to the women's camp. There was one woman on the lookout, and even though the men were staying back in hiding, she saw them coming. Then she spotted Old Man standing alone on a hilltop overlooking the camp. She hurried to tell the woman chief, who was butchering with most of the other women at the buffalo jump. For this job they wore their poorest outfits: just pieces of rawhide with a hole for the head, or maybe only a strap of rawhide around the waist. What little they had on was stiff with blood and reeked of freshly slaughtered carcasses. Even their faces and hands were streaked with blood.

"We'll meet these men just as we are," said the woman chief. "They will appreciate our being dressed like them."

So the woman chief went up to the hill on which Old Man was standing, and the other women followed her. When he saw the woman chief standing there in her butchering clothes, her flint skinning knife still in her hand, her hair matted and unkempt, he exclaimed, "Hah! Hrumph! This woman chief is ugly. She's dressed in rags covered with blood. She stinks. I want nothing to do with a creature like this. And those other women are just like her. No, I made no mistake putting these beings far away from us men!" And having said this, he turned around and went back the way he had come, with all his men following him.

Second Thoughts

"It seems we can't do anything right," said the woman chief. "Whatever it is, those male beings misunderstand it. But I still think we should unite with them. I think they have something we haven't got, and we have something they haven't got, and these things must come together. We'll try one last time to get them to understand us. Let's make ourselves beautiful."

The women went into the river and bathed. They washed and combed their hair, braided it, and attached their strings of bone pipes and shell beads. They put on their finest robes of well-tanned, dazzling white doeskin covered with wonderful designs of porcupine quills more colorful than the rainbow. They placed bone and shell chokers around their necks and shell bracelets around their wrists. On their feet they put full quilled moccasins. Finally the women painted their cheeks with sacred red face paint. Thus wonderfully decked out, they started on their journey to the men's camp.

In the village of male creatures, Old Man was cross and ill-humored. Nothing pleased him. He slept fitfully. He got angry over nothing. And so it was with all the men. "I don't know what's the matter," said Old Man. "I wish women were beautiful instead of ugly, sweet-smelling instead of malodorous, good-tempered instead of coming at us with stones or bloody knives in their hands."

"We wish it too," said all the other men.

Then a lookout came running, telling Old Man, "The women beings are marching over here to our camp. Probably they're coming to kill us. Quick everybody, get your bows and arrows!"

"No, wait!" said Old Man. "Quick! Go to the river. Clean yourselves. Anoint and rub your bodies with fat. Arrange your hair pleasingly. Smoke yourselves up with cedar. Put on your best fur garments. Paint your faces with sacred red paint. Put bright feathers on your heads." Old Man himself dressed in the quilled robe stolen from the women's camp which he had made into a war shirt. He wore his great chief's headdress. He put on his necklace of bear claws. Thus arrayed, the men assembled at the entrance of their camp, awaiting the women's coming.

The women came. They were singing. Their white quilled robes dazzled the men's eyes. Their bodies were fragrant with the good smell of sweet grass. Their cheeks shone with sacred red face paint.

Old Man exclaimed, "Why, these women beings are beautiful! They delight my eyes! Their singing is wonderfully pleasing to my ears. Their bodies are sweet-smelling and alluring!"

"They make our hearts leap," said the other men.

"I'll go talk to their woman chief," said Old Man. "I'll fix things up with her."

The woman chief in the meantime remarked to the other women, "Why, these men beings are really not as uncouth as we thought. Their rawness is a sort of strength. The sight of their arm muscles pleases my eyes, the sound of their deep voices thrills my ears. They are not altogether bad, these men."

Old Man went up to the mountain chief and said, "Let's you and I go some place and talk."

"Yes, let's do that," answered the woman chief. They went

some place. The woman chief looked at Old Man and liked what she saw. Old Man looked at the woman chief and his heart pounded with joy. "Let's try one thing that has never been tried before," he said to the woman new chief.

"I always like to try out new, useful things," she answered.

"Maybe one should lie down, trying this," said Old Man.

"Maybe one should," agreed the woman chief. They lay down.

After a while Old Man said, "This is surely the most wonderful thing that ever happened to me. I couldn't ever imagine such a wonderful thing."

"And I," said the woman chief, "I never dreamed I could feel so good. This is much better, even, than eating buffalo tongues. It's too good to be properly described."

"Let's go and tell the others about it," said Old Man.

When Old Man and the woman chief got back to the camp, they found nobody there. All the male creatures and the women beings had already paired off and gone some place, each pair to their own spot. They didn't need to be told about this new thing; they had already found out.

When the men and women came back from wherever they had gone, they were smiling. Their eyes were smiling. Their mouths were smiling, their whole bodies were smiling, so it seemed.

Then the women moved in with the men. They brought all their things, all their skills to the men's village. Then the women quilled and tanned for them. Then the men hunted for the women. Then there was love. Then there was happiness. Then there was marriage. Then there were children.[1]

What did you think of this story? It's an old Native American tale from the Blood-Piegan tribe. Forget for the moment some of the old role-stereotyping (we'll correct that later) and enjoy the humor of it. But as you do, notice that behind the humor are the old, old questions: Why are men and women different? Why two kinds of human beings? What gift does each bring to the relationship? What is sex all about?

The American Indians weren't the only ones asking these questions. From the time people first lived on earth they have wondered about sex, for sex is a deep mystery. Even today, when we know so much scientifically about sex, when we can draw diagrams and have courses for you in school and show you all kinds of sexual activity on TV and in the movies, can look at the growing baby inside the mother and talk about genes and make babies without sex and have sex without babies—even with all this explosion of information, the mystery remains.

The Bible's Quest

Even the Bible tried to find answers and came up with mystery: God made everything "and saw that it was good"(and that "everything" included the human body and the sexual parts), and Adam and Even ran around the garden of Eden naked "and felt no shame," no embarrassment at all. The Bible is firm on that. That's why we'll see later that there is no room for the Christian boy ever to think anything evil of his body or of sex. But, anyway, according to the Bible, something went wrong. God's good gift was somehow messed up. Whatever it was, in the confusion Adam and Eve wound up covering their bodies, especially the "private" parts because all of a sudden "they felt shame," and their relationship was strained. Even their children's relationships with each other often were hurtful (even, you might remember, to the point of murder) and everything seemed to go wrong. Strange mystery.

And so it is with every people and culture. They all have ancient stories that try to understand the mystery of sex. And sex is a mystery because, when you come right down to it, sex is about ourselves and our constant battle to want to be hugged and thought well of and to be important and wanted and loved by others, and yet, on the other hand, to want to be alone, to be oneself, apart, independent, "free." Sex is the mystery of our deep need for companionship, for someone to love us and for us to love someone, and yet it is also the mystery of never being perfectly one with another and of having to make room for differences. In fact, all the recent studies of what makes marriages successful say that it is precisely how couples deal with those differences. You see, marriage is a wonderful thing that fulfills your yearning for closeness and acceptance and love, and yet, for marriage to succeed, we must learn how to deal with the mysterious differences between man and woman, no matter how close they are. Sex is surely a mystery!

But I tell you this right off: Not everyone agrees. Some people think that sex is no mystery at all, but a simple appetite like eating and drinking and we should do it however, whenever, wherever, and with whomever we want. There is no God, no mystery, and no commitments—and therefore no real relationships. (Real relationships take time and are hard work.) People are reduced to objects like the sexy pictures of women you see in "girlie" magazines: just a picture designed to get you all excited, but no personality, no realness, no caring, no concern, no responsibility. And there is lots of money to be made from selling uncaring, unrelated sex. For some, babies in their mothers' wombs are not real people (even though they breathe, smile, suck their thumbs, remember later on music and sounds, react to light and do summersaults) but are called "fetuses." Of course, if such babies are not real, you can kill them. The fertilized eggs of women are put into other women's wombs to be sold later on to other couples.

In a word, for some sex is a commodity and babies are a commodity and people are a commodity to be bought and sold like any other object. But in this book, written for Christian boys like you, the understanding is that people are important, that they are not things or objects or to be used *but persons to be related to.* Above all, this book is written in the conviction not only that relationships are important but that sex is one of the most valuable and lasting and powerful relationships we can ever set up in our lives with another, and therefore, it is to be treated with respect, enjoyment, delight, and awe.

Wrong Turns

But I want to be honest and admit that the church has not always had such at attitude towards sex. Even though the Bible told us sex was good, the church became anti-sex. The church started out with that Bible-goodness of creation and the Incarnation (God coming into humanity, into our world, which we celebrate on Christmas). That was one side. On the other side were a host of Greek and Oriental philosophies at the time that said that matter and the body and sex were evil. The Bible said we were all of one piece. The Greeks said we were made up of two "pieces," body and soul. The body was a prison and evil, and the soul was pure and good, and the goal of life was for the pure soul to escape from the nasty prison of the body. That's why when told about Jesus, the Greek philosophers replied that if he is both God and man, then he must have only *pretended* to take on a body or the body was just make believe because no God would "soil" himself by associating with evil human flesh. The church vigorously said no to this. God really did enter fully into our human nature and creation. The world, material things, the body are all good, God-filled and blessed. But, still, would you believe, even after saying that, the church weakened and finally accepted the Greek notion that anything material was bad, especially the body and, yes, most especially sex, since sex produced more vile bodies!

So influenced by the Greek and Eastern philosophies and indeed with an eye to the awful misuse of sex by the pagan world, the church gradually began to see the Bible differently and said, Aha, the body and sex are bad because (1) you see what happened in the Garden of Eden? Adam and Eve hid their sexual organs; (2) John the Baptist, St. Paul, and Jesus himself were unmarried and that shows that renouncing sex is the only way to live a better, spiritual life; (3) Mary the Mother of Jesus was a virgin and that again shows God's preference for no-sex. So it soon became fashionable to think of sex as so sinful that even a husband and wife committed a venial sin by having sex and this was allowed only because children (which were good) were produced. St. Augustine in the fifth century was very influential in promoting and making official this kind of thinking (which had already been around a while) and he even said that original sin was passed on to the child though sex. In other words, in a few short centuries the Bible's attitude of the goodness of sex and Jesus' attitude of love and charity were changed to the church's attitudes of chastity, abstinence, and badness.

The church had become anti-sex. There's no other honest way to put it. That's why it praised celibacy and you might notice that out of the 174 official saints in our church calendar, 170 are unmarried! Being married (and having sex) was seen as an inferior, lesser state. That's why priests were commanded by law to be unmarried. That's why the church took a poor view of women. A woman was either, like Mary, a virgin with no sexual feelings at all, elevated to the highest heaven, or she was an Eve, going around seducing men to the lowest hell. Therefore she was a danger to be avoided. The unmarried monks were to flee women like the plague. Women were to be kept apart, down, submissive, in the home. (No wonder women are up in arms at the church today!) Also, married couples in medieval times were instructed to stay away from sexual intercourse three days before receiving Holy Communion on Sundays, which is why in those days the cry was "Thank God, it's Monday!" Yes, even though the church eventually made marriage a sacrament, it couldn't get away from its poor view of sex and sexual joy. We might say that it made a lot of the wedding and little of the marriage! The Protestants in the sixteenth century didn't do much better with their attitudes about sex. They too pronounced it to be bad.

Back to Basics

You can see with almost a thousand years history of anti-sex why there was a sexual revolution in our time. In their hearts people knew better. Then too the various sciences have come along and showed us a different picture of human nature and the workings of the human mind and body. And so, under their pressure, we are going back to our biblical roots and taking a second look and seeing sex as good, God-given, and a powerful force in our lives. We acknowledge that people today are free from the pressures to get married at all, free to have or not have children, free to talk about sex openly and publicly, free to ad-

mit that it's fun and funny. Women are seen, not as submissive to
men, not as Mary or Eve, but as companions and equals and,
what's more, with real sexual feelings, active pleasures, and
desires as much as men.

We recognize that the old foundations on which church
teaching was based have fallen, as well as the threefold
threat of conception, infection, and detection. The conception of
children is controlled by contraception, infection by antibiotics,
and detection in our world today is not a thing to hide but to go
on television with. These things, as we'll see, have bad sides to
them, but the point I want to make is that we have to put our
behavior on a better basis than these in order to help you find
out why you as a teenager should be chaste, why you should
save yourself till marriage. And the answers, as we shall also
see, will be found in trying to answer questions Jesus might ask,
such as: How can I love this person as I love myself? How are
my actions being true to another and to the child we may conceive? What effect does my sexual activity have on others, on
society? What do I think of the unborn? What are the safe-
guards against exploiting others? How do I gain and develop a
sense of responsibility? What are the ways I can protect myself
and others from the misuse of sex? How can my partner and I
grow in the love of God through sex?

And there are more questions we have to try to find answers
to because the freedoms of the sexual revolutions have brought
their own slavery. One man wrote: "The sexual revolution...has
freed America from her traditional puritanism with its accom-
panying guilt. But it has also turned love into a physical performance, a hygienic act from which mystery is excluded." Another comments about the disillusionment of young people
today who have unrestrained sex and find it empty and disap-
pointing. Another observes the terrible impact of the media
(television, movies, songs, rock star role models, MTVs) on encouraging young teenagers to engage in sex long before they can
take on the responsibility of it. And, sadly, there's the enormous number of out-of-wedlock births, the over one million annual abortions, and the wildfire diseases like AIDS.

The Call

So in searching for new answers we're the first to admit that we don't have them all. But there are some general guidelines that will pervade this book. (1) We will not advise that you withdraw from the world and go hide in a closet till you're ready to marry. You're here to live in the world and change it and help people learn to accept and love one another. (2) We're not going to warn of punishment and sin at every turn. Some things are sinful but only because love is hurt and not because some rule is violated. (3) We're ready to put the issue of sex out in the open. This is why I wrote this book, which I hope your parents or teachers gave to you and you can give it back to them to read as well. (4) We're convinced that no teenager should have sex, especially in grade or high school, for reasons we'll see. (5) We also want to go back and reaffirm the goodness of sex, the goodness that we detect in the creation and the Incarnation. (6) Finally, we want to offer a better way to loving human relationships than what's going on today on television.[2]

So let's get started. In the following chapters we are going to start out with the marvelous difference between boys and girls and then speak of the male "vocation." The word vocation means a calling, an invitation, a being-chosen. That's kind of important. You are not an accident. You are called, chosen by God, to be a male, as girls were so chosen to be female. You are to work out your love and life in a male way as she is in her female way. As we shall see, we call this process "sexuality." But for the moment, I just want to give you a sense of being chosen. "You have not chosen me," said Jesus; "I have chosen you." You're important. God has a plan for you as a boy-soon-to-be-man. In the next couple of years your growing and maturing mind and body are preparing you for your chosen task in life.

QUESTIONS FOR REFLECTION AND DISCUSSION

1. No matter how much science explains us, takes us apart and puts us back together again, there is still a fundamental mystery about us: who are we, why are we here, what is our destiny. Discuss. How would you express who we are?

2. Why are men and women different? What gifts does each bring to the other?

3. Why is human sexuality described as a "mystery"? Do you think it is? Explain.

4. What do you think the church's attitude is today?

5. The church's first biblical tradition about sex was positive, but later under Greek and Oriental influence, it became negative. What do Buddhism and Confucianism say about the body?

So God created man in his own image, in the image of God he created them; male and female he created them.

Genesis 1:27

2
LONG LIVE THE DIFFERENCE

Think of a little boy and girl we'll name Jim and Jean. They are six years old in the first grade. Like all of their classmates they have, for all practical purposes to the untrained eye, the same height, weight, shape, size, and build. In fact, if the parents wanted to fool you, they could dress them alike and you could hardly tell them apart: Who was the boy and who was the girl?

But if you saw Jean and Jim in, say, the eighth grade, you'd have no trouble telling who was Jean and Jim, who was male and female, even with unisex haircuts and clothes. Now, the question this prompts is: Why are the body structures of Jean and Jim so alike in first grade and so different in the eighth (and more so in the twelfth)? To press it further, why Jean and Jim at all? Why boys and girls? Why two genders? Two sexes?

And don't tell me the difference is to make babies. After all, God could have had babies grow on trees and drop off when they're ripe. No, the differences have something but not everything to do with babies. The differences have to do with both outside and inside responses and approaches to life, relationships, and responsibility.

First, the "outside." Look around you or your school or your cellar where perhaps your Dad may keep his tools. You know you don't write with a ruler or measure with a pencil. You don't hammer with pliers or saw with a screwdriver. Instead, you select the right tool for the right job. And the reason you have tools at all is because some engineers sat around a drawing table, looked at the task to be done, and asked the first sensible question, "What do we want to achieve?" Someone answers, "Well, there's this iron rod sticking out of a piece of wood— let's call it a nail—and we want to get it out of there because everyone's catching their sweater on it and tearing it. So, let's come up with a tool that will do the job, that will get that nail out of there." Guess what they invented? The claw hammer, of course.

Notice what they did. They looked at the job first and fitted the tool to the job. God is a great engineer. In the world of nature God too looks at the job and fits the tool to it. All the marvelous evolutions and adaptations of nature are evidence of this. God gives all of nature a job and then lets the divine inner force eventually provide the tools to carry it out.

The same with human beings. This may be hard to realize now because we're in another stage of development. We have invented machinery and computers so that heavy and muscular tasks can be carried out by anyone, boy or girl, man or woman, who can punch a keyboard. Anyone with training, however weak and small, can thrust a multi-ton rocket into space. But this is only very, very recent in our long human history, within the lifetimes of your mother and father and your own. It wasn't always that way.

Before that, most things pretty much depended on body design and power. Think of the Egyptian pyramids, the Great Wall of China, the Stonehenge rocks, the Roman Coliseum, the great cathedrals of the twelfth and thirteenth centuries. With some mechanical tools, they were built by sheer strength and muscle. Go back further to the prehistoric, living-in-caves times and think of battling mammoths and saber tooth tigers and other monsters. If there were only one sex spending all the time building, heaving, gathering nuts and berries, or slaying animals for food, who would carry, bear, and care for the babies? If there were only one sex spending all the time carrying, bearing, and nurturing babies—and helpless human babies take many years, as you know, before they can cope on their own— who could put up shelter, gather food, and provide protection from the wild animals and hostile tribes?

The Grand Design

So, God's engineering came to the fore in the special calling of a two-sexed world. One of these sexes, man, would have a body design for heavy work (notice, for example, the broader shoulders and chest muscles of the male). The other sex, woman— taken "out of the side of man" in the Bible account to show their equality—would have a body design for bearing children (notice, for example, the broader hips of the female for child-carrying space and breasts for child feeding). The physical differences were there for cooperation and mutual caring, sharing, and love.

And it would seem that "inside" differences were there too. This man and woman would have different perceptions, different behavior, different ways of looking at things, at people, at relationships, at life itself. Men and women speak in "different voices." We're not sure why this is so, whether this difference has to do with chemicals or nerve endings or hormones or brain cell connections or what. One woman, a professor of neuroanatomy (which studies the structure of cells and the nervous system) writes, "I think it is only a matter of time before technology allows us to measure precisely the differences in the structure of male and female human brains. Animal studies clearly indicate that such differences exist. With different arrangements of nerve cells between the sexes, there are undoubtedly different kinds of behavior that are inherent [that is, built in: you're born that way]."[1] Others disagree with this and say there are no chemical or brain differences that would account for behavior or intellectual differences between men and women. They believe it is how a child is treated and trained that creates differences. There probably will continue to be a lot of discussion on this whole issue of "inside" differences.

However, as scientists continue to explore the area of difference, can we come to any conclusion early on? Yes, we should
hold on to three understandings. (1) Everybody agrees that
there *are* physical and biological differences between men and
women;[2] (2) these physical differences, however, "have no
bearing at all on the great issues that face our society: how to
apportion power, work, and responsibility in late twentieth-
century America";[3] and (3) many functions in life, work, and
play are suitable for men or women, more than we have allowed in the past.

And while we're on the subject, we should mention too that
when we talk about those physical differences, namely, when
one person is in fact larger and stronger than others, the tendency is often to abuse the weaker. So maybe the bigger boys and
girls in your class pick on the smaller ones; some adults, men and
women, abuse helpless children; anyone with a gun has power
over the defenseless. People should not have run the Native
Americans off their land or pushed the blacks into ghettos because they were richer and stronger. Well, you get the point:
Being bigger in size (although not always in heart and inner
strength) men have had a history of using and abusing women.
It's not a pretty page on our record any more than racism and
slavery are, but it's good to be reminded of it as we discuss the
differences. It's even more of a shame for us Christians to ever
have abused women or kept them down, since Jesus came precisely to reach out to the downtrodden and abused and those no
one else had use for. He was very kind to women in an age that
thought little of them and gave them no rights.

The Challenge of Adolescence
Anyway, where do you fit in all this? Well, as a boy-turning-
man, you are right now in a very peculiar position. The adults
of your life, including your mother and father, are running
things in many respects, and this is as it should be. This is an
adult world which needs the wisdom, labor, and experience of
adults. But the simple fact is that this cannot continue forever.
Sooner or later (even though you may not like to think about it)

your mother and father will get old and die, just as, perhaps, their parents have and certainly their grandparents have died. What I'm saying is that some day you have to step into their shoes of responsibility. You have to get "tooled" for adult responsibility, to "take over" some day. Since you can't do that the way you are now (or were at eight or nine years old), you have to enter into a transition time, the difficult death-life period called adolescence. You might wish to call it teenage, but I don't care for the term (although I use it). That only means, technically, you're between 13 and 19. Big deal. By the way, you can figure out now why six-year-old Jean and Jim look alike and have little observable physical differences. There's no reason to be that different. They have no jobs to do that require different tooling— yet. But they will soon, and that's why adolescence comes in.

"Adolescence" has a nice Latin root. It comes from the word that has as its principle parts *adolesco, adolescere, adultus.* You can easily see where we get our English word. It means "to grow up" and when you in fact have grown up, you are an adult. An adolescent is one in the process of growing up, of becoming an adult, or in our terms, one slowly but surely (and gloriously) getting tooled for a calling to be a man or a woman.

I mentioned that this is a "death-life" period because you have to "die" to being a little boy and that's scary. It was nice to be looked after, fed, clothed, told what to do. But now that's becoming a pain. You're not old enough and big enough to be really on your own and your parents still think of you as "their little boy." Yet, you want to be let go, to stay out later, to have privileges, to act big, but in your heart you know you're not ready. So, it's a time of dying to your dependency and getting on your own; of dying to your parents in a way, and your home, to reach out to other friends. It's a time of dying to that "nice little boy" image, of becoming what is called a "teenage werewolf!" One day you're still that nice kid; another day you're a monster. It's a really hard time for parents and you, but, hold on, there's life after death! Once you pass through this transition, you'll emerge a fine and responsible adult. And this book will try to help you do this.

Meanwhile, we've got to look at you, at your transition time of mind and body, at your dramatic and confusing "time of tooling," so necessary even in this electronic, computer age. Let's see what will happen—is happening—to you.

QUESTIONS FOR REFLECTION AND DISCUSSION
1. Why don't ten year olds have the bodies of adults?
2. The difference between men and women are real, but differences don't mean inequality. Explain.
3. "You look at the job and get the tool that fits." Explain. Apply this analogy to sexuality.
4. Explain the origin and meaning of "adolescence."

*All things were created by him and all things ex-
ist through him and for him.*

3
THE MALE VOCATION

We must begin with a little science. Dotted all around the human body are chemical manufacturing plants called glands.
These glands make those chemicals or hormones that regulate
normal development, size growth, and even behavior. If the
right combination and flow of these hormones are not produced,
you will get an abnormality of some kind or another. Many deformed people, sometimes referred to as "circus freaks," have
glandular problems. The 17-foot giant, the 680-pound fat woman, the dwarf, all probably have some glandular defect that
caused or contributed to their condition. There are some scientists who feel they have found a link between certain hormone
levels and aggressive behavior. For example, the more a certain hormone (called androstenedione) there is in a boy's blood,
the more he tends to explode, be aggressive, and talk back to
his teachers and parents. Imbalanced chemical hormones can
sometimes give a girl something of a boy's type body and sex organs, and the boy something of a girl's type body and sex organs.
(Such people should go to the doctor for help, of course.)

The point is that these glands are important in your tooling
to become a man. Of the many glands in the body, the two we're
interested in right now are the pituitary gland at the base of
the brain and the sex glands in the lower trunk between your
legs. The pituitary gland is very important because, although
it is no larger than the tip of your fingernail, it does reside in

your "computer," your brain. As such, it is the master gland operating all the others. Other glands depend on signals from this gland.

To this extent we can speak of the pituitary gland as an "alarm clock." That is, it is programmed to "ring" at a certain time in your life and in the life of your friends and so "wake up" the sleeping sex glands. Every boy, of course, is born with sex glands but, for all practical purposes they do not work. They are "asleep." They wake up and go to work when awakened by the pituitary gland. For most boys this generally occurs in the seventh or eighth grade. But for other boys it goes off earlier or later. And this explains why, for example, you can have two boys in the eighth grade, one of whom looks like a hairy King Kong who already needs a shave and the other like Charlie Brown who could pass for a fifth grader. Look around your class and see the differences among the boys your age. The difference is simply that each boy's "alarm clock" went off differently. So whether you're among the early starters or late starters, it really doesn't matter. Your "alarm clock" will even things out. So you don't have to be concerned like "Dennis, age 14" who wrote to Judy Blume: "I used to wonder if I was normal when surrounded by the other boys, I would always compare my voice, my hair, my size and the rest of me, to them. Then I would worry."

The "Clock" Goes Off

All right, what happens when it does go off? Well, a chemical impulse goes from the pituitary gland, down the communication wires in your backbone (your nervous system) and wakes up the sex glands which in turn start manufacturing their special hormones called androgens which move into your boy's body to make something new of it. For from this point on, great changes will take place: a rapid, uneven, clumsy, exciting "tooling" into a man that will change your body and your feelings and indeed your whole life. It's a wild call from God. Anyway, in order to appreciate what happens, let's take a look at the boy's sexual organs and learn some technical terms.

There are three parts to a boy's sexual organs which are easy to see since your organs (unlike a girl's) are on the outside. First, there are the *testicles*, or *testes*. These are the sex glands themselves, the ones that are awakened and produce the androgens that physically change a boy into a man. They are the two round, ball-shaped parts (which is why some slang expressions for the testicles are "balls" or "nuts") about an inch in diameter. When they are awakened and begin to work they become larger. Often one hangs down a bit lower than the other. One reason is to keep them from bumping into each other when you walk. Sometimes, too, one testicle can be larger than the other. In any case, the testicles hang inside a thick-skinned pouch called the *scrotum*. The scrotum has two jobs. One is to protect the testicles from being damaged or hurt since, if they are, a boy might not physically develop satisfactorily. And, besides, the testicles are tender. If you've ever been hit there, you know what I'm talking about. And that's why, too, you should wear a protective cup over the sex organs in playing rough, contact sports, in case you get hit or kicked in the testicles. It's also a good idea to wear a jock strap in any kind of active sport just to keep the testicles from swinging around too much and getting hurt.

Sometimes boys ask, if the testicles are dangling around down there like that where they can get kicked or hurt, why aren't they tucked up in your body somewhere where they would be safe? The answer to that is found in the second job of the scrotum. You see, for the testicles to function properly they must have a proper temperature, must be within a few degrees of heat and cold. So, to insure this, the scrotum acts as an elevator: When it's too hot the scrotum stretches downward and gets the testicles away from too much of your body heat, and when it's too cold the scrotum wrinkles upward to get near your body heat. The easiest example of this is when you're swimming. When you take off your swim suit, you'll notice how tight and close to your body the scrotum is.

The final part of the boy's sexual organs is the *penis*. This tube-like, finger-like part hangs down over the scrotum. The penis itself has two parts, the shaft which is the long part, and the glans which is simply the acorn shaped tip or head of the penis. This glans is covered with skin called the *foreskin*, which, as we shall see shortly, is sometimes cut away in circumcision. The penis has two purposes also. One is that this is, as you know, the part a boy urinates from. The other purpose of the penis is for "communion," which means "union with." The penis will be a symbol of his committed contract that will someday unite him deeply with a woman he loves.

When a boy is born, this penis is covered with a soft folding of skin (called the foreskin). Some people, for either medical reasons (they think this skin might invite minor infections) or religious reasons, have this foreskin removed through a very simple surgical procedure called *circumcision* when the baby is two or three days old. (You can see the two root words there: "circum-" as in circumference means "around," and "-cision" which gives us our word "scissors," which means to cut. So the word means "to cut around.") Others don't feel this is necessary; that's why, in the shower room with other boys, you'll notice some who are circumcised (with the skin cut an inch or so down the tip of the penis) and others who aren't (with the skin almost completely over the penis tip). If you're not circumcised it's a good idea to pull back the foreskin when you shower and clean it because a secretion *(smegma)* collects there and can cause irritation or an unpleasant ordor.

On the Way to Becoming
So these are the three parts of the male sexual organs: the testicles, the scrotum, and the penis. Let's see what happens when they go into operation. Let me list these things in no particular order so that you can anticipate what will happen or is happening to you. As you go down the list, try to have a very positive attitude, that something good is happening, that God's hand is here, that God's calling you, tooling you for some work ahead, that this is fantastic and exciting. There's nothing dirty or evil or bad about sex, and anyone who tries to make it seem so is plain wrong.

1) Hair. Body hair begins to grow, usually first around your calves (lower legs) and under your arms, and then on your face as the first signs of a moustache begin to appear (and about which you may be kidded by your family). Some boys will be able to shave, at least occasionally, by the time they're fourteen, while others may not start shaving regularly for a couple of years. Mostly, though, the main sign that your glands are starting to work is the hair around your sexual organs, right above the base of your penis. This hair, called pubic hair, is coarse and is usually several shades darker than the hair on your head. Over the years it will spread, roughly in a triangular shape from the base of the penis up to the navel (belly button). Most boys worry a lot about the hair on their head and face and spend time to see if it matches all the other kids. But they also worry about the *amount* of body hair and pubic hair. Why? Because (as we shall see more fully later) they're caught up in the lie and untruths that television and magazines keep telling them: more of anything is always better. And so, if they have lots of body hair on their chest and legs and lots of wild, dark pubic hair, then they're more "masculine." Which is a lot of horsefeathers. The amount of hair on your body anywhere has nothing whatever to do with how much of or what kind of a man you are. Hair is a matter of heredity. Period. Whether you're full-headed or bald has nothing to do with being a man.

Whether your body is hairy or hairless has nothing to do with being a man, either. Hair, like fur and feathers, is left over from an age when people lived outdoors all the time and needed warmth and protection. As we moved more and more indoors and wore more and more clothes, then we needed hair less and less. And that's why scientists predict that in the future all people will be born and remain bald and hairless. (Guys who make a big deal of going around showing off the hair on their chests may be proud of this, but perhaps also unsure of themselves.)

2) Baby fat and bones. Under the pressure of the hormones, normal baby fat begins to work itself into muscle. The boy might notice his thighs tightening up and the back muscles beginning to develop and the waist beginning to harden. The point is, of course, that he is going to need strength to do responsible work. The bones of young children have certain slight separations in them. Now they'll begin to knit together and "lock" in. This means that the skeleton frame is on the way to becoming something like a one-welded car frame: a solid piece that can withstand stress, shock, and strain better. This is why coaches don't let kids under a certain age play football, even with proper equipment. Such kids are still too easy a target for a bone break or ligament tear.

3) *Growth.* Under the force of the new hormones pumping into him from the sex glands, the boy grows taller. Often he grows in spurts and can grow as much as five inches in height in a few months. In fact, he'll probably grow more in the next three to four years than he has in his whole life beforehand. And this explains, too, why his parents can't keep enough food around for him. He's always in the refrigerator looking for food and snacks because all those rapidly multiplying cells take a lot of fuel.

4) *Voice.* During this time the voice box *(larynx)* grows longer. The end result is a deeper tone of voice. But before that happens, it can be hard on both the boy and others because, on its way to a deeper tone, the voice can crack and screech and bounce between high and low notes much to everyone's embarrassment. It's hard on the ears, but it's only for a while.

5) *Sweat.* When a boy was little, he could get pretty hot and could perspire. But once he starts to mature he can really sweat. This may not seem like a great gift, but it happens. And not only can he sweat but he can smell! The reason is that the hormones activate the body's oil glands and if that mixes with bacteria, it can produce "underarm odor," or anywhere else for that matter. Like so many other things, of course, the amount of sweat and body odor (BO) depends on heredity and the type of hair and skin a boy has, but usually if you eat good food and are healthy your body odor probably isn't noticeable. In any case, it simply means taking more showers and using deodorants. If you sweat a lot, it's a good idea to wear 100 percent cotton undershirts and shorts since they are far more absorbent than the

synthetic materials. The same with pimples and acne. Your oil glands may stimulate whiteheads or blackheads on the face. This is usually temporary and you should wash with mild soap and cut down on greasy foods. Long-term or severe face pimples or acne should be brought to a doctor's attention.

6) *Breast change.* When a boy goes through puberty there are also certain changes in his breasts that he may notice. For example, that little ring of colored flesh around the nipple may get wider and darker in color and the nipple itself may get somewhat larger. Sometimes, too, you may notice that the breasts feel tender or sore, and you may notice even a small bump or lump under one or both nipples. That's OK and perfectly normal and a sign that the hormones are at work. Sometimes, too, some boys (maybe half or more of them) experience some swelling of the breasts at this time and the breasts feel sensitive and tender but this too is all right. It may last a while, but it will go away and it doen't mean (which worries some boys) that you're going to get female breasts and turn into a girl.

7) *Attitude.* This may seem farfetched but I tell you this: Your attitudes at this time of your life are more influenced by your glands and hormones than you think. For example, a mother says to her neighbor about her nine-year-old son, "Oh, Johnny's a real boy all right. He loves baseball, hates to eat his vegetables, and can't stand the girls." That's pretty true. Especially the last item, disliking girls. He teases them, wouldn't be caught dead playing with them, and has a sign on his hangouts, "No Girls Allowed!" (And the girls don't want him around either: "Mom, tell Johnny to stop bothering us!") But, take a look at the scene in the eighth grade or high school. Johnny can't keep away from the girls! He has become a professional junior wolf.

What's happened between nine years old and fifteen years old? What *hasn't* happened is this: Johnny did not sit down with himself one day and reason it all out. He did not conclude that since girls are going to be around on the planet for a long time he may as well learn to live at peace with them. Nothing of the sort. Rather, Johnny is a "victim" of chemistry, of hormones. You see, as he matures, some of those hormones sneak up to his brain and, in a chemical reaction, he begins—without any vote on his part—to tolerate girls, then become interested in them (and, of course, also in sex), and then gets to actually liking them! As time goes on he will go out with many girls, a few girls, and gradually with one special girl whom he will ask to be his wife forever. He thinks it's all his doing. But God had a hand in this. After all, if left to himself, a girl-hating nine-year-old Johnny would never be interested in girls and as a result they would never get together and love and marry and have a family—and so the world would end. So God has to throw some chemical magic around to get him interested in girls and girls in him, and keep things going.

Handing on the Tradition

8) Life carriers. Remember, we said that the testicles are like small round balls. Inside of them are small, bunched-up microscopic tubing which, if laid out straight, would stretch some 750 feet. These testicles, we said, produce the hormones that give the boy his masculine body and looks such as we just described in the five items above. But now we add one more most marvelous "product." The testicles also produce a boy's sperm—about 200 million of them are in about one tablespoon!—but they are so small that we can see them only with a microscope. They look like little tadpoles or polywogs swimming around this thickish white fluid called the *semen,* or sperm fluid. In fact, like tadpoles, the sperm have swishing tails that move them through the body ducts and eventually outside through the penis. What makes this awesome is that this is the boy's life-giving sperm by which he can with a woman produce a living baby; it's his contribution to the making of a child. Inside the sperm is his heredity or, if you will, his genes. The genes, attached on a kind of thread called chromosomes, are all his characteristics he has inherited from his parents and grandparents all the way back.

As you may know, for every general physical characteristic, you have a corresponding gene. Such things as your height, color, shape of your nose, the color of your hair and eyes, baldness or full headed hair—each of these has a representative gene in the sperm. Scientists, as you know from school, have discovered that some genes are stronger or more dominant than others and so the stronger ones will "outvote" the weaker ones when it comes to contributing to the making of a baby. For instance (everything else being equal), if a brown-eyed person married a blue-eyed person, the baby will have brown eyes since brown is a stronger gene or characteristic than blue. If a tall person married a short person, the baby will be tall since the gene of tallness will outvote the gene of shortness (which may pop out in another generation anyway). Scientists in the past years have done some remarkable things in moving genes around and this can be very helpful (removing sickness-carrying genes) or hurtful (creating a "super race"). But that's not our interest here.

What is our interest· is the incredible fact that when a boy starts producing that whitish fluid with its seeds of life, he can become a father! He can produce life. And not just life, but someday *his* life and the life of his wife, because his and her basic material and all of their ancestors will be in that baby. In a word, they hand on their joint heredity. No wonder grandma and grandpa love you so. They see resemblances in you, their own life continued long after they're dead. Family resemblances and characteristics are there so that you can often tell relatives a mile off. It's a unique and wonderful thing, because you have the power not only to create a baby but a family as well, an ongoing tradition of what makes you and your people special.

That's why I like a word that's not much used now. People speak of "making babies," but that sounds to me like making some kind of a product. Like, "When you get old enough, Johnny, and sexually grow up you can produce sperm in your testicles and make babies." I prefer the word "procreate." When you sexually grow up, you can procreate. Take the word apart. "Pro" means not an abbreviation for a professional, but "on behalf of." (When you study ancient Roman history you'll learn about "pro-counsels," people who "on behalf of" the emperor ruled in certain parts of the empire.) The word "create" means what it says. Put together, the whole word says that when you get old enough you receive the power of procreation, "to create on behalf of" God. Only God gives life. Thinking so much of you, God has entrusted some of the divine creative power with you. To say you have the power of procreation (rather than the power of sex) is to tie you into God and give the dignity and meaning to sex that it should always have. Furthermore, the word implies that creation is ongoing. That is to say, you not only create a living child on behalf of God, but you must continue to create that child every day. You must be there to raise the child, to love him or her, and give support, guidance, direction, and unconditional love. We call this family.

QUESTIONS FOR REFLECTION AND DISCUSSION

1. Do you ever think of yourself as having a "vocation," or a calling? How would you describe your "vocation"?

2. Teenage or adolescence is a crucial bridge between childhood and adulthood, not only in the sense of physical growth but also to settle values and ideals. Discuss.

3. Having children is not just a matter of making babies but of having a sense of history, of roots, of being a part of a larger scheme, an important link in the unity of humankind. As someone said, "A baby is God's vote for the future." Do you see it this way? Why? Why not?

*Did you not pour me out like milk and curdle
me like cheese, clothe me with skin and flesh
and knit me together with bones and sinews?*

Job 10:10

4
WHAT, ME WORRY?

This chapter title from *Mad* Magazine is Alfred E. Newman's
favorite question. The answer is always understood as "No,
nothing to worry about." I hope this might be your response too
as we examine seven areas that boys sometimes worry about, but
really shouldn't have to. The first three concern the penis and
the others the body in general.

1) The penis is normally in a soft and relaxed condition rest-
ing against the scrotum. Often, however, the penis can become
enlarged, stiff, and stand out straight and angled upwards.
This hardening of the penis (in slang sometimes called a "hard-
on") is called an *erection*. Boys have erections at an earlier age,
but now it becomes more pronounced, frequent, and obvious. The
medical explanation is that the penis is made up of sponge-like
cells and you know what happens to a sponge when liquid flows
into it. It swells up. The same thing happens to the penis.
When blood flows into it, it swells up, stiffens, and becomes
erect. The boy has an erection.

Many things can cause that blood flow and erection. Some are
directly or deliberately stimulating, and some are accidentally
stimulating. In the directly stimulating category are things
like touching or rubbing or playing with one's penis. Looking at
a sexy movie or reading a sexy book or just thinking or picturing

sexual things in your mind. That erection is always a sure-fire clue that the boy is getting sexually excited and aroused. That moving hard-on is a real signal flashing! In the automatically stimulating category, sometimes just the activity of your sex hormones does the trick. Or such things as fright, being nervous, tension, tight clothes, especially your underwear. Sometimes boys get erections playing or rough-housing or just having someone sit on their lap. One worried boy told me, "Sometimes when my little sister crawls up on my lap to be hugged, I find myself getting an erection. That bothers me. Am I normal? After all, she's only my little sister." The answer is that it's normal, a kind of automatic reaction that's not unusual. Or many boys tell me they have erections when they wake up in the morning. That's understandable. What happens is that during the night a boy, like other people, might have several dreams during sleep and frequently erections will accompany these dreams (which, of course, he is not aware of). If a boy awakes just after one of these dream episodes he will awake with an erection. As soon as he moves around a bit and gets more awake the swelled penis relaxes and becomes limp again. This is what causes morning erections and not, as some people think, a full bladder.

One thing you'll find out is that you cannot always control an erection, and much to your embarrassment, it can happen spontaneously at times. It could happen in class, in church, on the beach. The most embarrassing episode I know of concerns a 16-year-old boy who is very athletic and a gym instructor. He was taking a group of 12-year-old girls through their gymnastic routines before their proud parents when suddenly, in front of them all, he had an erection. If that weren't embarrassing enough, he nearly died when one little three-year-old girl, imitating her older sister's acrobatics, grabbed the "handle" to steady herself after having stood on her head. Talk about wanting to disappear! Well, some boys use all kinds of tricks to hide an erection when it happens. Some tell me they wear jock straps to "hold it down" (I have a feeling that doesn't work). Some resort to putting their hands in their pockets so that the shape caused by their fists will help camouflage the bulge caused by their erect penis. Some hold a school book in front of them. One of the best ways to treat it is to deliberately think of something neutral: the coming basketball game, tomorrow's exam, grandma's birthday present, or whatever, like counting backwards from 100, skipping every number with a 7 or multiple of 7 in it. As we'll see, our sexual activity is basically brain-controlled and you can discipline yourself in this area.

Since a boy's erection is a perfectly normal, common happening, there is nothing to worry about. A boy who knows that God is at work in his life might thank God for signs of his coming manhood. And having a sense of humor about it helps, especially when you know your buddies (who aren't telling you) are having the same problem.

Wet Dreams
2) The second thing a boy might worry about occurs when the testicles sometimes produce an oversupply of the sperm fluid (semen). Nature has a way of getting rid of this. What usually happens is that a boy has a sexy dream (no problem; that's a bonus for you from God) which becomes so intense that he suddenly wakes up and finds semen spurting out of his penis. And it's very exciting and pleasurable. This spurting or discharge is called an ejaculation, or *orgasm*. When a male is about to have an orgasm, whether awake or asleep, his penis is stiff or erect, his scrotum skin gets tighter and contracts close to his body, his heart starts beating faster, his breathing gets heavier, and even his skin may get flushed (called the "sex flush"). His nipples also stiffen, his buttocks may tighten and finally the penis muscles contract and the semen comes out in three or four spurts. Then everything gradually returns to normal. When this orgasm happens at night during sleep, some boys are both scared and fascinated, especially if no one's told them about it or prepared them for it. But it's a perfectly natural occurrence. When you have an orgasm during the night it is called a *nocturnal emission,* or *wet dream*. It happens to all males, to you (if you're of age) and to me, to your father, your friends—to all. It's just nature's way of expelling semen when too much has been stored up.

If you're embarrassed by this perfectly normal happening, you'll have a tendency to hide your pajamas which by morning are dry but starchy from the fluid. That's OK. You can go quietly and rinse them out yourself or throw them in the washer. If you're lucky enough to realize your parents know you're growing up and know a lot about sex, you may just leave the pajamas there and feel sure that they will understand. Either way, it's O.K. and a wet dream is a wonderful sign of becoming a man.

Here's an account of a farm's boy wild dream and his first wet dream. He's about 14 years old. In his dream:

A pack of boys was chasing him. They were yelling. Take his pants off and check him out...He was running as fast as he could, screaming with terror...Suddenly he ran by a tree and his father was standing there. He slowly handed the boy the long sword his great-grandfather had carried in the war between the States and said, Try this, son...[but suddenly] in his place stood his mother...Smiling, she reached out an arm and said softly, Why don't you give me that? He mutely shook his head and held the sword behind his back, whereupon his mother smiled, stretched her other arm to the side in a welcoming gesture and said, Well, maybe you'll give it to her. The boy faced around to the new arrival who was a tall statuesque woman with red gold hair. She was dressed in a toga which left one breast bare...the boy held the sword in front of him...As he took one step forward he recognized her and said reverently, You're Ceres, aren't you, ma'am, the head goddess of earth? [He had that in class recently.] The lady responded, Since you've asked I'll have to go, and [she] changed immediately into Marietta Marsengill [a girl he has a crush on in school]... As she stood there in a warm swirling mist, she slowly raised both arms and the blue dress parted smoothly right down the middle and dropped out of sight into the mist around her feet. The sword in his hands moved and became hot and he realized that it was really his penis. Marietta looked at him demurely and said in reverent tones, Do you have something for me?...

Lightning flashed through his loins, and he awoke to feel one irresistible shudder after another passing with inundating bewilderment through his penis. The boy lay for a moment in bewilderment and then exclaimed with surprise, "Hey, I've had one! I had a wet dream!"[1]

Size and Sense

3) The third area of worry is the size of one's penis. This, unfortunately, is another one of those worries that has no real basis in fact but is a part of the nonsense that comes from ignorance and the media. Once more the message is: Bigger is better. And once more the truth is: It's a lie. The simple fact is that the size and shape of the penis (and it varies somewhat in shape) is inherited. In general, a relaxed penis is from two to four inches long and when erect maybe five to seven inches long. But it makes no difference. A bigger or smaller penis works as well as a big or small eye or ear or anything else. Function has nothing whatever to do with size and the boy with the largest penis is not more manly or masculine any more than the boy with the largest nose is more noble or handsome or smart. Yet, boys will talk and continue to exchange ignorance and I know you'll get pulled into thinking that bigger is better. But at least you heard the truth and maybe deep down when you feel good about yourself you will be comfortable with the truth you know. Here's another passage from the book I quoted above. This time the boy is only eleven years old and he's living in the 1930s on a small farm in Georgia. It's a hot day and he and some bigger boys, both black and white, decide to go swimming down at the old water hole:

Within minutes they were all stripping off their clothes, taking care to fold them on rocks so that redbugs would not get in them. As the boy hopped on one leg divesting himself of his underpants, he became acutely conscious of his lack of physical development. He had never before been in a group of naked adults. Prepubescent [that is, before you start to sexually develop, when you're just a kid] nudity was commonplace on the farm...[but] among adolescents and adults, body consciousness appeared suddenly and demandingly.

The genitals [sex organs or penis] were called privates and were just exactly that. Modesty was an ingrained tenet of conduct...The boy, despite devious and ingenious curiosity, had never had a good look at an adult penis...Now, prancing unashamedly in the sunlight, his friends from town, older than he and fully matured, were exhibiting themselves completely. He was startled by the sight of flat, stark white bellies accented by the vibrant growths of rich curly black hair and decorated with swinging genitalia. They acted proud of themselves. James Kelly was even popping his [penis] between thumb and forefinger with a slapping sound against his belly to make it bigger. Try as he would to avert his gaze and pretend indifference, the boy felt surrounded by big penises...He looked down at himself. Well, he thought, it looks for all the world like a grub worm.

Fearful of attention and comment from his peers, he slid unobtrusively into the shallow water by Buddy. No one said a word to him, but the conversation on the sandbar was penetratingly audible.

"Look at old James, he done worked himself up a semi [an erection half-way up]," yelled Tom.

"Yeah," observed Warren. "Ain't he got a whopper?"

"You think that's something—you ought to see ole Dave Dillapree," responded James. "He's got the biggest one in town."

"How do you know?" asked Warren laughing.

"Yea, that's right," confirmed Tom, "He showed it to a bunch of us in the cemetery one day. When it's hard it's ten and a half inches long and four inches around the bottom. He measured it right in front of us."

"My God," said the minister's son, "How come it got so big?"

"We asked him," answered James, "and he said he puts nitrate of soda poultices on it....The farmers use it a lot....I don't know whether he's lying or not..."

"I believe he's lying," opined Tom, " but then he might not be. It sho is big. You oughta see Benton Bishop's though. It's crooked... ."[2]

And so it goes. A bunch of boys not quite sure of themselves and thinking that a big size is the important thing when it isn't and with no one to tell them any better, they try to hide their ignorance and fears (How does their penis compare to others? Are they normal?) by horsing around about it.

4) This area of concern has to do with simple information about the part of our bodies we sit down on. Common street terms are "butt," "behind," "backside," "ass," "rear-end," etc. These terms are all right except they show a lack of education and a certain degree of uncomfortableness. Anyway, the correct term is *buttocks*. The buttocks are two large muscles (not fat or flab, but muscle tissue) and form a perfect padding for sitting comfort. The opening between the buttocks is called the *anus*, or *rectum*. This is the opening which is the end of the large intestine from which solid waste matter or excretment is expelled. (Note that this large intestine that leads to the anus is designed to have things come *out* of it, not *into* it, at least not without danger, as we'll see later on.)

Even here there is a nice bit of design and kindness. For example, if you stand up and feel your elbows you immediately feel two sharp bones. If you put your hands on your behind or buttocks and press in, you can't feel any sharp (pelvic) bones even though they are there. Now if you sat down on those bare bones you'd be in agony. It would be like sitting on a picket fence. So these pelvic bones are covered with the buttock muscles that are so full and cushioned that you can sit comfortably and relax. Besides, the buttocks are a parent's gift in that they have enough nerve endings so that you can feel a good spanking, but they're bouncy enough and padded enough that you can't really be hurt.

5) The fifth area of concern might be one's body type. Most adolescents at some time or other hate their bodies. You're not good looking enough, tall enough, hairy enough, and so on. You measure yourself against the people you see on the television or

in the magazines, not realizing that lots of people spent lots of time trying to make *them* over. But we're not so much concerned about that here as we are to remind you of this: All people are born with certain body types or styles and it's just plain smart to know this and live with it.

For example, scientists say that people usually fall into certain body style groupings. They give them wild names like Endomorph, Mesomorph, and Ectomorph—which means they break people up into how round, muscular, or angular their bodies are. The endomorphs tend to be round and this person could be stocky with a large, round belly, short, thick neck, short arms and legs, with fat upper arms and thighs. This is the kind of guy that would be a great shotputter or wrestler or football player. The mesomorphs tend to be muscular, the kind that might develop into a strong build with broad shoulders and chest and little body fat. This guy would make a great baseball player. The ectomorphs tend to be tall and thin and wiry. This guy would make a good high jumper or tennis player or basketball player. One is not better than the other. They're just different, that's all.

The point I'm making is to learn to be comfortable with your body type and don't strain beyond it. If you're a stocky five-feet-two, you can still be a great basketball star by sheer determination, but it will be tough to work so hard to do what a six-foot-seven lanky guy can do with ease. If you're tall and wiry and skinny, weighing 127 pounds, you could, I guess, be a great fullback, but you might be crazy to try. If you're muscular and athletic you could do well at wrestling, but you'd be overwhelmed by a 280 pound monster and you better stick to soccer or baseball. In other words, learn to be comfortable with your body type and try the things and the sports that it's best fitted for, things you'll do well at. People don't have to be the same and make it a dull world. Your body type has great outlets and will fit in somewhere. Knowing and liking and working within your body type is a smart thing to do.

6) Some boys might worry about their image and the pressure it brings. That is, just as females are stereotyped or burdened

with the false image that they enjoy sex less or are undersexed or less sexually interested or inclined than males (all untruths), so males are burdened with the image of being oversexed and overly interested in sex. According to this stereotype, every boy, every man, is supposed to be constantly riveted on supersex, constantly thinking about it and ready in a moment's notice to have sex. This lie, of course, reduces males to insensitive machines that respond instantly when the correct button is pushed. The result is that boys often feel pressured to be macho, to pretend to be driven wild about sex all the time and, in relationship with girls, to make some kind of sexual move or else feel somehow inadequate or "less manly." And it doesn't help either that the girls themselves are saddled with the same stereotypes about boys and think that that's the way boys should be and act. As one boy wrote:

When I go out with a girl for the first time, I am often confused over sex. I feel pressured to make a move even when I don't really want to. Isn't that what girls expect? If I don't try something they might think there's something wrong with me or that I'm gay or something. I almost feel like I have to explain myself if I act uninterested in having sex.

So be forewarned. There is nothing wrong with you if you're not all worked up over sex all the time. There's nothing wrong with you if you're not interested in sex at every moment. There's nothing wrong with you—and everything right with you—if you just want to enjoy a girl's company and are not intent on having sex with her. There's nothing wrong with you if you restrain your sexual drives and save yourself for marriage. Yes, let the other boys brag about all their sexual adventures (mostly in their own minds). They're just playing out a role they think they're supposed to play, an unreal (and eventually hurtful) stereotype promoted by the movies and TV. The normal role is a healthy interest in sex but also a healthy and well-rounded interest in all that life and people have to offer.

7) Boys at times worry about the things that go on in their minds, that is, the dreams and the pictures and images of sexu-

al things that cluster on the TV screen of their imaginations. These are called sexual or erotic fantasies. Such fantasies are normal. Generally they are a healthy sign of being a sexual person and they can come and go without too much concern. However, too much or uncontrolled sexual fantasy is not good for it may lead some people to try to act it out in real life. Also such fantasies might take up too much time in your mind. So to this extent, sexual fantasies should be accepted but not encouraged, recognized but controlled.

QUESTIONS FOR REFLECTION AND DISCUSSION
1. I am my body. What does that mean?
2. The body-mind-heart changes are crucial and sacred. Why do most boy share a sense of shame rather than sacredness about what is happening to them? Where did they pick that up?
3. Comment on the "bigger, therefore better" attitude in general and then concerning the penis.
4. What is the true significance of calling the genitalia "private parts"?

Do you not know that your body is the Temple of the Holy Spirit who dwells within you and who was given to you by God? You do not belong to yourselves but to God. He bought you for a price. So use your bodies for God's glory.

1 Corinthians 6:19

5
MASTURBATION

There's a final worry that some boys have, the worry of masturbation. What is it? It is touching or rubbing, stimulating or playing with one's penis to cause an erection or an orgasm, the spurting of the seed fluid, which causes intense excitement. A boy can use his hand or rub his penis against something like the bed sheet and usually there are fantasies and sexual imaginations going on in his mind. Who masturbates? Probably most boys one time or another and sometimes it will be very frequent, from one to four or five times or more a week. It causes the average boy lots of confusion and guilt and parents lots of embarrassment, so much so that they seldom talk about it to him even when, like some parents, they probably know a boy's doing it. (They can see the dried "starchy" stain on his pajamas or sheets, which tells them that he either had a wet dream or masturbated.)

People in the past, getting some misinformation from doctors, parents, or educators, felt that it was horrible to waste the life-giving seed that was used to create life. Sometimes scientists in times past (who, after all, did not have our knowledge) thought that each sperm contained a "little man" inside and so to waste it was almost an act of murder. Also, since the sexual pleasure and attraction for the man and woman was put there in order to coax them into marriage and parenthood, it was terribly selfish to steal the pleasure without the responsibility. Then others said that masturbation would cause your hair to fall out or make you deformed, crazy, and lots of other things. So, a lot of confusion, ignorance, and guilt have surrounded masturbation. So, what about it? Well, the three most basic things we can tell you about masturbation is (1) it's not as bad as they say, (2) it's not as good as they say, and (3) what you can do about it.

Not as Bad
1) It's not as bad as they say. In the past the church concentrated on the biology. You shouldn't waste the seed that gives life. You shouldn't steal the pleasure. It's a mortal sin. Also, it will give you all sorts of ills and drive you bananas. That "driving you bananas" the church got from the medical profession which early on taught that masturbation would just do that. Did you know that's how Kellogg's Corn Flakes got started? Mr. Kellogg invented his cereal with the thought that if boys ate it, it contained enough vitamins and minerals and whatnot that would keep them from masturbating and getting all kinds of diseases. But all that was a case of overkill. We know better now. No, there are no physical or mental ills connected with masturbation, so you can forget about that. And morally? Well, the church doen't concentrate on the biology as much any more and sees masturbation as a temporary event in the context of a boy's larger development as a sexual being on his way to maturity. That is to say, the church is understanding. It knows the boy's under pressure and confusion at this time and so does not condemn the boy or say that masturbation's a sin. This is no excuse to do it casually, only the insight that it's not as bad as it seems. It's not as bad as they say.[1]

Not as Good
2) It's not as good as they say. Masturbation is not as good as they say. You have to be careful of people or books that say,

"Hey, masturbation is normal. Everybody does it. It's natural, so go ahead, do it whenever and however and as often as you want. It's a great feeling." Yes, it is a great feeling, but it really isn't as good as all that. It has its dangers. Not to the body, as we saw, but to the spirit, to good development. A couple of reasons. We're going to see later the difference between a symptom and a disease (which I suspect you already know). A symptom is a clue, an outward sign that something invisible (the disease) is there. So, the doctor checks all the signs, looks at your teeth, eyes, skin, ears and says, "Ah ha, you have bronchitis." The bronchitis is inside you, in your chest or lungs where he can't see it; it's caused by germs he can't see either. The doctor can see the *signs* of the disease but will waste no time working on those clues or signs, attacking rather the disease itself with antibiotics. Of course, when the disease is gone, so too will the signs that pointed to it in the first place.

Sometimes masturbation can be such a sign or symptom. Take an imaginary Joe. Joe's not too popular. He's a loner. He's not too sharp in school, can't play sports, and, let's really lay it on, he looks like Alfred E. Newman and has bad breath! Joe has lots of problems. Maybe inside himself, maybe at home. Now he could compensate for his defects by doing something well, but he doesn't. So Joe seems a prime target for masturbation. He'll probably masturbate several times a week, not because he consciously wants to (he will likely feel ashamed each time) but because masturbation represents a temporary forgetfulness of his problems, a release from the tensions of a poor self-image. But the not-so-good thing is that masturbation, used in this way, causes Joe to withdraw into a dream world and it becomes a symptom of his "disease" of not dealing well with himself, life, and the world in general. In other words, Joe is turning in on himself too much and that's not the best way to grow. The thrust of sex should be outward, to build good relationships. Masturbation may tend to turn a guy too much back on himself. And that's not good. And masturbation tends to be habit forming, and who wants a habit of self-centeredness? So it should be dealt with.

A Conversation

This conversation may help. Here's a scene of a young husband. Chris, who has taken his young teenage nephew, Andy, fishing. They're talking about life in general and about Chris and Sue's (his wife) forthcoming baby. Then in sudden change of conversation, Andy says:

"Chris?"

"Hm."

"What do you think about masturbation? Do you reckon it's wrong to masturbate?"

"Lots of boys do it. But if you're asking me if it's wrong, something or someone must have suggested to you it is wrong."

"Well, people don't exactly shout about it, so there must be some reason for keeping it quiet, as if it's something you're not supposed to do."

"That's not a bad way of looking at it because it's usually only a passing phase; eventually you will come to the stage in your life when proper sexual intercourse will take its place. It's a kind of 'comfort' thing. Little boys sometimes rub their penis in their sleep, or to get to sleep, because it is a pleasant sensation and makes them feel relaxed and comfortable. When they get older they sometimes do this for the pleasure of it, to reduce tension. It is a nice sensation or feeling to rub your penis up and down with your hand. The orgasm is the same kind of pleasant physical feeling you get in intercourse. I say intercourse because I can't call it making love. That has a special feel of its own. Making love is the physical pleasure plus the happiness of giving yourself to someone you love and receiving their love in return. That kind of loving is for two people and its direction is always away from you toward someone else."

"When you masturbate it's like turning the feeling round so that it faces you. It doesn't go out anywhere; it just turns back into you, so that in the end it becomes yourself loving yourself. That is why boys have this mixed-up feeling that it is partly enjoyable and partly bad or wrong."

"We are brought up to believe that we should be unself-ish and think of others and so anything that is completely self-centered and only for your own pleasures leaves us with a slightly guilty feeling and we don't want people to know."

"So you are saying that it is wrong?" [asks Andy].

"I'm explaining why it 'feels' wrong. You shouldn't worry about it because the desire to do this will probably pass as you grow older and manage your sexual feelings better. I used to have all those worries just like you but now I'm married. I don't even think any more about it."

"If a boy decided this was the great way for getting pleasure and settled for it as his way of expressing sexual feelings—that would be wrong. But as long as he is aware that this is not the true or proper way of gaining sexual satisfaction, then eventually he will get himself sorted out and he won't need to masturbate."[2]

That about sums it up. Masturbation has its dangers—the dangers of retarding one's development and movement toward others—and so it's not as good as they say.

What to Do About It
Here's some advice, our third point, that may be helpful in passing through any phase of masturbation.

1) Keep a balance. Masturbation is not as bad as they say. Other boys (and girls) do it. It is not uncommon. It does release tension. Still, pay attention to the other side, that little shame or guilt you feel is a sign that you know you should someday work through and pass it, that masturbation's tendency to turn you inward is not a good thing.

2) If you ever masturbate excessively, remember what we said: We may have here a symptom and maybe you need to talk over any problems you have with a trusted friend or adult. Something's not being dealt with in your life. Take a look at it.

3) Don't overtease yourself. That means, don't overstimulate yourself so that you can't help masturbating. I know that pictures of girls half dressed or undressed are exciting. Yes, the desire to look at them is exciting. Yes, the desire to masturbate with fantasies caused by these pictures is exciting. But it's all too much pressure. Try to keep away from the dirty pictures, and girlie magazines, and lurid rock videos (which, as we'll see later on distorts real people). If you stimulate yourself, you're asking for trouble.

4) *Practice charity.* I know that sounds strange, but what I'm saying is, be kind to others, reach out to others. In other words, practice your powers of love, of overcoming selfishness, of reaching out to others, of learning to relate. All this helps in any efforts to come to terms with masturbation.

5) *Have a sense of humor.* Enjoy being a boy and enjoy being a sexual boy. Realize you don't become a caring and sensitive man overnight. Don't take yourself or your failures too seriously, for time is on your side. Masturbation is a stage. It will pass.

6) *Pray.* Pray not "against" masturbation if you're troubled with it, but "for" the ways to become more loving and mature. Pray for the other kids in your class, especially the one no one likes or who is not very popular. And in the praying, know that Jesus loves you.

QUESTIONS FOR REFLECTION AND DISCUSSION
1. Masturbation is not bad. It is not good. Explain.
2. Masturbation's a stage; it is habit forming. How should you manage it? What should your attitude be?
3. Why is masturbation described as "yourself loving yourself"?
4. How might the habit of masturbation retard one's development?

"I enjoy being a girl!"

Linda Loo, *Flower Drum Song*

6
THE FEMALE VOCATION

If the design of a boy is marvelous, it may be even more so for the girl. Let's see why and follow the progress of her development from girl to woman. She too has her "alarm clock" system and when her pituitary glands send down the signal to her sex glands she begins to leave behind her little girl's body and starts to assume the body of a mature woman. Adolescence begins her process of tooling for her physically mature body. Moreover, since she has so much more to do in procreating, she has to start earlier to grow than the boy (usually two or three years earlier), but she stops two or three years earlier too; say, she might start developing around the fourth or fifth grade and stop at 18 years old and the boy might start in the sixth or seventh grade and stop at 21. Also, her sex organs, unlike the boy's, are inside her body.

All that can be seen on the outside of her body is a double soft padded mound between her legs (where her pubic hair will grow) called the *vulva*. Where this double mount or vulva meets there is an entrance to an opening like a pair of lips called the *labia* (the Latin word for lips, as a matter of fact). Inside these lips are two openings: one small opening from which she urinates and the other, a larger one, the *vagina*, or birth canal. This is a narrow tube about three or four inches long made of elastic muscle tissue that can easily stretch. At the upper end of the vagina is the *uterus*, or womb, which looks like an upside down pear. On either side of the uterus, connected by a long tube (the fallopian tubes) are the *ovaries*, or egg-producing glands. They have the same function as the male's testicles that produce the sperm.

When the girl's alarm clock goes off, she too begins to grow. Hair begins to grow more or less in the same place as it does for boys: on her arms, and legs, under her arms, between her legs and sometimes even on her face, though not nearly so much as on a man. In some cultures, you should know, body hair is much thought of on a female and is considered attractive, but in our culture it is considered unattractive on the girl but attractive on the boy! So, considering the pressures that come from society, many girls feel little choice about removing hair on the legs, face, and underarms by shaving, creams, or plucking. If you think that's strange, you should remember that back in the Roaring Twenties, women who wanted to reject the ways and values of their mothers cut their head hair short like boys and boys in the 1960s and 1970s who wanted to reject their father's ways and values let their hair grow long! And even into the 1980s you often couldn't play in a rock band unless you had long hair, but in the 1940s you couldn't play in a band unless you had short hair. (It's good to notice here that much of what we think is "manly" or "womanly" or "attractive" or "weird" or "in" or "out" depends on where and when you live.)

On Her Way to Becoming

Under pressure from her chemical hormones (called estrogen and progesterone) the girl starts to grow taller (sooner than boys her age), although growth does not last as long, which is why she eventually is smaller than the male. Her oil glands become active, and she, too, has trouble with acne, pimples, blemishes, and body odor. Her hip area becomes wider to make her body capable of carrying a baby and giving birth to it through the vagina, and her chest, which was as flat as a boy's, develops breasts.

I mentioned in the last chapter that boys, cruelly and un-wisely, worry about the size of their penis only because some not-too-bright person says they ought to. Well, it's even harder on the girls. They're made to worry about their breast size as if that has anything to do with its purpose, which it definitely does not. Our society is preoccupied with breasts and the advertising industry, television, and movies try to give the impression that girls with large breasts are more feminine and attractive to men and better able to have children than small-breasted girls. This is in the same category as the moon being made out of green cheese. Quite simply, the breasts are designed to produce the baby's milk when she gives birth, and breast size has nothing to do with the amount of milk there is. Anyway, at this stage, girls may begin to wear bras for the same reason a boy may wear a jock strap: They don't want their breasts to jump around so much when they dance or play sports or the like, since that can be uncomfortable.

The most important change of all is that now her ovaries (Latin for "egg containers") now produce the egg. Actually, eggs were always present but were inactive. Now they are activated. Of the tens of thousands of eggs in each one of the two ovaries, only about four or five hundred of them will ripen in a woman's lifetime. Like our testicles, the girl's ovaries contain all of her heredity, her genes, and chromosomes. This is her power of procreation, her contribution to the making of new life. We just mentioned that only four or five hundred eggs will ripen in her lifetime. That means that on a monthly basis, for much of her life, only one ripe or mature egg will be produced, and travel, and cause incredible changes. Let's look at this fascinating and complicated process.

Ovulation and Menstruation

When the girl starts to develop sexually, once a month one ovary on one side of her uterus or womb will produce a ripe egg. This egg (or *ovum*) falls into a tube (the fallopian) and travels up and around it, heading for the uterus. As this journey is taking place, her uterus, which is made up of spongy cells, is getting ready to receive the egg. It is getting ready by sponging up blood and other liquids to nourish the egg if it becomes ferti-

lized for a new life by the male seed (this is called fertilization, or conception). But what happens if the egg is not fertilized? Then there is no need either for the egg or that stored up
blood in the wall of the uterus and so both simply wash away
through the vagina. This is called menstruation, and the whole
process takes about a month. Ten days or two weeks later, the
ovary on the other side takes its turn and produces a ripened egg
and drops it into the tube and the wall of the uterus, now recov-
ered from flushing out the last blood-filled lining, starts all
over again to refill. This cycle is repeated month after month
with each ovary alternating in producing an egg and each
month, if the egg is not fertilized, the uterus emptying out.

This whole cycle has the technical names of *ovulation* and
menstruation. The word "ovulation," as you know, means egg-
producing, and the word "menstruation" is from the Latin for
month; this means the cycle we described happens monthly—
every 28 days more or less (although at the beginning this may
widely vary for a girl till it settles down). Therefore, frequently those days of the blood emptying-out time is called a
"monthly period." It lasts perhaps for four or five days and it's
a bleeding but not like getting a cut. To respond to this blood
flow, a girl begins to wear a sanitary pad or napkin (you see
them all the time advertised on television) to absorb blood.
These napkin pads are made up of absorbent material and are
worn over the opening of the vagina and are held in place by a
special belt or an adhesive that sticks to the underpants. Or a
girl may used a rolled up pad called a tampon which she can
insert into the vagina. Both help catch the blood and keep her
clothes from being soiled.

For some girls, there is pain and discomfort and cramps before or during the first days of each period. For others, there
also may be headaches, dizziness, or fatigue. Her moods may
change as she becomes tense before her period as her hormones
decrease, and charged up and energized after her period as the
hormones return to full strength. This is why some women, perhaps your sister (or your mother) or someone in school you've
been kidding around with or teasing, may not respond as she

usually does and appear somewhat different. She may be having her monthly period and not feeling well. In time she'll be back giving you a Karate punch, being her own fun self. A girl's monthly period is a fantastic sign that her life is constantly being recharged and renewed and that she is tied into a privilege that males shall never know, the possibility of carrying new life within them.

There's another episode that happens with women that we ought to be aware of. A man will normally produce seed or sperm till the day he dies but a woman, usually around 45 or 50, will *stop* having her cycle. She will no longer produce eggs and have her uterus fill up or have her monthly periods. She can no longer have children. This is what is meant by "a change of life" or menopause. Some women sail through this transition well, but others have a difficult time. There are a lot of chemical changes, for one thing, that upsets her system. For another, she can no longer have children and this may sadden her. Not that she wants them now, but it's just the thought, especially if her children are not going to have babies and give her grandchildren. For another, it signals that a woman is getting older.

In other societies this would be a happy event for she would then be held in honor and blessed for her experience of life and wisdom. For instance, in Old Russia (and many other places) the elderly would take long journeys or pilgrimages throughout the land and people would welcome them into their homes where they, the elderly, would tell wonderful tales and share much wisdom. And people felt blessed for having them. But, unfortunately, in America, the elderly are not really honored as they should be because the emphasis is on youth, on being young (even if, in fact, in America, the population is getting older so that by the year 2030, according to the Census Bureau, one-fifth of all Americans will be over the age of 65!). We tend to get rid of our elderly by segregation in senior citizens villages where they are out of the mainstream.

So all this puts pressure on men and women, especially the women. The change of life quite clearly tells them that no matter how much they color their hair or put on makeup, as they may have done in earlier years, they are getting older and this—again, in our culture—may depress some of them for a time, maybe for months or even for years. In time, however, most women learn what we hope most men learn (men also have life changes but not as outwardly physical as those of women): The mature years are but a stage of continuous growth of mind and heart for all pilgrims moving to the fullness of God's love.

QUESTIONS FOR REFLECTION AND DISCUSSION

1. Girls and women are more in tune than boys with the rhythms of nature, the seasons, relationships. Why?

2. How do we as a country treat the elderly? How about in your family?

3. Discuss society's preoccupation with breasts. What good or harm does it do?

4. What do you think is especially important for boys to understand concerning a girl's physical development? Emotional development?

"Haven't you read," Jesus replied to those ques-
tioning him about divorce, "that at the begin-
ning the Creator made them male and female
and said, 'For this reason a man will leave his fa-
ther and mother and be united to his wife, and
the two will become one flesh'?"

Matthew 19:4

7
COMMUNION

What happens when an egg is fertilized? Fertilization usually happens as a result of sexual intercourse. Sexual intercourse is difficult to talk about because it involves the deepest emotions known to people, the emotions of intimacy and love. At your age—any adolescent's age—you very likely haven't grown into any kind of deep love yet. No one really should expect this of you now. Love has to be learned and it has to grow and be refined with experience. Your understandable lack of experience makes it hard to get across the act and full meaning of sexual intercourse. But I will at least try on the basis of what you do know.

Let me begin by pointing out that a synonym for sexual intercourse is "sexual love" or "sealed love." Good phrases. Sometimes people also use the more common phrase of "making love." This one I distrust because most people mean "having sex" and that may have nothing to do with love at all. If they're going to use the phrase, I'd rather they would tell the whole truth and say "making love grow." Imagine how that would sound: "That night we were making love *grow*" catches

---

63

you up short and forces you to realize that love must in reality be there first, before sex—and afterward. Sex is something that comes *after* love and is the wonderful seal of love, and when it comes after love it makes love grow. Why? Because the whole purpose and direction of love is union, togetherness.

Let me show you what I mean. You have a buddy, your best friend. Every time we see him we see you, and vice versa. At school you're together, at recess, after school, on outings; maybe you're on the same team. You go to the movies and perhaps even on vacation together. And why not? If you really like someone, you like to be with him, close to him. That's a built-in instinct. If you have a little brother, you see him run and throw his arms around Mommy until he nearly chokes her or takes her breath away. ("Hugs are better than drugs," as the bumper stickers say.) You did it yourself and are probably too self-conscious to do it anymore now. But it's an honest and human instinct: to want to be together, one with the person you love. Maybe when you were an infant or one or two years old you had a toy, a horsie or Teddy Bear, that your mother gave you when she put you in the crib. And how you hugged that toy! Your mother had a tough job getting it away from you so she could clean it. Silly? Not at all. The old truth is there: If you love someone or something you want to be one with that person or thing, just as if you love apple pie or a baseball glove you'll do what you can until you have it.

The Drive to Union
We see this in Jesus' life. He wanted badly to be at one with us. So much so that he gave us the sacrament of togetherness, Holy Communion. Communion comes from joining two words in Latin: *cum* which means "with" and *unio* which means "union." So Jesus wanted to have "union-with" us and so dearly did he love us that he found a way we could "eat him up." You've heard women use that expression when admiring and cooing over a baby. "Oh," they exclaim, "he's so cute. He's so precious I could just eat him up!" And they may even lift the baby and make smacking noises with their mouths! It's a very graphic and powerful

expression of very graphic and powerful feelings. They're acting out in words and body language their natural urge to be as close as they can to someone they find so darling and lovable. "Eating a person up" is the closest thing you can come in creating togetherness.

But not quite. God invented an even closer expression and seal of love. As the Bible expressed it, a couple who truly already love each other and are willing to stick with each other forever could become "two in one flesh." Jesus repeated the Bible's words when he reminded us of the close union of two people who are in love, that they "are no longer two but one flesh." That's a pretty close union: two separate people who in one way will always remain separate, yet blend as one. And that's precisely what is expressed in sexual intercourse.

Let's backtrack a little. There came a time when a young man and young woman asked each other to do something extremely difficult and only their love for one another would enable them to do it. They asked each other to leave their own homes, to leave their own brothers and sisters, to leave their own parents, to leave their own ways of doing everything, coming and going as they pleased. They asked each other to leave all this and more and come and live together and start a new family unit. So they did because their love for each other was strong and they wanted to be together. They got married and now that they were together they wanted to—needed to, had a drive to—express that togetherness every bit as much as a child who throws his arms around his mother. They would partake of the holy communion called sexual intercourse. At night, with no interruptions to bother them, they would tell each other of their love, kiss, and lie down together. They would not only hug but their hugging and touching and kissing would arouse them. Her vagina would become moist and his penis would harden and then, in the moment of greatest warmth, his erect penis would be inserted into her vagina (moist to make it easier to slide it in) and then and there, in that "two-in-one flesh" embrace, they would be truly one and love would be satisfied. Just the way God intended it and is pleased with it. The husband and wife were now doing in great depth and beauty what they did on a less important level from the time they hugged their teddy bears to the time they put their arm around a friend.

The Bonding of Sex

This sexual intercourse is intimacy because it unites two people, and not just for now but forever. This sexual intercourse is responsible because it's the seal of their agreed on promise to love each other even when they argue, are sick, or poor. This sexual intercourse is blessed because it fulfills God's plan. It is not making love. It is making love grow. And, finally, this sexual intercourse can not only be spiritually life-giving but also physically life-giving since from this act can come a living child made in the image and likeness of God and of the parents. How would this happen?

It can happen because in sexual intercourse the husband has an orgasm (remember, this means his penis and pelvic muscles contract until he spurts out his semen. The wife has an orgasm too, wonderful feelings of warmth and closeness and pleasure.). He ejects millions of sperm into the vagina of his wife and now, with their tails swishing and propelling them along, they go in search of an egg. If there is no egg in the fallopian tube then the sperm will eventually just die out and no child will be conceived or born. But if there is an egg or ovum present, then eventually one of the sperm will penetrate it. Just one sperm can enter. The rest die off. It's a case of the first sperm to reach an egg wins. The egg may still be traveling along the tube but eventually, if fertilized by the sperm, it will lodge within the lining of the uterus. Of course, as you recall, the uterus lining has been filling up with blood and this gives the wife the first clue she is pregnant. She misses her monthly period. Of course, we might mention in passing that there are sometimes other reasons why she could miss her monthly period: upsetment, illness, and so on. That's why she will eventually consult her doctor. But normally, if the blood is staying in the uterus, that can mean only one thing: there's a fertilized egg there that needs the blood's nourishment. She is pregnant. She is going to have a baby.

The Gift of the Child

Then, right after fertilization, something marvelous happens to the tiny egg cell. It begins to split and multiply. It splits in two, then four, then eight, sixteen, thirty-two, and so on. Moreover the fertilized egg is programed to split into various types. Some cells turn into skin cells, some into tissue, some into bone, hair, etc. Meanwhile, during all this multiplication of the cells, the elastic uterus is stretching to accommodate them. As you know, it normally takes nine months for all the cells to be developed into a baby ready to be born.

Inside the mother's womb the baby is normally situated upside down, its head at the mouth of the womb. This makes it easier for the baby to slide out of the womb through the vagina. The baby is also encased in a sack of fluid that has the same purpose as the fluid in a door jam: it absorbs any shock. During the nine months, as the tiny person grows, he floats or swims in the fluid. Note also that the baby is not a part of the mother, like an arm or an appendix, but has its own complete independent life, even its own bloodstream (the baby does not share the mother's). But the baby is dependent on the mother because he or she gets food and oxygen through a tube (the umbilical cord) from the wall of the mother's womb directly into his or her body through a main blood vessel. Which is why it is important that the mother does not smoke or take drugs or alcohol or have a disease because the harm from these can be passed to the baby through that tube. So, there is the baby, snug as a bug in a rug. He is getting free food, free air, free warmth, and free transportation. But after nine months it's time to be born.

The mother goes to the hospital where the doctor can help her; he has examined her and knows the exact position of the baby. In fact, these days the doctors can even take a picture of the baby inside the womb and show the baby on a monitor screen so that everyone can see it moving, sucking its thumb, turning over, and the rest. When birth nears, the upper muscles of the womb begin to contract and start to force the baby out through the vagina, or birth canal. It's like squeezing a balloon at the back end forcing the air out of the opening. These contractions of the womb are called labor pains. Gradually, the vagina stretches wide, the baby passes through and is born. And there is joy. The umbilical cord is cut (like cutting a piece of hair: it doesn't hurt) and the little remaining cord on the baby's midsection will eventually form into a kind of scab and fall off. What is left is the scar or "belly button," or what the doctors call a navel. All the other organs inside the mother's body that were pushed aside to make room for the baby growing large in her womb fall back into place and in a short time mother is herself again.

And so is father. For he has been anxious and nervous. These days, fortunately, more and more fathers are with the mother when the baby is born. Some families even have the children in to watch. This really bonds a family together. I hope some day, when you are married and if you become a father, you are there with your wife, giving your love and support, for both of you had a hand in procreating new life.

Breasts: Where the Tenderness Begins

Meanwhile, while the mother was carrying the child in her womb, her breasts were getting larger and filling up with a special formula baby milk. When the baby is born, the mother feeds him or her at her breasts as the baby sucks the milk, the best baby food in the world. We've already noted that our society is kind of crazy about a woman's breasts, promoting the old lie that bigger is better or more feminine. No, size is unimportant. The smallest breasts can feed the child well. But there's more to the mother's breasts than that. Doctors and psychologists say that a mother must hold the baby close to her breasts to cuddle and let the child know that he or she is wanted and loved. They say that if the baby is not wanted and loved, then she may die or grow up with severe mental and emotional problems. Mother's acceptance and love are even more important than her milk. Even small children lay their heads on mother's breasts and tell their joys and sorrows and receive warmth and assurance. That's what breasts are about.

It's too bad that unlike most other societies in the world we in the United States do not witness mothers publicly and openly nursing their babies. It's a very beautiful and common sight elsewhere. When you don't see this, then of course you're left to all of the silly nonsense about a woman's breasts that afflict our society. And, saddest of all, is when the girls themselves get caught in this nonsense and try to be "sexy" by showing part of their breasts (better to show all), or take injections to make them larger, or cry if they're "too small." This is only giving in to male chauvinism and fantasy and making the male-female relationship always a matter of body and shape and not of spirit and love.

Anyway, it really takes three to create a baby. The father who gives the seed, the mother who gives the egg, and God who shares his life-giving Spirit. Actually, none of this should be strange to Christian boys. You've been hearing about such things all of your lives without knowing it. Every Christmas you hear St. Luke's Gospel, which has a lot to do with sex.

Our Joyful Tradition

Now in the sixth month the angel Gabriel was sent from God to a town of Galilee called Nazareth, to a virgin engaged to a man named Joseph...and when the angel had come to her he said, "Hail, full of grace, the Lord is with you... .Do not be afraid, Mary, for you have found favor with God. Behold, you shall conceive in your womb and shall bring forth a son and you shall call his name Jesus..." But Mary said to the angel, "How can this happen since I do not know man?" And the angel answered and said to her, "The Holy Spirit shall come upon you and the power of the Most High shall overshadow you and therefore the Holy One to be born shall be called Son of God...." Mary said, "Behold the servant of the Lord; let it be done to me according to your word." (Luke 1:26-38)

Notice several things. First of all, the angel used sex terms like "conceive" and "womb." Mary was not shocked. She understood perfectly well God's plan for children (and had no television to make her snigger). Therefore she didn't get upset and grab a broom and start chasing the angel around the room crying, "Get out of here, you dirty thing! Mom!" No, she understood sex, so well in fact, that her first recorded words are a sex question: "How can this happen since I do not know man?" The tricky word here is "know." It doesn't mean knowledge in the original language, but rather, sexual intercourse. (As in, "Adam knew his wife, Eve, and she bore a son.") Mary is saying in so many words, "Yes, you are telling me that I'm going to have a baby, but I'm not married and I have not received any sperm to make my egg grow." And the angel is saying, "Well, that's a good observation but, you see, in your case God is going to perform a miracle and have your egg grow without a sperm. The Holy Spirit will come upon you." And Catholics repeat all this sex talk every time they pray the popular prayer, the "Hail Mary," because in that prayer we pray "and blessed is the fruit of thy womb, Jesus." Jesus is the fruit or result of Mary's womb as we are of our mother's. Once more, sex comes to us as holy, a message from heaven through the role of one of our favorite saints, Mary. It takes a lot of work to make sex sound evil or bad or dirty or a mere plaything, but people have managed to do this. But you're not a lot of people. You stand in a tradition of the holiness of sex, of relationship, of love.

QUESTIONS FOR REFLECTION AND DISCUSSION
1. Love demands union. Discuss.
2. Sexual intercourse has a lot of "hard" slang synonyms: knock up, screw, fuck, etc. Why or how have these "hard" words come into use for something God-given and love-unifying?
3. In most countries mothers openly and publicly nurse their infants at the breast. Why not in North America?
4. Compare these two descriptions of sexual intercourse: "making love" and "making love grow." Comment on each and paraphrase each.
5. How is sexual intercourse a "seal"?

8
TIME OUT 1

Pretend that we've been in a classroom situation and the chapters so far in this book represent a course you're taking in sexuality and sexual behavior. Say I'm the teacher, a priest in your school or CCD class, and today—as we're going to do a few times— we're going to have a short, free-for-all-discussion and, just to break things up, we're going to dip into our Question Box and try to field what's there. OK? The only condition is that you have to put up with my limericks. Do I hear groans again? OK, for being so smart you get to hear this one:

> An accident really uncanny
> Befell a respectable granny:
> She sat down on a chair
> While her false teeth were there
> And bit herself right in the fanny.

Pretty bad, huh? OK, any questions? Joey? "You talk about all those changes during puberty. I know when I was starting to go through them I felt like I did not want to go through all that. I liked the way I was. You know, who wants to grow up and get big and hairy and pimply?" Well, the first thing, Joey, understand that puberty isn't a disease. It's a perfectly normal and God-given way that we move from childhood to adulthood. I know at times it's a mess. It's awkward stumbling over big feet or having your voice crack and getting pimples or acne. But look on the other side. You're on your way to becoming a man. You won't have to wear braces much longer, you'll get to stay out later, more privileges, soon you'll be able to drive, and go to college, and all the rest. So puberty's got a lot going for it too. I like to see it like it happened to Jesus. There's a place in the epistle to the Hebrews where it says:

When Christ came into the world he said, "Sacrifice and offering you did not desire, but a body you prepared for me. With burnt offerings and sin offerings you were not pleased. Then I said, "Here I am—it is written about me in the scroll—I have come to do your will, O God." (10:5-7).

See what Jesus says? God gave him a body so he could do God's will. "Here I am," he shouts. So with you. After puberty, that should be your cry, "Here I am, Lord! Here I am with the body you prepared for me. How can I love and serve through it?" Mike?

Mike: "You say some boys start earlier or later than others because their 'alarm clock' goes off at a different time... " Here I interrupt: Yes, the pituitary gland, and when it goes off depends on your background, your family heredity, and so on. "Yes," continues Mike, "but how late can a late starter be? I mean, how old?" Well, most boys start to develop between 12 and 14, so I would say that if a boy hasn't started to develop by 15 he should see a doctor. And this does not mean he has a medical problem. No, not at all. It is just a precaution that he *may* have and it's good to check it out...Kevin?

Kevin's got a sly look, so I know he's up to something. "You know, you were taking about erections. I nearly split when you told of that poor guy in the gym class. But I get them sometimes when I'm out jogging. That's how come I always wear a pair of gym shorts over my sweat pants. You get a hard-on and it sticks out like a tent pole in those baggy sweats!" This breaks up the class and Ray yells out, "Yeah, I remember last summer I was on the beach in my nylon bathing suit and I saw this fantastic girl wearing a bikini. In a second I got so hard I had to run into the ocean so no one would see me!" More howling.

OK, OK, quiet down. We don't want to start a "Can you top this?" marathon...Bob? "Sometimes I get itchy down there. You know. Is that what they call 'jock itch'?" Yes, sounds like it.

Jock itch or I've heard "jock rot" too. Anyway, it's a fungus infection usually caused by wearing your clothes too tight so that
air doesn't circulate freely. Then your sex organs become red,
sore and itchy. Wear looser clothing, keep your genitals clean,
and then rub some cornstarch on them. If that doesn't do it, see a
doctor and he'll give you some medication. That will clear it up
quickly...Pedro? "What would happen if a boy had only one
testicle?" What happens in a rare case like this is that the
other testicle takes over and still produces enough sperm.

Any more questions? No? So let's look at the question box.
Here's one: "If a boy masturbates a lot, can he run out of sperm?"
The answer is no. Remember, the testicles are constantly making millions of new sperm every day and no way will you ever
run out. While we're on the subject, some boys ask if masturbating too much will hurt your penis or body. The answer is also no.
You may make your penis sore from rubbing it too much, but
there's no way you'll hurt it or your body or your health.

Here's another one also on the subject of masturbation: "Can
masturbation affect the way you play sports?" No, in general it
doesn't affect your athletic ability. Let's see, this one asks
something along the same line: "If a boy masturbates a lot, will
it affect him when he's older?" I presume this question means
will it affect his sex life later on and the answer is a simple no.
Here's a question on a different subject: "Can a woman have intercourse when she's having her monthly period?" Yes a woman
can have sex while she's menstruating and no harm will come to
her or her husband. She can do anything at this time she could
do at any other time of her life.

This one asks "Is sex painful for a woman, you know, having
something pushed inside of her?" Well, the word "push" sounds
harsh, but the answer is no. Even though the penis gets thicker
and larger when erect, as we've seen, a woman's vagina is very
stretchy (remember it has to stretch to let the baby through)
and it can accommodate any size penis. Besides, the penis produces a certain amount of lubricating fluid and so does her vagina and that makes the insertion comfortable. Of course, if a
husband and wife try to have intercourse before those lubricat-

ing fluids are there, it could be uncomfortable.

All right, another question. This one says, "I remember I was masturbating and I didn't want to get the stuff all over my pajamas so my mother would see it, so just as I was about to come I put my finger over the tip of my penis so nothing would come out. And nothing did. But then for the next few days I got a pain in my penis and this milky stuff has come out. What happened?" What happened is that since the sperm fluid was prevented from coming out it backed up and was forced either into the bladder or into the prostate gland. If it got into the prostrate gland, it can cause pain. Sometimes this will clear up by itself, but if not, you should see a doctor who will give you antibiotics to prevent infection. And, of course, you should learn that what you did is not such a good medical idea.

This question asks: "I heard someone use the expression 'blue balls.' What are they?" I'm not sure but I think it refers to what they call "aching balls," by which most guys mean his testicles or sex organs ache. This isn't any kind of disease or medical problem, it's simply a strain problem. It happens when a boy has an erection for a long time. Remember, when he's stiff like that, the scrotum is pushing the testicles close to the body and so putting pressure on them. Well, if that erection continues, as I said, for a long time without release, then the pressure on the testicles of the stiff penis eventually will produce "aching" or 'blue balls."

This card has "down there" written in big letters and underlined. Here's what it asks: "How come we grow hair down there?" Which shows that we haven't gotten used to the proper terms yet. Anyway, the questioner wants to know why we grow pubic hair, hair around the sexual organs. And, by the way, pubic hair and underarm hair are the two places both men and women share. People may get bald and have little hair on their bodies, but both sexes have hair in those two places (although women, as you know, shave off their underarm hair). I discovered the answer to this in a neat book called *Why Do Clocks Run Clockwise and Other Imponderables*. It says that the most likely explanation for pubic and underarm hair is that such hair traps the milky fluid secreted by special glands and when broken down by bacteria it forms an odor that *attracts* the opposite sex! How do you like that? That means that all those ads aimed at getting us to use deodorants and antiperspirants are covering up the very odors that can attract people! On the other hand, the people who study animal behavior also say that many animals, especially the primates like the monkeys and baboons, have very flashy visual features around their sexual organs in order to attract a mate. So that wide patch of pubic hair on us is for the very same reason, to attract people—except, again, we wear clothes. OK? I'm sure you all feel better now that you've learned that piece of trivia.

All right, one last question. Oh, this is a doozy. It asks, "How does it feel to have sex?" You're asking me? OK, laugh, but I'm going to get off the hook and let someone else answer that one, a lady who makes some good points:

It's hard to answer. Sex feels different to different people. But, most people agree it feels wonderful. Of course, how it feels depends a lot on the situation. If you're having sex with someone you love and the two of you both feel comfortable about what you're doing, then sex can bring pleasure, fun, passion, and joy. There's a rush of good feeling when you share a good sexual experience with someone you truly care about. Sex can be a very special way of being close to someone and discovering more about each other.

But sex can also bring sadness and emotional pain. If you don't truly care about each other or you don't feel it's right for you to be having sex, intercourse may not be a pleasant feeling at all.[2]

Enough already! We got to go. Time's up. You know what that means? Go ahead, groan away, but here's one you've got to hear:

> There was a young lady named Stella
> Fell in love with a bowlegged fella
> The venturesome chap
> Let her sit on his lap
> And she plummeted down to the cella.

How about this?

> There once was a maid in Siam
> Who said to her boyfriend, Kiam,
> "If you kiss me, of course
> You will have to use force,
> But thank goodness you're stronger than I am."

OK. See you soon....Oh, I forgot. One more thing that's serious, but nothing to be alarmed about. There is such a thing as cancer of the testicles. Actually, it makes up less than one percent of all cancers but, on the other hand, it is one of the most common concerns for males between the ages of 20 to 35. If caught early it is very curable. But the point in my telling you this is that you might start now getting into the habit of checking. Just once a month will be enough. The best time to examine your testicles is right after a hot bath or shower when the scrotum is soft and you can feel the testicles more easily. Also it's a good idea to get used to feeling the skin at the back of the scrotum so you won't confuse it with any sign of a problem later. What you do is roll each testicle gently between your fingers and thumb. What you're feeling for is any lump about the size of a pea and if there is even such a lump there it will most likely show up on the front or side of the testicle. As I said, there is nothing to get excited about, but it's a good idea to get in the habit of checking.

PART TWO
THE CHALLENGE

What I guess the adult world has failed to realize is that we are more sophisticated now, whether they like it or not. They expect us to view the world in black and white, and they give us as examples the extremes of abstinence and promiscuity. But they don't tell us that there's something in between.   16-year-old Boy

9
GOOD FEELING, FEELING GOOD

Have you ever stopped to think just how much sheer joy there is in having a human body, *in being a human body?* In fact, there are so many pleasures and joys to the human body that we take them for granted.[1] Such as:

Eating. If food tasted awful, we would not eat well or as much as we do. And, if no one ate, people would soon become weak, sick, and die. Maybe our parents would have to hold us down to force food into us. Even now, when food really does taste good, people put it off a bit. Your mother calls from the kitchen, "For the last time, turn off that television and come and eat!" Or the mad scientist down the cellar gets so wrapped up in her work that she forgets to eat. So the stakes are high. We need to eat to live and live healthily. So God provides. To get us to do what we ought to do anyway, God comes to us with a clever idea: making food taste good and that is usually a pretty good inducement for us. We usually don't eat because we check out those scientific mineral and vitamin labels; we tend to eat because food tastes good and therefore we enjoy it. We get the pleasure and we stay healthy and alive. Good bargain.

Or sleeping. Without sleep our body would not have time to repair itself and if that went on for a long time we would die. That's why one of the cruelest forms of torture is to keep the prisoner awake. His dead cells don't have the rest time they need to be replaced so they back up on him in his system, bringing death. So we need to sleep, and once more, to get us to do so, God makes sleep feel good. Think how good you feel when after a hard day playing soccer, you snuggle into bed on a cool night and fall off to sleep. And, of course, how you hate to leave such enjoyment by having to get up in the morning!

Or going to the bathroom. There's relief and pleasure in going to the bathroom, in eliminating the waste matter of your body. Your body takes in the food-fuel, burns it up, and leaves the "ashes," or waste. This waste is poison and if it were to remain in your body it would eventually kill you. So it must feel good to eliminate it so that you'll do it. A body pleasure with a purpose.

In fact, as you can see, all of the body pleasures are related to the body's health and to coaxing people into taking on the responsibility of keeping well. And, moreover, these pleasures carry with them a real positive drive to seek them. You not only enjoy the pleasure, you seek it out. It draws you like a magnet draws a metal pin.

Sex: God's Invitation

And so it is with sex. There's a joy and pleasure to it and such pleasure is among our most intense because the job it's meant to call us to is the hardest. So the "come on" has to be the strongest. To see what I mean, try this: Take a piece of paper and fold it in half. On the one side write down some of the freedoms you will have to surrender when you get married and on the other side some of the obligations you will have to take on. On the surrender side I can think of five items.

1) Money. Whom can you spend all your money on when you're single? Yourself! Numero Uno. You can buy a Jaguar, have the latest clothes, skip work, and all the rest. But when you're married, there's someone else to consider, perhaps even children. Even if your wife works outside the home, the rent has to be paid, the kids need clothes, there are doctor's bills. In a word, there is another or others to consider. You are being called to share and, all of us being somewhat selfish, we don't always like to do that.

2) *Going Out.* Before you're married you can go out every night if you want to—and without answering to anybody, coming and going as you please, staying over and not coming home, and all the rest. But once you're married, there is another or others to consider. It doesn't mean that you can't go out, but it does mean that you have a responsibility to others about where and when you go and how long you'll be gone. And you will have to, want to, go out with them very often to bond your love and family community.

3) *Playing the Field.* Before you're married you can play the field. You can be the town's greatest Romeo: a brunette one night, a redhead another, a blond another. You can be God's gift to women! But once you're married, it's one woman and one woman only "until death do you part" because you want it that way and because that's the way love is.

4) *Family Life.* Before marriage, there is really only yourself to worry about (more or less). No baby disturbing your sleep, no flushing toilets in the middle of the night, no kid throwing up at the table. But after marriage, there is much concern about taking care of others (not a burden if you love them, but nevertheless, a concern). Your daughter is ill and you're up with her half the night. Your wife calls you on the phone telling you that Johnny's smashed his finger in the door or the dog's been hit. You and your wife will feed the baby who spits food all over you; you'll wipe the baby's behind and help your children do homework.

5) *Companionship.* Here's the fifth, final, idea I want to share. It's somewhat difficult to grasp but I must mention it here because it is very important. We human beings are not really fulfilled if left alone. We're kind of "half" people by ourselves. Left alone, we can so easily turn selfish and even sick. Loneliness is a terrible thing and many psychologists say that loneliness is one of the biggest problems (and sicknesses) in

America. There's an ache in our hearts to be with someone, to be close, to care for another, to be cared for. We yearn for someone to understand us and to accept us as we are. We want someone to hug, to fulfill us; we want to fulfill them. We want desperately to share ourselves with another. Yet, we're scared. What if someone really gets to know me and then rejects me or makes fun of me? What if who I am is not accepted? What if I get hurt? So we stand on the brink. Should I entrust myself to someone? If I don't I'll die of loneliness (rejected babies often do). If I do, I may get hurt. I need something to give me a push.

Well, you get the point. There's a lot to surrender when you get married and a lot of responsibility to take on (as well as simply marvelous times and experiences) that some people, looking at both sides of our paper, might hesitate. And if everyone hesitated and if no one got married and wanted to care for others (even babies produced in a test tube need someone to care for them) that would soon end the human race and God certainly did not want that to happen especially when God told Adam and Eve to "increase and multiply and fill the earth." And so to urge people out of loneliness God decreed that "a man and woman shall leave their own father and mother and cling to one another so that they are no longer two people, but one."

We have more than a divine decree to get us moving. God did the same for sex as for eating and sleeping and all the rest. God made sex pleasurable and in fact, as we mentioned, extra pleasurable, because God wanted us to use it and take the risk of caring for others, of family life, and of love. God used the drive and force of sexual pleasure to push us over the brink of lonely hesitation and to take the risk of sharing ourselves with another. In other words, the pleasure and the drive of sex is a strong, healthy force *leading us out of ourselves toward another person.* This is why sex is good and enjoyable and so strong. It has a purpose. It is a force pulling us beyond ourselves.

Sex Is for Others
And yet, after I've said that, immediately I must make the sad statement, evident all around you at times, that people can

frustrate this whole plan of God. For example, they can become so attached to the eating itself that they direct it to the pleasure alone without the responsibility of good health. They steal the joy and harm the body by overeating or overdrinking. They can so seek the pleasure of sleep that they do not renew their bodies but make them soft and flabby. And they can so seek the intense pleasure of sex that they enjoy it for its own sake, for themselves, and *never connect in love with another person.* That's sad and hurtful.

The television production "The Death of a Porn Queen" (we'll talk about pornography later) is about a sweet sixteen-year-old girl from the Midwest who gets caught up in having men use her to get sexual pleasure for themselves, without ever caring for her, reaching out to her, bonding with her in love. She was only a "thing," and she was enticed to make movies showing men having sexual intercourse with her. She became somewhat famous, but she was so hurt that she was being used, that the pleasures of sex were deliberately one-way and cut off from all personal relationships, that she sensed she was no longer a real person but was being turned into a thing. She turned to drugs. And when that didn't help, she killed herself. Sixteen. Dead of a sexual drive that men turned back on themselves.

Yes, sexual pleasure is strong and intense (as you may be discovering). It is meant for intense bonding, for caring, for support, for affirmation, for love, for moving beyond yourself to another. You see this most of all, of course, when a child is conceived and welcomed. That's really proof that sex is for the sake of another, that it went forth from you to new life and new responsibility. Anyway, these are the words therefore that must always be present to the Christian boy when sex is discussed: a joyful force toward another, bonding, and responsibility.

QUESTIONS FOR REFLECTION AND DISCUSSION

1. "It's so pleasurable it's sinful!" Explain where expressions like that come from.

2. "Sex is God's invitation." To what? Explain.

3. What is the relationship between sex and companionship. Explain.

4. How would you explain the statement, "Sex is for others"?

5. How would you connect these to a discussion of sex: a joyful force toward another, bonding, responsibility?

A very popular videocassette in my area is "Risky Business," the 1983 film about a high school student's experiences with call girls. I have to let them see that real people don't live this way. Sex Education Teacher

10
SEX: DISCHARGE OR SYMBOL?

If the sex drive is a drive to closeness and intimacy, then there is only one question for the boy who wants to use this gift well: What shall I make of sex, a discharge or a symbol? Or, What do I want to do with sex? How can I use it as a sign of caring and not of selfishness? What do I want it to say about me?

These are not really new questions, just more urgent ones now that you're growing up. For the truth is that your or any boy's sexual feelings and emotions and drives did not just arise. You didn't just become a sexual being when you turned 12 or 13. Rather, as the famous sex doctors, Masters and Johnson, point out, with adolescence, reproductive and glandular sex emerge but also as a "further dimension of an already existing sexuality." What do they mean by this? They mean that a boy is a boy all over from the time he's born. Inside and out. "Sexuality" refers to his total state of being a human being in a male way. He is male in the way he thinks, acts, and feels (and she is female in the same way). There is as much "sex" in his fingernail as in his sexual organs. That is, a boy's "maleness," his sexuality, is himself all over and he expresses his sexuality every minute of every day.

Again, sexuality is the way people live as men and women.

Men and women bring different attitudes and insights and richness to the world that is shaped by their being men or women. We are sexual people all the time, not just when dealing with our sexual organs. Our sexuality is seen in the ways we are creative and life-giving as a man and woman, male and female persons. Mother Teresa of Calcutta is expressing her sexuality when she accepts and is moved by the poor people she rescues from the streets. The priest bringing the life-giving Word of God to others is working out his sexuality. Sexuality is not the same as using your sexual organs, not the same, as we say, as genital (sex organ) sex. It is the *complete you* all the time as a creative, relating male or female.

You see, the only thing that happens at adolescence—and it's a dramatic "only" to be sure—is that a boy's sexual drives add a new thrust of sexual emotion and power to his already existing state as a masculine sexual being. His new sexual urges, like all of his other feelings of anger, fear, hate, etc. affect him as a person and prepare the whole person for action. Let's put it this way: It's like driving a car for the first time. The driving is new and exciting, and the boy who's now driving has been around for 17 years but is now using his total abilities and emotions in the new thrust of driving. His old personality has found a new and exciting means of expression. In the same way, sex is a new and exciting way of expressing who and what you are and always have been.

Sexuality
But that brings us back to our question. A boy has this new drive to his sexuality, to his personality as a sexual male. Now, what shall he do with it? Shall he merely discharge his new sexual drives whenever he feels like it, like he might discharge his drive of anger by punching out his school friend whenever he feels like it? Or, shall he make of his sexual drive an expression of himself, of his personality, of the kind of person he wants to be? In short, shall he use it as a new source of power and relating? You have to come to terms with these questions now. You can't wait until you're in the midst of a sexual

situation, or horsing around with the guys. You have to make up your mind *now* as to what meaning you want sex to have in your life. What do you want it to say about you? In a word, do you want sex to be a discharge or a symbol?

Let's take a look at sex as a simple discharge. We take this first because a lot of people who write the television scripts or who put out the sexy magazines take this view. It's a short-term, "fun" view, but a long-term destructive one. Joey is getting real "horney" as they say (getting sexually aroused, getting an erection and feeling the tension of it). The pressure is there because he's making out with a girl, not necessarily his girl friend, but one of the girls he goes out with now and then. He touches her breasts and in general touches her until he reaches a climax and has an orgasm and the semen is released in his pants. It was exciting and fun while it lasted. Now that it's over, what did his sexual activity with this girl really say? Well, it said that Joey, like all other males in the world, is easily excitable in matters of sex. Yes, but what else? It also says that Joey had sexual tension and he released it and used this girl for this purpose. He would deny he's using her, but the fact is, let's say in this instance, there's no serious commitment to this girl who herself doesn't mind making out with Joey. They both think this is the expected thing to do, since the movies and television tell them so. Joey never even gave it a thought that he might discipline or delay his drive. His making out was only a way of discharging a feeling, and if he continues to do this he will make of sex just that: a discharge of tension, a way to have excitement—*but that's all*. It is not "saying" anything about Joey except perhaps that he is selfish. It has no meaning. It is not building an honest and deep relationship.

Let me remind you of something. Every time some of these psychologists take polls on how to get along and what are the most important aspects of good human relationships, this one fact always keeps coming up, namely, that of the ten most important aspects of a good adult relationship, sex is number nine. (You'd never think that from what you hear.) Love and caring are number one. Number two is a sense of humor. Number ten is sharing household tasks together. Well, you could figure that out. Sex alone, without meaning, without "saying" something about your commitments and honor and love and caring and sticking it out with another through thick and thin—sex becomes just a discharge of pent-up feelings. It is not a sign, a symbol of who and what you are and want to be. It is not a sign that you had a drive to make your beloved more loved and loving. And all this lack of real meaning began with our friend Joey who as a teenager used sex for self-fun because he wasn't ready to take responsibility for another.

The Primacy of Love

Sex isn't, or shouldn't be, just a discharge. You are hungry, you grab food; you are angry, you hit; you are fearful, you run; you are tempted, you steal; you are sexy, you have intercourse. No, if people are creatures whose lives and actions have deeper meaning, they will often discipline their natural urges so that they may say "something more" about themselves, the something that is truer and deeper.

Even if you are hungry, you may go without food for a higher cause, as Gandhi did when he fasted to free India from British rule or as Walesa did to protest Communist rule in Poland. They were saying there's more to life than food. (As Jesus, quoting the Bible, said, we do "not live by bread alone.") Even if you are angry, you may hold your temper and your fists as Jesus did in the Garden of Gethsemane. He was saying there's more to life than revenge. Even if you are fearful, you may stick around like Sydney Carlton in Charles Dickens's *A Tale of Two Cities*, who took his friend's place on the gallows. He was saying there's more to life than saving your own skin. Just what Jesus taught us when he said, "The one who loses his life for my sake will save it." And again, "No greater love is there than this, that one lay down his life for his friend." Even if you're tempted, you leave the ten dollars where it is, as Frodo did, who was tempted to keep the magic ring in *The Hobbit*, but gave it back. He is saying there is more to life than material things. Even if you feel a strong sexual urge, you distract yourself like Thomas Aquinas, who ran from a woman who was sent to have sex with him. He was saying there's more to life than genital sex. In fact, as we saw above, there are eight other things more important.

So, if you want a quick rule that Jesus gives us about how to act in every area of life, you might note that sex is not the first language or final proof of love; no, for Christians, the greatest proof of love is caring for others even to the point of self-sacrifice, just like those people we just mentioned.

A famous psychologist, Erik Erikson, wisely says that adolescents like you have two choices about sex. One is what I described above about Joey: just discharge it. The other choice, he says, is a "disciplined and devoted delay." That's a great phrase worth memorizing because the one truth we know is that today, while a teenage boy is biologically ready for sex-organ sex, he rarely is emotionally and spiritually ready for relationship-sex. I don't mean to imply that he can't be loving and caring. Of course he can, and beautifully so. It's just that at this stage in his life he can't love and care *to the fullest*, to a promised and honored future that a girl deserves and love demands. And so you must admit this to yourself in the boy-girl relationships, and so plan ahead how you are to keep free of genital sex and put the energy into practicing and exploring those valuable and lifelong skills of communication and self-sacrifice. And remember, too, the fact is that many young people do abide by the "disciplined and devoted delay" rule—the majority of them. Many, many young people do not have sex before marriage. They just don't talk about it because they wouldn't sound "cool."

Sex Turned Back on Itself
And those who do? Very few, so intent on self-pleasure or self-need, form lasting relationships. Dr. Sol Gordon, who's written many books on sex, reminds us of statistics that show that less than one percent of the boys ever marry the first girl they had intercourse with. How's that for "hit and run"? How's that for a discharge and not a symbol of one's self-givingness and faith-

fulness? The Rolling Stone Press's survey called *Sex and the American Teenager* shows that only 14 percent of teenagers' sexual relationships last more than a year and about the same percentage last only a week! And, of course, once they start relating only through sexual-organ sex, the same kids pick up the habit of having temporary sexual activity with other partners. By the time they do marry they have had so many sex partners that they're an easy mark for a divorce since they've had so much experience in breaking up—and so little experience in sharing themselves on all other levels. That's why I'm not surprised to read of a study conducted by Planned Parenthood in Chicago which surveyed a thousand young men and asked them if it was okay to lie to a girl and say they were in love with her in order to have sex. Seventy percent said yes! And that makes you wonder how they got that way and also about the girls who believe such a lie.

The answer is not hard to find. All the studies show that teenagers who use sex, drugs, and have antisocial behavior usually in fact *do all three* and reflect the very same pattern of fractured lives and homes and poor self-esteem. As one research team (the famous Search Institute that does a lot of study about teens) wrote, "All three factors [sexual intercourse, chemical use, and antisocial behavior] are tied to similar family and value patterns—young adolescents who are deeply involved in any of these three behaviors tend to place less emphasis on church and religion, to have lower achievement motivation, and to receive less nurturance and support from parents."[1] So, as we'll see so many times, your values and your self-esteem are far more critical in how you'll act about sex than any amount of hormones or sex urges in the world. Remember that.

That's why one professor of psychology who specializes in the problems of adolescents say that what's really behind the sex drive are three more basic drives.

1) The Drive for Acceptance. Young people are really concerned about being accepted. They want very much to belong. Sometimes in their confusion they will use their sexual behavior as a way and a means to belong, a way of finding acceptance with the group. The professor suggests that such young people need to find self-respect and self-esteem in ways that they can value themselves as people and not mere sexual items.

2) *The Drive for Intimacy.* Some adolescents may mistakenly equate sexual activity with emotional intimacy. They need to learn to expand their idea of intimacy, that it is something far more and far wider than genital sex (like sharing silence or a beautiful scene with your best friend or just sitting in the same room with your folks).

3) *The Drive for Pleasure.* Some adolescents he has dealt with say it's the pleasure they want in sex and he confronts them with their self-centeredness and tries to help them see that sex is a *gift* and like all gifts is to be used for the benefit of all, not hugged to oneself.[2] So, what do you think? Maybe in coming to terms with sex you have to look and see whether these three more basic drives are operating. Or, to put it another way, maybe you have to sit back and ask yourself if your sexual activity is really covering up other issues, other problems.

Consequences of Selfish Sex

And remember the consequences of acting out one's problems through sex. We'll talk about terrible sexual diseases like AIDS later on. Here we just mention the out-of-wedlock pregnancies. More than one million teenage girls get pregnant each year. About 400,000 of them have their babies killed through abortion. Of those who do give birth, most of them drop out of school. Their babies are much more apt to have physical and growing-up problems and, if they are female babies, raised as they were, they will much more likely repeat the pattern and have babies themselves out of marriage. The care of such teenage mothers costs the government (and you and I) hundreds of millions of dollars a year. And, of course, there's the greatest tragedy of all: the lost opportunities for these girls and their children.

The girls get pregnant. But what about the boys? What about a sense of responsibility for the children they brought into the world? Do they just go on to other girls? Tell more lies? Is their relationship just limited to their sexual organs? Will they ever learn to love? Well, some guys say, I'll settle down later and be responsible later. But Dr. Evelyn Duvall reminds such guys:

But wait, you say. "Sure I'll settle down when the time comes, but right now it's only natural that I get some release." You may just do that. But, remember that the overwhelming tendency is to continue doing what you have done before.

The chances are that you speak much as you have been doing through the years. You can tell a man from New England from a fellow from the deep South, as soon as you hear him talk. Why? Because each man tends to speak as he learned to talk when he was growing up. Is there any reason to believe that the same thing does not happen in sexual expression? If a fellow always has played fast and loose with girls, is he sure to drop all these habits once he gets married? Will he no longer be attracted to other women? If he is, will he not want to do as he always has before, and make a play for them? What assurance have you that the marriage ceremony will change the kind of thing you always have done?

The only thing you can be fairly sure about is that you will probably be very much the same person after you marry that you have been before. Getting married is a big step, but it cannot change human nature. You need not kid yourself when you marry, either you or your mate will all of a sudden be something neither of you has been before. You cannot hope to reform your partner or yourself. You both may become more mature. You may settle down, at least for a while. But you will always be the kind of personalities you brought to your marriage in the first place.[3]

Dr. Mary S. Calderone of the Sex Information and Education Council of the U.S., in a talk to Vassar freshmen said:

There is absolutely no possibility of having sexual relationship without irrevocably meshing a portion of your two non-physical selves. Sex is each time such a definitive experience that a part of each of you remains forever a part of the other. How many times and how casually you are willing to invest a portion of your total self and to

be the custodian of a like investment from the other person
without the sureness of knowing that these investments
are being made for keeps?

Quotes like that and the truly awful statistics—and remember
these "statistics" are real people who have been hurt by irresponsible sex—are the result of what was once called the "sexual revolution," when some people said that now that you have
birth control, you can have sex whenever, wherever, and with
whomever you want. This is fun and it's freedom! It would be fun
and freedom if you were talking about machines. But no matter
how much some people tried, they couldn't be machines and the
whole thing backfired:

> Our children proudly announce that they are growing up in
> the "sexual revolution" as though that implies an exciting
> breakthrough! Each year there are more than a million
> pregnancies and half a million unwanted births among
> teenagers. The Center for Disease Control estimates that
> ten to fifteen million Americans develop a sexually trans-
> mitted disease each year. (STDs are the most prevalent
> teenage disease, second only to the common cold.) There are
> an estimated two million abortions annually. And half of
> all married couples suffer from some sort of sexual problem.
> This so-called revolution is hardly a cause for celebration.[4]

That's right. So far there's been neither fun nor freedom in the
sexual revolution, certainly not for many divorced, the out-of-
marriage pregnant, the unwed fathers, the children with one
parent, the poverty and welfare, and the diseased and dying. In
a word, sex that is supposed to drive one toward honest and en-
during relationships has, when used wrongly, put a wedge between people and made them suffer in untold numbers. That's
one of the mysteries of sex. It's like a powerful and fascinating
waterfall. If you channel the rushing water into turbines, it can
light up hundreds of thousands of homes. If you don't channel it
(or it overflows its boundaries) it can run wild and drown whole
towns. Like the water, the creative use of sex is found within
limits.

So, when someone asks you, "How's your sex life?" you

should immediately know it's a dumb question if that person is referring only to the activity of your sexual organs. This is like asking: how many times did you score? How many girls did you fool around with? How "good" are you? and so on. If your questioner means that, I suppose you can answer with some list of statistics. But you know in your heart that that really is a dumb question. The real question about sex is not "How's your sex life?" The only question that matters is "How is your relationship life?" Or, more precisely, "How have the limits you placed on sex made your relationships full of light and life?"

Anyway, when you look around and see so much sex-love power gone astray, overflowing the limits, so to speak, and drowning people in broken and betrayed relationships, you wonder what reasons people would have for not waiting for the bonding of marriage. It's those reasons we want to look at next.

QUESTIONS FOR REFLECTION AND DISCUSSION

1. What's a symbol? What symbols are you using, wearing right now?

2. Do you see sex as a discharge or symbol? Explain.

3. In what sense do you express sexuality "every minute of the day"?

4. What is the meaning of "disciplined and devoted delay" concerning sexual activity?

5. What are the three more basic drives behind your sex drive?

6. A survey showed that 70 percent of boys lied to girls to get them to have sex. What do you think of that behavior?

When it comes to sex, my mother doesn't know what to say. She's really uptight about it; that's just the way she was brought up. But nowadays, if you're not sexually active, you're, like, you know, Nerd City.

15-year-old Boy

11
THE URGE TO MERGE

Am I oversexed? Boys ask that often because it seems that all they think about is sex. Girls who date wonder too. "Why is it a lot of guys I date want to neck and pet all the time?" Boys are curious about sex, they are drawn to girlie pictures and have a hard time keeping their hands off themselves or the girls. Why this craziness? Why is sex so hard to handle? Thinking himself a victim of the "urge scourge," a boy might complain, "Am I normal to have this drive all the time?" The answer is that the urge scourge is normal. The answer is also that the urge scourge has to be recognized, admitted, and dealt with, because, as we shall see, other people will exploit the urge and that's bad news. But, first, some answers.

Let's start off by saying that girls too are also highly sexed and once aroused and ready for sex they desire it every bit as much as boys do. But it takes a girl longer to get interested in and aroused by sex than a boy. There are biological reasons for this. First of all, the boy begins storing up those bodily hormones that keep pressuring him about sex. He is quick to notice an attractive girl or one wearing tight clothes because his hormones are more intense and his millions of active sperms are being produced every single day. Girls on the other hand are less quick to notice, or at least to react as physically to a good look-ing boy because their hormones are not in the same amount or in-tensity as the boy's.

Remember, they produce one ripe egg a month while the boy produces countless sperm all the time. Besides, the girls' psy-chology is different and is perhaps best summed up in a popular way by a 16-year-old girl who said, "Girls use their bodies to get love—boys use their bodies to feel power." So the girls will get aroused more by an emotional context of caring than merely the physical context of body display. Many girls and women re-port that, unless sexually aroused by necking or petting, they may go for weeks or months without thinking of sex. Most guys can't go beyond a day. (Try an hour?)

Second, as we have seen, boys' sexual organs are on the out-side and they are sensitive. Your clothes may rub your penis (es-pecially the sensitive tip) when you walk. You can easily press it against the mattress in bed or anything else for that matter. You hold it when you go to the bathroom. So the boy's external sexual organs, unlike the girls' internal ones, are within easy reach and easy to arouse.

Finally, there's a time gap between males and females. Males can reach the peak of their sex drive around 18 and then it tapers down a bit after that. For females the sex drive is less powerful in the teens but grows in intensity over the years, reaching its peak usually after 30. This means there's about a ten-year difference between boys and girls. And this is why the teenage girl may think she's out with a sex maniac. Or, on the other hand, why the guy is confused that all he's thinking about is sex and she seems so uninterested.

The Challenge of Being Different

This also poses a challenge for both. The girl has to understand that the guy is not a maniac but does have real pressures and, if she loves him, has to guide him to other wider areas of devel-oping their relationship. The boy has to understand that she is coming from a different place and wants sensitive, emotional approaches to the relationship, not a hot and heavy physical

one. I think they could work it out and reserve sexual intercourse for marriage if it weren't for the other pressures that
give more scourge to the urge, pressures that have led boys and
girls into premature sex.

For example, the simple fact that boys and girls sexually
mature earlier than ever before. In medieval times, boys, let's
say, would become sexually mature (reach puberty) at 14 or 15,
marry at 17 or 18, and die at 25 or 30. So there wasn't much time
to live with sexual pressure. But today that's different. Because of improved diet, vitamins and so forth, boys can sexually
mature at 11 or 12. Because you live in a very complex society
you need much more schooling and you're not ready to graduate
until you're 17 or 21 or 24, if you go on to graduate work. It will
take you a while to get enough money to marry which may be
around 24 or 26 or later. So that means you may have perhaps
15 or more years between sexual development and marriage.
Certainly this puts pressure on controlling the sexual urge, especially at the peak years.

The Cost of "Scoring"

Another example: conditioning. From the beginning boys are often unconsciously (sometimes consciously) conditioned to deny
their dependency needs because, the reasoning goes, to be dependent on someone else is to be weak. Even to ask for help is made
to seem like a sign of weakness. This is not true, of course, for
everyone needs someone else at one time or other. That's what
makes for friendships and family and growth. But somehow
the idea got around that that's all right for girls but not for
boys. So a kind of "code" comes in early and this code includes
four principles:

1) *No Sissy Stuff.* No effeminate behavior or behavior that
one might be taught to associate with girls, like hugging or being passive or liking poetry.

2) *Be a Big Wheel.* High status (owning a sportscar, making
megabucks, living in a home with more rooms than you can fill
or use) is the mark of "success." Anything less is failure (even
though you might be happier).

3) Be a Sturdy Oak. Be tough, confident, self-reliant. Everybody leans on you and you lean on nobody (which can be pretty lonely, especially when you need someone to hug you).

4) Give 'em Hell. Be aggressive, driving and, if necessary, violent.

So, you see, the male is brought up to pay little attention to or express his real feelings. Rather he is taught to function like a machine, designed for work, to be independent, in control, and, of course, know that he is superior to women. He pays a price in many ways for keeping down, or ignoring his real needs and feelings:

> The death rate for males is 200 percent higher in the early 20s than for females. From 30 on it is twice as high. Boys outnumber girls by nearly 50 percent in state and county mental hospital children's units. Men are four to five times more likely to die from bronchitis, emphysema, and asthma than women... Men also have much higher death rates from hypertension, from pneumonia and influenza, and from cancer. Men do not cope well with severe emotional problems either.[1]

I mention this because the training of the male gears him so much toward control on the one hand and, on the other hand, toward repressing his feelings of tenderness, concern, and sensitivity that he approaches a girl with attitudes of dominance and the need to "score" bodily, sexually. Our culture trains him not to take time for significant ways to relate to her on many other levels. He automatically moves his "machine," his body, into sexual gear so he can feel "manly" and be in control and "prove" himself. All this means that it's not only the natural hormone urge the boy has to deal with, but the scourge of a whole bunch of baggage he has inside his mind and heart from a male childhood that makes him relate to a girl machine-like, as Big Wheel, Sturdy Oak, Rambo. He has to prove the power of his body instead of the tenderness, concern, and caring of his heart. This leads to sexual activity long before he's ready to invest it with the full meaning of commitment. And the sexual activity in turn becomes so dominant that it takes the time away from developing relationships on a more basic and lasting basis and prevents him from seeing a girl (and wife to be) as a genuinely equal partner in the covenant of marriage.

For you must remember this: Far more basic than any of these biological or cultural reasons for feeling "oversexed"—in fact, in back of all of them—is God. That urge scourge, as we called it, is more properly called the "urge merge." God has a plan that man and woman should become "two in one flesh," that separate people should be joined in love. They should merge in the convenant we call marriage. So every time you feel horny, every time you feel the urge, remember that's an invitation to merge. It's a pressing reminder, a nudge from God for you to get about the business of learning to grow in love so that one day you'll be ready and worthy of the one you will marry. The urge to merge—it's all part of God's plan.

So you have to think about your real feelings, your needs, your dependency. You have to ask yourself, who's telling me that to be a man I can't cry or want to be held or be ministered to? Or sing or dance or look at the birds overhead? or that I have to be such a big shot and get ahead by dominating or "scoring" or stepping over people? Maybe your parents, the school, the culture. Certainly the media is. I think of one of the brands of scotch that advertises, "As you are fighting your way to the top, it helps to have a taste of what's up there." Fighting? And what good's the "top" if no one's there with you, if you can't say to someone, "I love you" or even "I'm sorry"? So the pressure to have sex and to be a "man" according to some stupid pattern that leaves you lonely and ties up your emotions and shortens your life is real. But if you know such pressures exist, you can at least challenge them and get a better glimpse of the man you would like to be.

QUESTIONS FOR REFLECTION AND DISCUSSION
1. You are swayed but not determined by your impulses. Discuss the meaning of this in concrete terms.
2. What roles are males and females pressured to play?
3. Why do males find it so hard to express their feelings?
4. Who is your hero? your role model? Why?
5. Why is the connection between self-esteem and sexual conduct so crucial?

As the years wear on, you stop compromising your principles.

> Football star Bubba Smith, refusing to do any more beer commericals affecting teens.

12
SELF-ESTEEM

Another critical pressure that leads boys and girls to sexual activity too soon and unwisely is, believe it or not, self-esteem. You'd be surprised how much this is at the bottom of so many problems. Self-esteem simply means, "How do you feel about yourself? Do you like yourself?" If boys or girls hate themselves, think they're unimportant, stupid, ugly, unloved, and so on, they are prime targets for acting out their self-hate. They'll steal, do drugs, show off, act like big shots—and have sex with themselves (excessive masturbation) and others. In other words, sex becomes a symptom. You recall the difference between a symptom and a disease. The disease is the invisible sickness itself, but the sympton is the visible clue and sign that it's there somewhere. So the doctor checks your skin or blood or whatever for clues as to the real sickness. She is playing detective. She knows, for instance, that yellow skin is a sign of liver infection. So she doesn't waste time treating the skin, but rather treats the liver. When the sickness (the liver) is cured, the symptom (yellow skin) will disappear.

Behavior Clues
So it is with much of our behavior. The outside acts are often hiding an inside hurt. Maybe the big bully is really insecure inside. Maybe the show-off has nobody at home who tells him

he's important. Maybe the girl who lets every guy paw at her body doesn't have a father who ever put his arm around her and told her she was special. Or a father around at all. That's why you can sense danger ahead in this letter from a girl to Judy Blume, "Dear Judy, I love your books! I can really relate to them. My mom has been divorced twice and she is only 29. I have a little brother. I'm interested in sex. I am ten." There is so much truth to this that nowadays more and more psychologists and social workers say that the key to preventing all that teenage pregnancy is not just to hand out condoms, but to deal with teenagers as people. Try to see what makes them tick. Help them with their home and school problems. Help them take a good look at themselves and learn to like what they see. Why all this? Because the Big Truth is that if you think well of yourself, if your self-esteem is high, you don't *need* to go in for behavior that is destructive.

That's why experts from all over the country, meeting in Washington, D.C. in March 1984, reported:

The key ingredient to success, conference participants overwhelmingly agreed, was the ability to weave the topic of adolescent sexuality into the broader context of teen age life, not separate it from education and job preparation or from the family, school and church...[Said one expert] "Everything we know about teen pregnancy tells us that young people who have little self-esteem, who cannot envision alternatives for themselves, are a risk for irresponsible sexual behavior. So it's not a question of knowing how to use a condom; it is about knowing that you can do something about your life."

I think of one guy I know who had been suspended from school and who refused to talk to me or anyone at all for that matter. But we gave him a camera and within months he was winning photography awards. Now he plans to get his high school equivalency degree and go on for visual arts. Most of all, he is no longer trying to prove he's macho by fooling around with sex. You see, as so often in the case of teenagers, sex is a symptom. His real disease was his poor self-image, so he tried to hide it

by proving he was a "man" by having sex. When the disease
(poor self-image) was cured, the symptom (irresponsible sexual
behavior) disappeared.

One very successful program in preventing teen pregnancy is in
South Carolina and it is interesting to look at the five points of
their successful program: (1) to improve decision-making skills;
(2) to improve interpersonal communication skills; (3) to en-
hance self-esteem; (4) to align personal values with those of the
family, church, and community; (5) to increase knowledge of human reproductive anatomy, physiology, and contraception. Notice that the first four, before you ever get to the body, concern
the mind and personality: how to resist pressure, how to really
communicate, how to learn to love and respect yourself, how to
have values. This is where it's really at, where the real problem is. That's the trouble that many of us have with just handing everyone condoms in school. Condoms don't address values.

Loving Yourself
But you can see why there are in fact so many teen pregnancies:
because there are so many who think so little of themselves or
so many to whom no one has given the message, "You are special." Think of the kids who are physically or sexually abused.
What do you think they'll do about sex when they grow up?
They likely will repeat what's happened to them.

Think of the kids of divorce, from broken homes.[1] They need
special concern about their self-image since every study shows
that kids of every age, even in their 20s and 30s, are badly affected by divorce. Although the parent they're living with is
often not only trying to hold down a job and give them care with
splendid heroism and sacrifice, the kids need this extra concern
because they are still more vulnerable than most to lower self-
esteem and to "acting out" their anxieties. And, of course, even
more so if they're not lucky enough to have such a devoted and
concerned parent but are bounced back and forth from one parent
to another with the invisible message that they're not wanted
by either. That will do a job on their self-esteem!

Think of all the latchkey kids who come home to an empty

house. Again, in so many cases, this can't be helped, and the kids make creative and responsible use of their time. They know that their parent or parents are doing their best. Both have to work just to keep the family together. Still, all that I'm saying is that, once more, special care and caring must be there for these kids so that the extended, adult-free house doesn't cause special anxiety and temptations. I may have even more of a concern about self-esteem for those latchkey kids whose both parents in fact don't have to work—and this seems to be a growing majority[2] —when such well-off parents hand them over to all-day baby sitters or day care centers or otherwise leave them alone for long periods out of convenience rather than necessity. What message do you think they're getting? What kind of self-image of unimportance is being formed?

Think of the kids you know who don't get hugged at home or cuddled or kissed, who are not listened to, appreciated, believed, and affirmed. Such kids grow up suffering from "skin-hunger." There are healthy and unhealthy ways to feed "skin-hunger" and sexual intercourse for a teenager is always the unhealthy way. But you can see why it may happen. For them, sex is not for sex's sake; it's a symptom and a substitute for the hugging and closeness they never got at home. Sometimes girls who have babies outside of marriage will say they wanted a baby so they could have someone to hug. Unfortunately, as they find out, the baby is not a teddy bear and needs more physical and emotional care than they can give.

Anyway, good self-esteem is probably the best way to handle sexual pressures. Knowing that, you don't have to steal to be popular or talk dirty to be one of the guys; you don't have to give into the lie that a girl won't amount to anything unless some boy wants and loves her, or the lie that a boy has something wrong with him if he doesn't have sex in high school. If you think well of yourself, you'll do well with yourself. If your "skin-hunger" is taken care of, you're free to be yourself and explore other avenues of care and communication. Now, how about taking care of that "skin-hunger," that need to be touched and affirmed? There are several ways to handle this.

Valued Friends with Values

First of all, there's friendship. And it's about time we've revived that. It seems that in our society, in a relationship with another person, you either have to be romantically or sexually involved or a complete stranger. Why? What about that wonderful and rich middle ground called friendship? Why can't you be good friends with another person of the same or opposite sex? But you can't it seems. Kids tell me that every time they really like or want to be close to or go out with someone, everybody right away thinks a romance is going on, or that they're boyfriend or girlfriend, or going steady. Even with another boy, some guys are afraid to be too close or even express affection or give a birthday gift or a real hug because the others might think they're gay or something like that. How sad and how depriving! How much poorer people are without having cultivated friends. Yes, it seems to be true: Our society just won't allow for being friends.[3]

What a loss, because to cultivate and have a friendship is one of life's greatest gifts. A real friend means: being able to be yourself with no pretense, not having to weigh your words or be careful of stepping on toes, not having to put on a mask, knowing that he or she is there for you whenever you need them, saying what's in your heart, expressing your fears and, above all, knowing that what you are and do and say will stay forever locked in your friend's heart, for a true friend keeps secrets and confidences. Yes, friendship is a great gift at any time of your life. Grab it, work at it, and forget what the others say.

And, in the line of friendship, I have one more bold thing to say. In an interesting experiment a few years ago parents were asked what was the greatest need they felt about their teenagers. They replied that they wanted to be close to them, to talk with them and understand them, but that the kids didn't seem to want this. Teens were asked what was the greatest need they felt about their parents. They replied that they wanted to be close to them, to talk with them and understand them, but that the parents didn't seem to want this! So, here we are, two groups who desperately want to connect, but nobody knows it or knows how to do it. Furthermore, the same survey showed that of all the friends teens wanted to share with and tell their secrets to and ask advice from, their parents were first. So you might cultivate your parents, who love you and want to talk with you. Try it even if you have to get out of the house for privacy. Or there may be an aunt or uncle, a brother or sister, a teacher or priest you can trust. Or you just may make a pact with a buddy, swear him to secrecy, and then be able to tell your feelings to him with the understanding that if there's a question too big for either of you to handle, you'll seek adult advice.

Furthermore, *having friends with values* is the best gift a guy can ever have. You may do all kinds of crazy things, but the invisible value system among you draws lines for you and helps you to stay clear of trouble. For example, if your friends are not potheads, do not use drugs simply because they don't need to—they're comfortable enough with themselves that they don't need an artificial high (in other words, their self-esteem is OK)—then that's an automatic support to you. If drugs are being passed around at a party, a look across the room at your buddy or hearing another buddy say "no thanks" makes it much easier for you to say no as well. They give you the energy to say no and you give it to them.

The same works for sex. For example, in northern Virginia there is an organization of teenagers called the Catholic Life Communities. It's a support group. The president, John Sutter, said, "The eighth grade retreat got me interested; the main reason I joined was because of God. I think CLC helps me spiritually, and I've made many friends....CLC is a safety valve in case you get tempted, something to back you up because you've made a commitment....People in school respect me for the commitments I've made—and CLC helps you to avoid some situations." Notice his words, "CLC is a safety valve in case you get tempted." That's the idea. The kids look out for one another. They give invisible support when somebody is tempted to use sex in a wrong way. They're there to talk things over, which is easy to do because they share values. Here's some of the values that members pledge themselves to: (1) the eucharist at Mass twice a week, (2) a life of prayer, (3) making an effort to build a positive family life, (4) abstaining from marijuana and other drugs; no drinking to get drunk, and more to our point here, (5) willingness to declare a belief in premarital chastity, to develop sexual controls and purity of intentions. It can be done, is being done. Try it.

Creative Activity

Creative activity is always a self-esteem builder. Maybe you can play ball well, or play the guitar, or make something with your hands, or raise the best petunias in town. Look for something that gives you satisfaction, that you get a kick out of, that people admire, that you can stamp with your own personality. Work is a good builder too, whether it's for pay or not. I know many teens who get a charge out of working or volunteering in hospitals or as religion teachers or as day-camp help. I have two young friends who, on getting out of college, are giving a year of their lives in living among and helping the poor in Appalachia before they go on to their careers. Dating is another way to fulfill a need to have company and, in the process, learn how to get along with girls. Very often you can help to satisfy skin hunger by holding hands, hugging, kissing, or just sitting beside one another and feeling each other's presence.

But, sadly, you never hear about things like this because the media doesn't find good family life or friendships or sexual self-control "saleable." What they do find saleable goes against every decent thing we know. The media glamorizes sex outside of marriage, gives one constant, consistent message: "Do it!" When teenagers follow their advice and do it, the media is not there to help with the babies, the poverty, or the death-dealing diseases. The media, in fact—television, magazines, videotapes and the movies—are so powerful that they form a unique pressure on the teenager. The media industry needs a special chapter all by itself.

QUESTIONS FOR REFLECTION AND DISCUSSION
1. How does self-esteem relate to sexual activity?
2. Do you agree that friendship is fading in our society and that you have to be either romantically involved or a stranger? Explain your opinion.
3. Bubba Smith says that somewhere along the line you stop compromising your principles. Do you know anyone else who's done this? a friend, a role model, a hero? Share their story.
4. There's nothing so valuable as a support group. How would you go about starting one?

*You walk down the escalator in Bloomingdale's
and you see a huge ad for Obsession—this lady is
standing there without a shirt on, and this guy is
kissing her breasts. It seems like things are just
becoming more obscene.*   Teenage Girl

*Item: Calvin Klein's 1986 budget to sell Obses-
sion: 23 million dollars.*

13
THE RIVER'S EDGE

"It no longer," intones *The New York Times*, "requires access to a
blue movie TV channel to find a semi-naked couple... Turn on
the set any time, any channel, and there are—consenting adults
(and teenagers) consenting like crazy....Not everyone who tunes
in to watch is over 21...On the contrary, a lot of those TV fans
are teenagers...." And Planned Parenthood, in one of its ads,
says that "In 1978 researchers reported some 9,230 sexual acts
took place on prime-time network television. It's even worse today." In one of her medical columns, Jane Brody reports that
more than 3,000 studies have linked the effect of repeated exposure to televised violence to increased aggression and violent
behavior in children. Moreover, kids who watch a lot of television regard the world as more violent than do lesser viewers
and also that television can give children a highly distorted
view of life about the elderly, the sick, the handicapped, and
minority groups. She also reports that "depictions of sex and especially of sex in casual relationships have increased dramati-
cally (the number of sexual references on television jumped

nearly sevenfold between 1975 and 1979 alone)... "In fact, they talk today about some 20,000 sexual messages by way of the media each year.

The famous Pulitzer Prize psychiatrist Dr. Robert Coles, whose main work is children's development, comments on their television viewing:

> I have many times wondered what in the world they are making of a particular television program we are watching. Sometimes I myself don't know what to make of it—the crude violence, the increasingly explicit sexuality, the selfishness and meanness that I see worked into one program after another.

Then there's the studies that have shown that films that portray violence against women sexually aroused nearly a third of the men who watched them and that repeated viewings of such films as *Friday the 13th* and *The Texas Chainsaw Massacre* instill attitudes in the minds of the viewers very similar to those found in rapists. Even women who watch such films become less sensitive, more indifferent to violence toward women, and even more likely to believe that a woman who was raped wanted to be! "Teenagers are inordinately influenced by the media. They have less interaction with real adults than ever before, and so their friends, and the 'models' presented in the media have an even greater effect."

TV or Not TV?

Well, that's a lot of input to open this chapter with, but on the other hand, the media is a lot of input. You are the first complete generation to grow up with total television, VCRs, videotapes, and widespread, common "adult" movies. These things are the very air you breathe and, without even meaning to, you draw in the media's values and are often made to believe, "This is the way to live." Your outlook and your behavior is molded by the media, especially television. There's no doubt about that, any more than there is a doubt about the study that showed that most television people who write and produce the programs are not Christian and therefore do not have a Chris-

tian viewpoint or outlook (understandably) and are promoters
and advocates of attitudes and values that we consider wrong.
And those attitudes and values get into our bloodstream
through television just by sheer force of volume.

The maddening thing is that there is so much good on telelvi-
sion. For every Sonny Crockett of "Miami Vice" blowing away a
bad guy with a shotgun blast, there is a documentary on hunger
in Ethiopia. For every cartoon showing laser guns, antitank
weapons and routine deaths, there are shows like "Reading
Rainbow" devoted to encouraging children to read. Or there's
the story of the Civil Rights victory or the wonderful "Wonder-
works" series or afternoon specials for children, Mr. Roberts, The
National Geographic specials, "Nature," "Nova," Bill Moyers,
and all the rest on the Public Broadcasting Televison stations.
There's sports and the Olympics, great movies, and dramatic
newsbreaking scenes we'd never see otherwise. Or there's the
"Bill Cosby Show," "Family Ties," "Growing Pains," "My Sister
Sam," "Mr. Belvedere," "The Honeymooners," and others (I
hope they're still on as you read this, even as re-runs) showing us
all real live characters trying to live lovingly in family. Yes,
there really is so much that is good and enjoyable on televison.

Teens in Dialogue
On the other hand there are real problems. Problems about the
attitudes and values TV can instill. Let me give you a case in
point since it deals with teenagers. Consider. In 1987 a one-hour
documentary, "Hollywood's Favorite Heavy," portrayed how
businesspeople were portrayed on prime time TV: making an
awful lot of money without ever having to work hard or produce useful products. To succeed, all they had to do was to be
liars, cheaters, blackmailers, and murderers who would do anything to get what they want. In fact, on prime time television,
business men and women commit more crimes than any other
group. Did you know that? Who are they? They are the businesspeople in popular shows (some are re-running now) as "Dynasty," "Falcon Crest," "Hart to Hart," "Dallas," and others.
Here's a part of a typical script:

When the going gets rich, the rich get going. Of course, I
had to bump off a few people along the way and a mess of
cattle. But $250 million is a mighty worthy cause, mighty
worthy.

Businesspeople on TV, then, are unscrupulous and out for two
things: money and power (which are pretty much the same
thing in our world), and they'll get what they want even it it
means killing. Now in real life understandably they might cry
(maybe your Dad or Mom if they're in business), "Wait a minute! We're not all like that. We don't all have evil values or no
values at all. Don't portray all of us like that, because if you do
you'll fill the minds of people and of kids with bad images.
You'll teach them it's all right to do anything, however bad, to
get a fast buck." Really?

Really. Let's go on further in the documentary. An investigator named Herb London (actually he's an author and dean of
New York University) went to some high schools to interview
the teens about all this. Here's part of the interview:

Herb London: How many of you are influenced by what
happens on television programs you watch? (Kids shake
heads.) No one here is influenced. O.K., are businessman
and women more greedy than other people or is greed in-
trinsic to human nature and businessmen and women are no
different from any other group of people?

Girl 4: I don't think a businessman is ever satisfied.
He's got more money than Rockefeller and he's still going
to try to get more money and more power.

Herb London: You agree with that position? (Kids say
yes.) Then all of you agree with that position. Do you
think that businessmen break the rules to accumulate
wealth and power?

Boy 1: When it comes to your business and your morals,
they usually become separated when you see the money. If
you see that you're going to make a quick buck and it might
not trace back to you, you're going to take the chance that
nothing will happen.

Herb London: How many of you agree with that posi-

tion? (Kids say yes.) Most of you agree with this position—that there's a separation between morality and
business. Now you say—or you said—that much of what
you see on TV is unrealistic. Now if that's unrealistic,
that appears on television all the time. That's what J.R.
[Ewing] is all about, isn't it? (Kid agrees.) You told me
that wealthy businessmen were more greedy than other
people. Now I want to know where this view comes from.
Please, Allison.

Girl 5: Well, I guess we get the ideas from TV programs
that we watch, but everybody...

Herb London: But you just told me that TV is unrealistic.

Girl 5: It is, but I guess it does give us ideas.

Herb London: Do you believe you should do everything
you can to keep your business in existence, even if it means
doing something immoral?

Girl 3: Yes.

Herb London: If you were in the position of saving your
business by selling drugs, or delivering drugs, would you do
either act?

Boy 1: There's no doubt about it. If I was in the same situation, I would definitely do it. I'd like to say that I
wouldn't, but that would be lying, knowing true human nature...

Herb London: Would you, if you owned a chemical business, allow toxic waste to get into the sewer system, even
if it meant a lot of people would be harmed?

Girl 3: If they offered me a certain amount of money...

Herb London: Well, I'm going to give you a lot of money
on this option. You're going to make ten million dollars
with this chemical company.

Girl 3: Then I would.

Herb London: You'd dump the chemicals even though
you knew it would cause harm to other people? And what
would you be thinking about? You'd say, "I have to make
profits"?

Girl 3: I'd think about the money...

Herb London: If it is the last resort to keep your business functioning, would you lie, steal, blackmail, and cheat? How many of you would be willing to do that... You're half way up [to one girl who hesitated and half raised her hand]... Unanimous. This is mind blowing. Unanimous.[1]

And there you are. As the narrator of the documentary remarks, "...people get many of their values from entertainment, especially young people...With TV as their guide, today's young people may become more and more confused." Why not? In this particular instance, by the age of 18 the average kid has seen businesspeople on TV attempt over 10,000 murders.

About eight months after the television show we just mentioned, the investigator, Herb London, after reflecting on his experience with teenagers, wrote a piece for *The New York Times* (August 23, 1987) in which, among other things, he said:

What I heard was, and remains, astonishing. Based on the limited sample of students with whom I chatted in a pair of four-hour conversations, I am convinced that television is having a profound effect on the values (I prefer the word principles) of young Americans... their opinions regarding behavior, to a surprising degree, are clearly influenced by the characters and plots they had watched on television. Seemingly, today's heroes—and heroines—whose immoral behavior is often sumptuously rewarded have become role models for many young Americans...[A professor] George Gerbner, dean of the Annenberg School of Communications at the University of Pennsylvania and a longtime analyst of the relationship between television and society, has observed, "...television is the most pervasive medium we have and most people consider what they see on television as the norm, as the standard."...After talking to these high school students, who were charming, resourceful and typical in most respects, I was shocked how far down the slippery slope of moral relativism we have come. More importantly perhaps, I had not appreciated the degree to which television influences adolescent principles. Seemingly, television creates a moral reality of its own through its indirect and occasionally direct attack on the Judeo-Christian tradition.

"I had not appreciated the degree to which television influences adolescent principle," writes Herb London. Is this just
his opinion? No, an article on the 22nd annual survey of entering college freshmen conducted by the American Council on Education and the Higher Education Research Institute at the University of California at Los Angeles and released in 1988 states:

A record proportion of more than three-quarters of college
freshmen surveyed around the country feel that being financially well off is an "essential" or "very important"
goal. At the same time, the lowest proportion of freshmen
in 20 years, only 39 percent, put a great emphasis on developing a meaningful philosophy of life.

In addition, the number of freshmen saying that a key
reason for their decision to attend college was "to make
more money" has reached a new high of 71 percent... .[In
1966] 83 percent thought that developing a meaningful
philosophy of life was an essential or very important
goal. The percentage has dropped in all but two years
since then, to a low of 39 percent in the latest survey. "Students still see their life being dependent on affluence and
are not inclined to be reflective," Dr. Astin [director of the
survey] said...and noted that it was unusual to see a trend
continue unchanged, as this one has, for so long a period.
"Obviously," he said, "we are seeing something very profound in the society."[2]

Plainly you can see documented how much the media affects
your sense of values, of what's important in life, your relationships and your morals. As Dr. Astin remarked, "Despite Newsweek's announcement that greed is dead, our data show that
it's alive and well." Looks like J.R. has triumphed. And as far
as sex goes, so have his morals. For that same survey also found:

Despite widespread publicity about AIDS, an increase of
freshmen agree that if two people genuinely like each
other, it is fine for them to have sexual relations, even if
they have known each other only a short time.

The Medium's Message

Surely this reflects the success of the constant message of the media: It's OK to have sex anytime you feel like it. You don't have to be married. It's casual, it's expected, it's normal, and everyone does it. Certainly all the movie stars and rock stars do and so does everyone in TV land. Television and the movies take for granted that every unmarried person, every teenager, will have sex. So they show it all the time and, as each year passes, it becomes more frequent and more explicit. The result is that you become more and more aware that to be "with it" you, a boy, have to have sex too. You don't want to be left out. God forbid someone should find out you're a virgin—a compliment in your parent's day, an insult in yours, especially for boys. (See how things can change!) It is not surprising then that in a study spanning some 25 years it was noted that among the eight thousand adolescents surveyed there was a significant drop in the number who viewed premarital intercourse as wrong.[3] Nor is it surprising that statistics show that more and more kids are having sex and starting younger.

And not only does the media give you the message that you should have sex, but it excites you to do it. Look at all the nudity on TV and in the movies. The commercials on television are sexually suggestive, going into more and more nudity. Jeans commercials on television and in magazines are highly sexual. Listen to all of the double meaning jokes and comments about sex. Even radio has now gone into shocking, sexually explicit language.

As I write this there are an estimated 37 million homes with VCRs. This means that videotapes are accessible to everyone. What worries some is the availability of extremely gross and violent horror films that any kid of any age can get and watch, especially the ones that show violence toward women in a sexual context. These are called in the trade "slice and dice" films and you can understand why. Some contain actual footage of human executions, violent deaths, autopsies, cannibalism, and animal slaughter. The grosser the better, seems to be the motto. So what? Sounds neat. Except for the long-range influence. If kids can have their values changed by watching TV films that show murderous businesspeople (and, as we saw above, it happens), then the same can happen—and does happen—with other values. Kids become desensitized to pain and hurt and other people's sufferings. Some even learn to enjoy other people's sufferings. What a twisted value that is. Then there are studies that show that viewers who are shown rape scenes in which the victim comes around to enjoy it come to believe that rape is not bad as a crime. Another change of values brought about by media.

Media Pressure

Movies too are mixed. Some are positive and show commitment and caring. They're well worth seeing. Others, unfortunately— often the box office hits—cater to a sense of violence and sex. Take, for example, *The River's Edge*. It's an especially interesting movie because it attempts to show the roots of violence. It's based on a true incident. In California a teenage boy kills his girl friend for no particular reason down by the river's edge and brags about it to his buddies. Several of them come to look at the body, but nobody does anything. No one calls the cops, tells the girl's parents, nothing. The movie tries to explore why these teenagers just stood there, looked, and went home. Why? Because the kids are alienated; that is, they're morally dead. They're separated from any value system whatever. They have watched so much TV that they think in TV terms. There is no caring relatedness to others. The girl's death and her dead body are just something they've always seen on television. So, what's new? How values can die!

We haven't even mentioned the MTVs and punk rock and the heavy metal bands that show and promote explicit violence. And then there's sex. Sex is so often taken out of any loving and caring context and is made to seem like so many casual connections with people who basically use each other. The net result is not only to give you a message of sex as mere physical discharge (not, remember, as a symbol of committed love), but to pander to you and get you stimulated a lot. Look, here's a report from a professional magazine called *The Medical Aspects of*

Human Sexuality (I hope you're impressed) which says:
Television puts the greatest pressure on younger teenagers
for premature sexual involvement. Fully 90% of 1,043 surveyed adolescents, most under age 16, said that they'd seen
between one and nine TV shows in the past week or so that
pressured them about sex. The next greatest pressure on
them is from pop music—81% said they'd recently heard
songs that emphasized sex Ranking third (80%) was pressure from peers, either from general teenage attitudes or
from personal acquaintances. Other frequently cited sources of sexual pressure were movies (70%) and TV commeri-
cals or magazine ads (64 %).

When you join such crude sex to violence, you can make a terrible impression on young people's minds. There are lyrics about
whipping a girl before intercourse (Ted Nugent's "Violent
Love"), comparing the penis to a sword that cuts or a gun that
shoots (Motley Crue's "Ten Seconds to Love"), or a knife that
slices (Kiss's "Fits Like a Glove" or the Who's "You Better You
Bet") A psychiatrist, Dr. Stuessy asks:

But what if I were an impressionable fifteen-year-old boy
today? My rock heroes have told me that sex on a date is
expected and that it is a violent act. My penis is a knife, a
gun, a rod of steel. Intercourse involves thrusting, plunging,
screaming and pain. My date is to be the object of my sexual cutting, slicing and shooting. I must be very conscious of
exerting my masculinity. I don't want my date, who, for
all I know, is "experienced" to think I'm a wimp! I will
nail her to the bed and make her scream in pain! Boy, this
sex stuff is great![5]

You say, "Well, I know that stuff is for the birds. It doesn't affect me." But the truth is that it does. It certainly affects lots of
other teens. (Remember, once more, *The River's Edge*.) The statistics show that. Sexual abuse, murders, rapes, teen pregnancies, broken homes—they're off the walls, right off the charts.
There has been an increase in all of these things. It's not just a
matter of better reporting. If your notion of human relationships
comes from the media that routinely show sex outside of marri-

age, violence, infidelity, abuse, murder, embezzlement, and
rape—how can you know about the ideals of marriage and self-
control and true love? It has to get inside of you whether you realize it or not. I just want to emphasize the media's influence on
you, to remind you of its power to form your values. Maybe, also,
I'd like you to examine your values and see what they are and
where you got them. Most of all, I'd like you to remember that
there is another source of values of how to treat and relate to
people: Jesus and his teachings.

Who Are These People?
Meanwhile, before we end, did you ever stop to think about the
people, the programers, the celebrities, who peddle this kind
of stuff in the media? Do they follow their own advice? Obviously. I say "obviously" because their ability to sustain long-
term, honest, and loving human relationships is notoriously
poor. The pulp magazines and the sensational newspapers—you
know, the ones with the headlines, "Three-Year-Old Child
Gives Birth To Twins," or "107-Year-Old Man Abducted By Beings From Outer Space and Returns Pregnant," or "Why My
Marriage to Hollywood's Sex Symbol Broke Up"—thrive on
these people's inability to love. Their divorce rate is routine.
So we chuckle that Liz Taylor's been married eight times or
Joan Collins or Sylvester Stallone four times. But is that funny?
Are there no tears, no pain, no shame, no sense of commitment?
Yes, movie stars and celebrities have babies without being married and have enough money to raise them or have someone else
do it. But did anyone ask the baby if he or she wanted to be deliberately raised without a father, without grandparents,
without a heritage? And what of the children of such celebrities? The drug use, the alcohol, the suicides? What was behind
rock stars Janis Joplin, Jimi Hendrix, or Elvis Presley overdosing
on drugs?

Why did Marilyn Monroe, the sex goddess herself, take her
own life? In her book entitled *Marilyn*, Gloria Steinem relates
a brief conversation Marilyn had with her maid near the end
of her life:

"Nobody's ever gonna love me now, Lena. What good am
I? I can't have kids. I can't cook. I've been divorced three
times. Who would want me?"

"Millions of men," answered her maid dutifully—and
correctly.

"Yeah," said Marilyn, "but who would love me?"

Ah, there it is, the old question. Poor woman. She was not
blonde, she was not happy, she was not even Marilyn Monroe.
She was a creation of the media. Her real name was Norma Jean
Baker, born out of wedlock to a mother soon to be institutional-
ized, who sought acceptance and love in drugs, alcohol, sex.
Marilyn died at 36. The sad thing is that not only did she not
find love but that she, like her mother, was made an object, even
though a more famous one. The real shame, therefore, was that
the world, seeing her as a thing, failed to love her as a person.

QUESTIONS FOR REFLECTION AND DISCUSSION

1. What are the predominant images of man-woman relationships you find on television?

2. What kind of videocassettes do you watch? Precisely what
attracts you?

3. What would have been your responses to the Herb London dialogue? What did you think of the 1988 survey on the values
and attitudes of the college freshmen?

4. How do you think the media influences your values, the way
you dress, the music you listen to, how you act and think? Explain.

5. In 1987, advertisers spent 19 billion dollars. Does advertising
pay? Explain.

14
TIME OUT 2

All right, another time out. Discussion time or question and answer time. And this time I think we really need one. That last section we just finished, I admit, was a little heavy and I know that I've been hitting pretty hard at some issues. Maybe a little too hard? You're nodding yes, I see. Well, even if you didn't I can see in your faces that "Give us a break" look. OK. Who wants to start?

"What's the problem? Joey?" "Well, for one thing," Joey responds after thinking a minute, "you're pretty rough on television and the movies. They're not that bad. We get a kick out of them." Well, maybe you're right, I answer, maybe you're right. Maybe at my age I see it differently. There is a lot of good stuff on TV and some great movies around. I know I enjoy them. It's just that...well, it's those constant messages and images about sex and violence and materialism that I think get to us all. Look, here's a nifty comic strip, Lynn Johnston's "For Better or For Worse." Michael who's about 12 is watching television with his nine-year-old sister. Panel 1: coming from the set, two characters are saying, "Oooh, Chad!" and "Oooh, Melanie" and the background sounds are: lust! ahhh! Kiss! Oooh! feel! Passion! ahhh! In panel 2, the sister asks, "What's the movie called?" and Michael answers, "First Date." They click the remote control and the TV is blasting out, "One more move, you %%#&&@, an' I'll slit your +&*^% throat!!" Panel 3: another click to another channel. "Oooh! Groann! Heave! Pant! Yes, Rubert, Yes! Before I go crazy!!" Panel 4: click: Couple number 2! "Stephanie, on your wedding night, would you say your husband was most like a floppy disk, a power drill, or a refrigerator?!!" Panel 5: click: "Hey, man, you calling me a #$%^&— well, suck lead, you %&%$#%% son of a $%^^$#!!!" Panel 6: click. "Ka-baam! Rattatatatrata. Kapfoomoommmm! Blang! Tataratrattat" In panel 7 Michael says to his sister, "Well, there's one thing I know for sure..." and in the last panel he finishes his sentence, "...I'm never gonna let my kids watch stuff like this!!!"

But I think what bothers me even more than such non-stop sex and violence is the job the media does on our thinking. I guess I do get a little hyper about that. For example, I keep thinking of how the media did a job on those kids' thinking, you know, the ones who would allow toxic waste to go into the sewer which would maybe give cancer to a lot of people—and they'd do it for money! That frightens me. I react and I think to myself, My God, would any of the kids in my class...would you...do that: make money at the expense of people? I react too—maybe overreact, do you think?—when I think of something we have just seen; you know, those freshmen who said that if you really like someone it's OK to have sex even if you've known her for a short time. That's amazing to me. Sex becomes so casual and, for after a while, so meaningless. Or that for 20 years in a slow steady pattern those same college freshmen, 71 percent of them—as you're going to be in a short time—feel that the main reason for going to college is to make more money, that being affluent, rich, is what life is all about. That boggles me too. Making money is what life is all about? Where'd these values, if you want to call them that, come from, if not from TV and its lifestyles and commercials and the materialistic culture we've created? Look, when I was doing my homework for this course, I found that in one year, 1987, advertisers spent 91 billion—not million, but billion dollars!—on advertising. Naturally, of course, they must get that back and lots more, right? Which means they got to you and me and others like us... Mike?

"Yeah," Mike says, "but we know that stuff's fake. It doesn't affect us." Ah, reply I, you say that, Mike, but in spite of what you know in your head, it gets inside your heart, your feelings. Did you ever hear the story of the man on a hot summer's day at the beach who went to a local bar to get a cold beer? When he got there the crowd was so dense he couldn't get in. So he yelled at the top of his voice, "Hey, everybody, there's a big white whale that just beached up on the sand out here!" So everybody rushes outside and down to the beach, leaving the place empty. So our friend saunters in, orders a beer, and leans against the bar smiling to himself. But then he hears the crowd roaring and roaring and the excitement and noise keeps going on outside and getting louder all the time until he can't stand it any longer. He puts down his beer, says to himself, "Damn, maybe there *is* a whale out there," and rushes out to join the crowd. So, that's the way it is. Advertising doesn't appeal to the head, it appeals to the feelings, to the insecurities.

You don't believe me? OK, try this one, I reply as I dig though my files. Let me ask you this. How many of you drink Coke for breakfast? Out of a class of 35, nine raise their hands. OK, let's see, about a third of you. So let me show you something. About ten years ago, almost no one would drink Coke for breakfast, but in ten years from now almost all of you will. You don't believe me? All right, here's a clipping from the paper I'm passing out to you.[1] Everybody got a copy? Follow along with me as we jump around a bit. The soft drink companies are out:

> To persuade young adults to get their morning caffeine and sugar fix from cola instead of coffee. To this end, the Coca-Cola Company is undertaking an advertising campaign aimed at increasing the morning consumption of Coke. The "Coke in the Morning" campaign has been tested.... Morning consumption now accounts for 12 percent of total soft drink sales....

Kevin, suppose you read the next paragraph to the class. Kevin, who's been mentally floating, looks flustered, gets a hint where we are from the guy next to him, and reads as follows:

> These statistics are but one more sign of how influential sophisticated advertising can be, analysts say. In recent

decades the soda companies...have poured vast amounts
into ads intended to persuade young people to down more
of their products...People between the ages of 24 and 44
are the largest consumers of soft drinks...Robert Baskin, a
spokesman for Coca-Cola, USA, added, "The fact is we're
in a post-industrial society and people want things quickly...A Coke is immediate gratification."
All right, I add, look at the strategy outlined down further.
Here, let me read: "In stores the reminders are subtle and—some
say—seductive. Advertising is often near breakfast foods, a
marketing technique known as 'cross merchandising.' " You see?
In a few years they'll get you. It's the power of the media. You
might notice, by the way, in the last paragraph that Coca-
Cola has no intention of replacing orange juice since it also owns
Minute Maid! All right, I don't want to get "heavy" on you
again, but that's why I come on so serious and pound away so relentlessly. I want you to be alert to how easily we're all manip-
ulated, who's shaping our values, and that often these values
are sometimes against what you and I are suppose to be, as
Christians.

And all this really does have its effect. Look, here's another
report from the papers[2] about you people. Teens who work after
school That's great. Some of you do and I did as a kid, but now
there's a big difference. The difference is not just working to get
a little spending money. No, the difference is what the article
calls a whole new "work-and-spend ethic." Listen:

More than their predecessors, today's adolescents are
likely to work long hours during the week for hundreds of
dollars each month. They spend the money on themselves
rather then contributing it to their families. "I earn it and
I spend it and I spend it on me," is the credo of today's
teen-agers... in a 1987 survey of 16,000 high school seniors
nationwide, [they] found that 80 percent of student who
work spend their earnings on their own needs, such as
clothing, stereo equipment, records and movies... .

And one psychologist who wrote *When Teen-Agers Work*
said, "Now there is more for teen-agers to buy and having

things is a much more important part of being a teen-ager. Compared to several decades ago, kids are more materialistic now." Well, you see? That shows up in what we saw already, doesn't it? Going to college means getting the money to buy more things—because that's what life is about.

And what's all this have to do with sex? Well, remember, basically sex or sexuality has to do with relationships. That's the whole crux of the matter. That's what makes sex work and makes it satisfying. But in this work-to-get-money-for-me system, human relationships themselves tend to fall into the same category: They tend to become objects, acquired "things"; and sexuality, instead of meaning relating lovingly and caringly for another as a male, becomes simple sex-organ sex whose activity is to what? *To score!* Notice the word. It's a quantity word. Sex becomes "scoring"—a word that has to do with totals and sums and adding up how many conquests you've made, how many girls you've acquired. I think that's why some kids I know, Kathleen Kane or Jim Gallagher, for example, are such good witnesses against all this materialistic philosophy, this thinking-only-of-myself. Kathy and Jim have joined the Jesuit Volunteer Corps and they're working for simple justice and assistance and the health of the people in this and other countries. They've taken a year out of their lives to share their gifts and concern for others, and...and there I go again, starting to preach and getting heavy, heavy! Sorry about that...Pedro?

Pedro stands up, shuffles his big feet, looks down at the floor with that silly grin of his and says, "Yeah, OK, that may be true, but you sorta want to take all the fun out of it." It? I ask. "Yeah, you know, it—sex." Hmmm, I think a minute, I don't know, Pedro. I don't want to take out any of the fun. Lord knows that but some of this stuff *is* serious. I mean, those statistics are people: people with babies, people with diseases, people with broken homes and that's why, I warn you now, we'll be mighty serious about the STDs and abortion and things like that, because they're not funny. But I know what you mean.

But we should make a distinction between pleasure and fun. Sex is pleasurable, one of our keenest, our most intense, and it's natural to want it. Sex is enjoyable. It feels good (though not in every instance). But all I can say now is that love is beyond pleasure. Love takes in pleasure but at times postpones and sets it aside if a higher value is at stake—which often it is. As one famous psychiatrist says, "Love, beyond pleasure, is a dedication of the self through trust...In our willingness to sacrifice pleasure for service and obligation to others we will be rewarded. We will discover a form of pleasure beyond comfort and vanity."[3] That's all I can say for the moment without going overboard again. But as for fun? I don't want to give the impression that sex isn't fun. It is. And sometimes it's downright ridiculous and outrageous, which is why we have those bawdy stories and jokes and bumper stickers.

That was a mistake. I knew as soon as I said "bumper stickers" I was in for trouble. Soon the kids were having a ball yelling out, "Mountain climbers do it on top...Divers do it deeper... Plumbers plunge further... !" Hold it, hold it! I shouted. You'll have the principal in here. That's all right to laugh. We don't want to become too serious, and people have always had great jokes and stories about sex. Which is a way at laughing at ourselves and in effect saying, there's mystery here we don't know how to completely handle, so, like whistling in the dark, we have to have some fun to take the tension off. Jeff shouts out, "Hey, do you know any of those stories?" Silence. A slight embarrassment they're quick to notice.

Well, I hesitate, I know a few. I sense them waiting, all attention. Well, how about his one I heard from a Jewish friend of mine: Mrs. Moskowicz was having her house painted, and between the smell of the paint and the hassle, she found life hard. It was the last straw when Mr. Moskowicz forgot himself and leaned against the wall and left a distinct hand mark on the fresh paint. The Mrs. made her feelings clearly known and the husband tried to calm her down, "What's the fuss?" he said, "the painter's returning tomorrow so he'll paint it over." Nevertheless, Mrs. Moskowicz found it difficult to sleep all night. The thought of that hand mark bothered her. The next morning then, the painter had hardly stepped over the threshhold when she was upon him saying, "Oh, I'm so glad you're here. All night long I've been thinking of you and waiting for you. Come with me. I want to show you where my husband put his hand." The painter blanched and stepped back horrified, "Please," he said, "I'm an old man. A cup of tea and maybe a cookie is all I want."

Loud laughter from some and then the rest as they caught on. Then I know some more limericks like:

> There was a young laddie named Claude
> A sort of society fraud.
> In the parlor, 'tis told,
> He was distant and cold,
> But on the veranda, my Gawd!

And that reminds me of the one about the modern kid saying to another kid, "Look what I found on the veranda. A condom!" The other kids says, "What's a veranda?" How about this one?

> A mischievous lad from Woods Hole
> Had a notion exceedingly droll:
> At a masquerade ball
> He wore nothing at all,
> And backed in as a Parker House roll.

OK, keep it down. One more and that's all:

> There was an old monk in Siberia
> Whose existence grew steadily drearier.
> Till he broke from his cell
> With a hell of a yell
> And eloped with the Mother Superior.

After things died down, Al raised his hand and wanted to know, "Well, if we're supposed to save sex till marriage, what about all those feelings?" What feelings? I asked. You mean, sexual feelings, getting horney all the time? Heads all around shake yes. OK, just one more discussion. Our time's almost up.

The first thing to know is that feelings are. That's it. They just are. They are neither good or bad in themselves. They are just there like your skin is just there. Feeling angry, anxious or nervous, feeling hurt, sad, envious, ashamed, happy, guilty, feeling sexy—these are all normal feelings that everybody has from the pope on down. Sexual feelings are a part of being human. So it's all right to have feelings. It's more than all right. It's normal and it's healthy. All feelings, any feelings. But, of course, it's what you do with your feelings that count. Feeling angry doesn't mean you have to punch somebody. Feeling sad doesn't mean you have to walk around with a long face. Feeling horney doesn't mean you have to have sex. But the feeling itself is all right. No problem here.

Anyway, our time is up and I'll see you guys next week. And then, as I told you, it's back to the serious stuff. We'll be beginning with the STDs and move on to homosexuality, abortion, and pornography. Heavy stuff, but we've got to talk about things that normally you don't hear about and, most of all, we've got to see where we all stand as Christ's friends. See you next week. One more? OK, and that's it.

> God's plan made a hopeful beginning
> But man spoiled his chances by sinning.
> We trust that the story
> Will end in God's glory
> But, at present, the other side's winning.

PART THREE
THE QUESTIONS

Cartoon: Grandson speaking to Granddad:
Grandson: Gee, Granddad, your generation
didn't have all these social diseases. What did
you wear to have safe sex?
Granddad: A wedding ring.

15
THE STDs

Once upon a time the title of this chapter would be called "Venereal Disease" (VD) but we don't use that term so much any more because it might imply that you can catch such diseases only by having sexual intercourse. Which is wrong. So we use the initials STD, which stands for "Sexually Transmitted Diseases," and this lets you know that you can catch them by other bodily contacts that originate from any of the body openings such as rectum, vagina, mouth, or penis. The big disease, of course, is AIDS, and even though you probably get information on that in class, we'll talk about it later. First, however, I want to mention other diseases. I do so because with all of the publicity about AIDS you might overlook—much to your peril—other highly infectious, dangerous, and even deadly and incurable diseases.

Likewise, before we get into this chapter, let me tell you one truth that, if you live by it, you won't have to read further. If you are chaste, that is, if you control your sexual urges and do not make contact with the sexual parts of anyone's body or, of course, catch anything from a blood transfusion or needles, you will never get any sexually transmitted disease. Guaranteed. As the old and wise saying goes, the best oral contraceptive is the word "No!"

Why do people get such diseases to begin with? The United Nations World Health Organization (WHO) gave a report years ago that is still true today. It is said that the causes of the spread of these terrible diseases are:

1) Ignorance of the nature and meaning of sex and of the dangers and abuse of the sexual function.

2) The decline in religious faith [which gave some good guidelines and help].

3) The emancipation of women [in the sense that more of them wanted to have sex outside of marriage, as the men—with the same results].

4) The lack of discipline in home life and of parental supervision [which results in low self-esteem].

5) The failure of fear as a deterrent [teens especially think they are invulnerable].

6) The emphasis on sexuality in books, plays, and films, on television and advertisements [the ones who wrote this years ago should see today!].

7) Misinterpretation of psychological teaching.

8) Earlier physical development.

You see, sexually transmitted diseases do not just "happen" to a person. They are not caught from things, but from people through sexual contact with them or, as in the case of AIDS and other diseases, contact with the infected fluids they left behind, such as on a needle or in blood.

Common STDs

There are all kinds of sexually transmitted diseases. Perhaps the most common are gonorrhea, herpes (non curable), and syphilis. They are dangerous and are easily passed from person to person. Such diseases can cause heart trouble, blindness, and insanity. They kill. They also can mimic other diseases so that you don't know you have them.

1) Gonorrhea. In slang this is sometimes called "clap" or "the drip" or "strain." There is only one way to get gonorrhea: by an infected penis entering the vagina (or when the vagina is infected)—sexual intercourse—or any other openings such as the mouth or rectum, where these germs can also reside. What happens to the boy if he gets it? He will get a drip from the penis or feel a burning sensation while urinating (for some, quite painful). Sometimes he will discharge a lot of pus. If someone has forced his penis into a rectum there may be a discharge from there; if the mouth was involved at all there may be signs of a sore throat and swollen glands. On the other hand, sneakily and dangerously enough, there are no signs for some boys; they continue to carry the disease, give it, and eventually get sick from it. The girl may have a slight discharge from the vagina, also with a burning feeling (especially during her monthly period), but the sad truth is she may show no signs—almost 80 percent show no signs—and so carry the infection for weeks and even years. If she gets pregnant, this could cause the baby to be born blind.

There are no perfect tests to see if you have gonorrhea, and if you ever had sexual contact you should be checked for this disease. Gonorrhea can be cured and doctors are even trying to develop a vaccine that can immunize people. Penicillin can do it. Or used to do it. What has developed lately is that a sharp rise in penicillin-resistant gonorrhea has been reported. Like the mosquitoes that develop a resistance to chemicals that used to kill them, so the gonorrhea virus has done the same. It can still be fought by other more expensive drugs, but often they are out of the reach of many people. And besides, how long before they too build up a resistance to new drugs?

2) *Syphilis*. Some slang terms are "bad blood," "Old Joe," or "lues." This disease is always spread by sexual contact and, please note, this includes kissing (the "French" kiss) when you put your tongue into the other's mouth. This disease can last a lifetime and there are over a half million people in our country who have it and don't know it. And it's on the rise. In 1987 syphilis cases increased 35 percent over the previous year nationwide and more so in the big cities: 50 percent in New York City, 97 percent in Los Angeles County, and 86 percent in Florida. Such victims may be in line for paralysis, heart trouble, skin disease, and insanity. Syphilis also can be cured by penicillin,

but the damage already done cannot be repaired. This disease progresses in stages. Most often the first sign of the first stage is a sore (called a "chancre" and pronounced "shank-er") on the tip of the boy's penis or the girl's vagina or inside the vagina. Or, if the mouth is used, on the lips. Then the sore goes, but you're not free. Stage two is coming up: a rash, moist-looking welts around the sexual organs, low fever, hair falling out, sore throat, swollen glands. These signs too go away, but you're not free. Stage three is coming up. In this state you can't pass it on to anyone—except that the girl, if she's pregnant, can pass it on to her baby who may be born deformed or handicapped. But the syphilis germs inside you are at work and maybe for five to twenty years; but it will catch up with you, reaching your heart, brain, and other organs and even causing your death. Moreover, studies have shown that people with the genital sores of syphilis are more likely to catch AIDS because the sores serve as an entry for that disease. For the present, syphilis can be cured (although newer and tougher forms are appearing that might not be), but only if you know you have it and seek treatment.

3) Herpes. It is estimated that over 20 million Americans have herpes and a half million are added each year. There are two varieties of herpes, Herpes I and Herpes II. Herpes I causes cold sores and fever blisters around the mouth but is usually not classified as a sexually transmitted disease. But Herpes II is; it causes sores in the sexual area or rectum or sometimes on the mouth. Such sores are easily spread through sexual contact. They can break open and are very painful. There is no known cure at present for Herpes II. A pregnant woman with herpes may infect her baby.

4) Papilloma Virus. You don't hear much about this strange-sounding virus (usually connected with harmless warts) but you will definitely hear more about it in the future, for it is only recently that this virus has caught the attention of the doctors. Why? Because of its increasing connection with cancer, especially cancer of the vagina, the penis, and the rectum (which is why scientists have recently concluded that "homosexual behavior in men is a risk factor for rectal cancer.") This virus is easily transmitted through sexual intercourse. Condoms offer some protection but not totally since the virus may be present in areas not covered by a condom. This virus does not seem directly to cause cancer, but rather is a very strong contributor to it.

5) *Chlamydia* (pronounced "clam-id-ia"). This is a very widespread disease and can lead to inflammatory pelvic diseases in women and NGU disease in men, that is, infection of the urinary tract.

Some sexually transmitted diseases are at present incurable, like Herpes II and AIDS. But those that are curable can be caught over and over again as often as you have sexual contact with an infected person, who may not know he or she has any disease.

AIDS

6) *AIDS* (acquired immune deficiency syndrome). This disease was pretty much unknown before 1981 but by mid-1987 more than 32,000 Americans had been diagnosed as having it (we don't know how many more) and nearly 60 percent of these have died from it. Unless some cure or treatment is found, predictions are that by 1991 there will be over a quarter million such cases with over half of them dying. In fact, in 1991 alone, some 54,000 Americans are expected to die from AIDS, which is about the same death toll as in all of the Vietnam War.

AIDS is caused by a virus that destroys part of the body's immune system (defense system) and leaves people unable to defend themselves against infections and certain cancers. Some people who have this virus get sick and some die; others carry the virus and stay all right but pass it on to others. So far, there is no cure for it. Furthermore, at the beginning of 1988 a second type of AIDS virus was discovered in this country. This discovery underscores the scary fact that the world faces two distinct AIDS epidemics.

The educated guess is that AIDS first appeared, at least in this country, among homosexual men in New York and San Francisco in the mid 1970s, especially through anal intercourse, or sodomy (inserting the penis into the rectum), which is common among homosexuals. It also was appearing abroad in Africa. Nobody really knows where it first started or its origins. It soon also appeared in the (contaminated) blood of drug users, in New York and other northeastern cities, who shared contaminated needles, sadly among babies infected by their mothers who used drugs from contaminated needles or had sex with infected bisexual men (men who had sex with both males and females) and, finally, among those who already were carrying some other form of STDs. And all this rapid spread was accelerated by promiscuity, that is, a person having many, many sexual contacts. The knowledge of how it was spread came too late for many and in the 1980s it swept through the homosexual communities. Michael Bennet (of *Chorus Line, Dreamgirls* fame), Rock Hudson, and Liberace are among the more famous homosexual victims.

To this day, AIDS remains mostly confined to these four groups: (1) promiscuous homosexual men who have or have had high rates of anal, or rectal, intercourse; (2) those already infected with other STDs; (3) users of contaminated needles; and (4) receivers of contaminated blood products. The first three groups make up "about 90 percent of cumulative AIDS cases. It is likely that these groups will continue to be at highest risk for infection and disease because this is where the virus was first established in this country."[1]

The reason for the first group is that the cells of the rectum rupture very easily and so let in infection. Also, since there are no real lubricants to any extent in the rectum, even using condoms is not effective since they readily tear. Anal sex, therefore, which is a common way some homosexuals have sex, is an extremely high and risky means for transmitting AIDS and other diseases. The lesson is that you should never let any object, whatever it is, be inserted into your rectum.

You do hear a lot of alarming figures that AIDS will significantly spread to the heterosexual population as well. No doubt there is danger but the danger is exaggerated. The numbers of AIDS victims among heterosexuals is "projected to increase from 4 percent of patients in December 1986 to 10 percent in 1991,"[2] which is bad enough but not an "epidemic." It is possible to get a sudden surge in AIDS because the disease can linger or incubate anywhere from five to seven years or longer before it breaks out and the sudden appearance may sound like an "epidemic," but that's just an average expectation. As Dr. Harold Jaffee from the Center for Disease Control in Atlanta says, "Those who are suggesting that we are going to see an explosive spread of AIDS in the heterosexual population have to explain why this isn't happening." Randy Shilts who wrote a very popular book on AIDS says the same thing: "In two or three years heterosexuals are going to wake up and see that they're not getting the disease. Then what?"

That both men are right is easy to verify. As you read this now, almost ten years after AIDS began showing up in the United States in 1981, there is still no epidemic among heterosexuals. I live near New York City which not only has probably the best tracking and identification system in the world but also has the unhappy distinction of being the nation's AIDS capital (more cases than San Francisco or Los Angeles), and that city relates that as late as the end of 1987 there have been no second-generation heterosexual AIDS victims. Where there are heterosexual victims of AIDS, they represent a very small portion of the population.[3]

I write this simply to keep the record straight and to prevent you from being scared to death by those TV spots and school lectures about catching AIDS, as if almost all of the general population were going to catch it. Nevertheless, although difficult to catch, AIDS can be a danger, and a heterosexual AIDS epidemic, though not likely, is always possible. Actually, you are in far more danger from the other STDs than from AIDS. In any case, whatever the future history of the disease, you should know that AIDS is not spread through casual contact in school or on the job or even in the swimming pool. It is not spread by toilet seats, handshakes, hugs (I remember hugging an AIDS parishioner of mine in his mid-twenties who did die and at whose funeral I officiated), eating from the same dish or drinking from the same glass, or by food handlers in restaurants and not even by mosquitoes—although if one plans to get his or her ear pierced or be tattooed, he or she should insist on a sterile needle.

Nor, contrary to widespread believe, can blood donors get AIDS, but it is remotely possible for those receiving blood transfusions to get it. In short, AIDS is infectious, not contagious, and there's an important difference. Contagious means you can catch something just by walking into the same room with the sick person. You can't get AIDS this way. Infectious means you have to go out of your way to have direct contact with the sick person. In other words, you can get AIDS, like any other STDs, only by intimate contact with another person, such as sexual contact or by unsterilized drug-used needles or contaminated blood. If someone suspects that he or she may have AIDS, that person should go for testing, inform his or her sexual partner, keep away from sexual activity, and do not donate blood.

Reaction to AIDS

Meanwhile, because of special reactions and feelings towards the victims of AIDS, we ought to add the following comments. For some reason, people have at different times associated some diseases as God's punishment for sin. For example, back in 1831 and again in 1849 in our country there was an epidemic, cholera, caused by a virus that gets in the digestive track (through food, water, hands). It claimed relatively few lives but many Americans back then said that the disease was the scourge of the sinful and the dirty. Respectable people didn't get cholera. God punished the "unrespectable." The same attitude was associated with the STDs. Victims were being punished by God for their sinful lives. The result was that people afflicted with sexually transmitted diseases suffered doubly: from the disease and from public shame and disapproval. Today some people react the same way to AIDS. They link sin and the disease and say that AIDS is God's punishment. To this notion is added discrimination, thus compounding the hurt.

People with AIDS were fired from their jobs, evicted

from their apartments, denied medical insurance payments, deserted by their friends, and abandoned by family members. Funeral directors refused to handle their bodies. Nurses, medical technicians, and physicians refused to care for them... People were told to avoid contact with stereotyped gay service providers: hairdressers, florists, designers, waiters. Children with AIDS were sent home from their schools.[4]

Such attitudes and discriminations frequently cause feelings of rejection, loss of self-esteem, depression, and thoughts of suicide—all this in addition to dealing with the fear of dying.

The boy who believes in Jesus cannot believe that AIDS is a punishment for sin since even innocent babies are born with this terrible disease. Nor should we forget that one group that no one thinks of, the hemophiliacs, people with a severe bleeding disorder. If they get a small cut on the finger, for example, they would bleed a great deal and may even die. As a result, they need many blood-based thickening products. However, prior to 1984 some of these products used to thicken and clot their blood was unknowingly contaminated with the AIDS virus, and so large numbers of hemophiliacs were exposed to the disease, perhaps, it is estimated, as many as nine out of ten. Despite their innocence, many hemophiliac kids have been thrown out of schools and sometimes their families have been harassed. Such kids, without their wanting it, have contracted AIDS and on top of that are rejected by their friends and neighbors. They've committed no sin—which perhaps cannot be said for those who have been cruel to them.

Besides, if God is going around inflicting diseases on sinners, then none of us are safe. Nor can the boy who believes in Jesus share those attitudes or discriminations. Jesus broadened the ways we are to love; we are to love not just our friends, but our enemies and even pray for our persecutors. There must be no limit to our love, for we are to be perfect as God is perfect. We must follow Jesus' example, who greeted sinners, searched for them, welcomed them to his table fellowship, and touched them, so much so that he was accused of being the associate of outcasts and sinners. He loved those whom others rejected and spoke movingly of paying attention to the more important issues of the law: justice, mercy, and good faith. Jesus showed us therefore the correct attitude toward people with AIDS: compassion, acceptance, love, and assistance.

It is therefore instructive to listen to some of our church leaders who take Jesus seriously. Archbishop John Quinn of San Francisco (which has a large number of homosexuals) wrote, "The Christian—the church—must not contribute to breaking the spirit of the sick and weakening their faith by harshness.... . Persons with AIDS and ARC are our brothers and sisters, members of our parish."[5] Cardinal O'Connor of New York committed his diocese "to do its best to minister to every person who is ill, of whatever disorder, because of our commitment to the belief that every person is made in the Image and Likeness of God."[6] And the cardinal himself, once a week, visits AIDS victims. Leaders like these show us how to react to the victims of AIDS. Moreover, since AIDS is infectious but not contagious, these bishops and many others allow kids with AIDS to attend school.

Anyway, getting back to practical matters, you must try to take in this truth: You increase the danger of getting any STD with each additional sex partner, and every time you have sex with another you are having sex with everyone else they ever had sex with. I can't emphasize this too strongly. If a boy, for example, has sex with a girl who has had sex with twelve guys, she is carrying the history of all twelve guys, and their potential for infection (including AIDS).

The Superman Complex

Unfortunately but understandably, people your age have the Superman Complex: Nothing can get to me. I am immortal and invulnerable. But that's not quite so. So vulnerable is your age group that it is the only one since 1960 whose death rate has risen. Why? Because adolescents are prone to take foolish risks. As one psychologist said, "The three biggest killers of young people are essentially psychological. They're dying of their own reckless behavior." And a vice president of children's programming on CBS television comments, "Teenagers tend to be more promiscuous and they are often drug users as well." So, to counteract this, I want to remind you that you really can get any of the Sexually Transmitted Diseases and they are painful, life-limiting, and even deadly.[7]

Unfortunately, the only "solution" to your risk-taking that many offer you is condoms. They do not say, don't have sex outside of marriage, but use condoms—those rubber or latex sheaths you can put over your erect penis before inserting it into the vagina. The girl is urged to use a back-up cream or jelly that contains nonoxynol-9, a chemical that kills the sperm. The condom prevents contact with infectious fluids and, of course, catches the sperm fluid so that there will be no fertilization of the girl's egg and therefore no baby. There's pros and cons here.

On the pro side: Although teenagers should not have sexual contacts outside of marriage, because they are really not emotionally and spiritually ready for such intimate and deep relationships, the problem is that some do. For whatever reason— the pressure of the moment, the need to "prove" themselves, lack of self-esteem, the media that stresses individualism, selfishness, greed, envy, and self-centeredness—some teens do have sex outside of marriage. What about them? If they won't stop having sex, then, as the lesser of two evils I would agree that it is better that they use condoms which will reduce (*but not eliminate*) the risk of infection. Our Catholic bishops have reluctantly said the same thing. They will allow the mention of condoms simply because, as they say, "Some people will not act as they can and should," but they emphasize that the only "morally correct and medically sure ways" to prevent AIDS is "abstinence outside of marriage and fidelity within as well as the avoidance of intravenous drug abuse."[8]

Still, even with this concession, teens will ignore the warnings. (The Superman Complex again!) For example, students interviewed at one high school said that no girl on the pill (the usual method of birth control among middle-class high school students) is going to ask her boyfriend to use a condom just to be safe about AIDS. One boy puts it this way:

Teenagers avoid thinking about AIDS because it scares them. I hear girls who are on the pill say if they're going to have sex with a guy a lot, that it's not worth the trouble of using a condom every time. A girl who has sex with a guy without a condom a few times simply feels, "Whatever he's got, I've got," and just doesn't think about it any more. They don't like to face the fact that the person they're having sex with could have slept with someone who has AIDS.

Another girl says, "It would be insulting to the guys, implying that they were cheating on you or were bisexuals." Another says that "it would break the mood" to ask a boy to wear a condom. The reality is, as the boy above admits, that the guys (and girls) are cheating. The tendency for those teens having sex outside of marriage is, as we have seen, to continue the same pattern when away to school or for a long summer vacation. Here they can easily pick up some disease and bring it back to their home town again. The trouble is, given the five to seven years before AIDS breaks out, these students will never see the harm immediately before them, but harm's been done and it's eventually fatal. It's hard to know what to say to such short-sighted teenagers, but surely fearing "insult" or fearing "breaking the mood" are gross and selfish trade-offs for the possible death of someone you would call a girlfriend or boyfriend.

Condoms: Untruth in Packaging

On the con side, I share this worry with the bishops. In all of the understandable anxiety to control a deadly disease through the use of and promotion of condoms, there is a real danger that the constant condom-use message will undermine the guys who can be, should be, and want to be chaste. Those promoting condoms will say to you, "Oh, yes, abstinence and restraint are better," but then go on to give such a heavy push on condoms that this message gets lost. You can wind up with the impression that being "sexually active" (as they put it) is just a mere preference, like preferring vanilla to chocolate. I can even see the kids eventually comparing condom brands. And how far behind can designer condoms be? The tragedy will be not only that one more pressure is put on you, but also that other values behind being "sexually active" are not explored. Such as what? Such as the well-known reality (as we have seen so often) that such sex is a mask for what's hurting or lacking inside a person. As one writer says, summing up all that we know about young people like you:

> Teens experiment and take risks. Their basic motivation springs from basic psychological needs such as the desire to be accepted, peer pressure, and the need to establish their independence. But the strongest motivating factor for sexual activity is the need to love and be loved.[9]

That quotation's truer than the writer may realize. The need for acceptance, the need to love and be loved—they're all a part of that God-given plan we mentioned. But that's just the point. They're a part of the plan, the getting-ready time, the preparation, and shouldn't be confused with the real thing. Premature sex confuses the issue. Therefore, mere condom promotion, while perhaps needed for others, doesn't deal with that most basic thing, your life. You get the impression that such values as acceptance and love and saving sex till marriage when you are really committed are for the "nerds" or, worse, for "religious" kids, but not for real teenagers rolling on movieland beaches. I fear that not much time will be spent in teaching teens moral values and the meaning behind sex. And that's too bad because that's where the real victory is. But it's also hard to do and it takes time. So why should people try when there's such an easy solution at hand such as condoms? And, besides, truth to tell, there's lots of money to be made from their sale.

I have another worry too, a worry in the form of a question. Will those who promote condoms tell you with full emphasis that while condoms may help lower the risk of infection, they are not foolproof? A fresh press release reports this (emphasis mine):

> Intensified government testing of condoms underscores a fact *well known* to health officials: they do not provide sure protection against AIDS, pregnancy or anything else.

While the odds of any particular condom being leakproof are impossible to determine in random testing, Food and Drug Administration inspections over the past four months found that roughly 20 percent of the 204 batches tested failed to meet government standards.[10]

Recently, the very respected *New England Journal of Medicine* stated, "It has recently been shown that condoms failed to prevent HIV (human immunodeficiency virus—AIDS virus) transmission in 3 of 18 couples, suggesting that the rate of condom failure with HIV may be as high as 17%."[11]

A female doctor is so upset about women being fooled into thinking that condom-sex is safe sex that she recently wrote a book, *The Real Truth About Women and AIDS*. She tells women that they have been dangerously misinformed about AIDS by not realizing that condoms may reduce the transmission of AIDS but by no means do they make sex "safe" by eliminating the possibility of catching the disease. And in the case of anal intercourse, condoms are only 50 percent safe. So note these warnings. Otherwise the bad joke is that the publicity blitz about condoms can give such a false sense of security that it may wind up promoting the very thing it is trying to prevent: pregnancy and the spread of a deadly disease.

No, look. The better way of dealing with the epidemic of AIDS and STDs is a basic reshaping of our attitudes and values. We so easily tolerate a decline in the standards of truthfulness and honesty—remember Watergate and Irangate?—and we so easily let babies die in abortions and take for granted that promiscuous sex is the right thing, but we have to change these non-values. We have to take a firm stand on the old value of chastity before marriage and fidelity in marriage. We can do it if we're motivated enough. Look at how many people were addicted to nicotine but lung cancer deaths and high-powered education and Smoke Enders programs freed hundreds of thousands from smoking. Years ago there was no hope for the alcoholic but someone came along with Alcoholics Anonymous and today there are millions of people who might have been slaves to alcohol who are now happy and free. So, too, if they really wanted to, our teachers and our media people could get together to help us change our attitudes and values. They're trying it with drugs. Don't scramble your brains, they say. They could do it with sex. Don't use sex, don't make it cheap, don't run the risk of giving or getting death. Give life.

So condoms can never, should never, be on the same level as abstinence and moral principles. For a boy like you, it should be a matter of that "disciplined and devoted delay" that makes your covenant with your beloved special and unique, not shared with anyone else, something that you both grow into, an outward sign of the deep and abiding and faithful love you have for one another. That dream is worth waiting for.

QUESTIONS FOR REFLECTION AND DISCUSSION

1. What are the eight causes of STDs, according to World Health Organization? Do you agree with each of them? Why? Why not?

2. AIDS has the spotlight, but name some of the other common STDs and how they are caught.

3. What is the "Superman Complex"? Does it play any role in your life?

4. One in 61 babies in New York City is born with AIDS, which means their mothers are infected and they are carriers of this disease. How did this happen?

I knelt and asked Christ to come into my life,
and to forgive me, and to be my friend and my
Lord. And I knew, in that instant, that getting
right with God was more important than any-
thing else in the world.

                              David Sheppard, Teen Athlete

16
GAY OK?

The rapid rise of AIDS has given new focus to homosexuals because they are by and large the most affected. As we saw, in
this country AIDS probably started with homosexuals and
spread among them in alarming numbers and has depleted their
ranks. Homosexuals in the once bustling Castro center in San
Francisco, for example, a large homosexual area, can no longer
count the number of friends who have died from the dreaded
disease, there have been so many. One resident says, "You're
always in mourning for someone and you know there's going to be
more." Another said that he stopped counting the number of his
friends at 30. Understandably. Since 1981, 3,402 cases of AIDS
have been diagnosed in San Francisco and of this number, mostly all homosexuals, 2,030 have already died.

Who are these people and what is homosexuality? Homosexuality is an attraction to, and sometimes sexual activity
with, members of one's own sex. A male homosexual, for example, may have the same sexual feelings and arousal from seeing
another guy, as you would from seeing a girl. It's hard to tell
how many there are, but guesses range from 4 to 10 percent of the
population in our country. History has been hard on homosexu-

als and much of the old laws punishing homosexuals are rooted in our Jewish-Christian heritage.[1] The Bible gives us a story of Sodom and Gomorrah which has often been interpreted as condemning homosexuality—whereas another possibility is that the story is really about condemning gross inhospitality (a major fault in the East). St. Paul is often quoted as saying that homosexual conduct and being a Christian could not go together and that homosexual acts are "against nature," but another possible translation of those words is that such acts are "not our custom." In any case, the Christian tradition has been generally condemnatory of homosexuality. Orthodox Judaism holds that it is prohibited by the Levitical laws.[2]

Causes

What causes homosexuality? No one knows for sure. We know that everyone has some degree of it in him or her. Sometimes before adolescence or between 11 and 14 some boys may engage in some occasional sex play with other boys, but this doesn't mean they are homosexual or will become so. They may even have a "crush" on another boy. But they may just be going through a phase, a curiosity, and there's nothing to be alarmed about. But as to the causes, no one knows for sure.

One guess is that homosexuals are born that way. That is, there may be some different chemical balance, some hormone arrangement (called the LH hormone) that makes a boy (or a girl) a homosexual. Others say no, it's the way he's brought up and the key figure is the father. If he's not around too much for the boy to identify with, then his mother becomes his role model. He begins to identify with women and takes on the female temperament and preferences in his feelings and emotions, even though his body is male. Recent research at Boston University Medical Center has found that homosexual men are five times more likely than non-homosexual men to have a brother who is gay. That's interesting but it still doesn't answer the basic question: Is homosexuality due to inheritance or upbringing? Maybe it's a combination of both. No one knows for sure. The doctor who led the study says, "We suspect that these results are due to some combination of environmental and biological causes."

Five things we do know: (1) Homosexuality is not deliberately chosen. It is something that happens to a boy. A boy is already that way by the time he begins to suspect that he's gay.(2) Many experts believe that sexual preference may be determined before eight. (3) Homosexuality is not contagious. You don't become a homosexual by knowing someone who is. (4) Homosexuality is not the result of some short-circuited or interrupted sexual development but seems to always have been a natural form of sexual development for a standard percentage of the human race in most cultures during the course of history. (5)An occasional sexual encounter or activity with another male does not turn you into a homosexual. If you have had some experience along these lines that worries you, it is important that you talk them over with someone, with some trusted adult just to clear up your own mind.

Anyway, whatever the cause, homosexuality exists. The homosexual soon learns to think of himself as different. He is not accepted by society and if he has a lot of "girlish" ways, he can be the butt of cruel jokes and taunts from others. He can become angry and frustrated, and all the more since he didn't choose to be this way. He may try to hide it (go in the "closet"), but the tension is there. In a popular novel years ago, *The Devil's Advocate*, a homosexual named Nicholas Black expresses his anguish to Monsignor Meredith this way:

I know your whole argument on the question of the use and misuse of the body. God made it for the procreation of children and then for the commerce of love between man and woman...[But] to want a boy in the same fashion is a sin against nature...But there's the catch and here's what I want you to tell me. What about my nature? I was born the way I am...It was my nature to be drawn more to men than to women...This is what I am. I can't change it. I didn't ask to be born. I didn't ask to be born like this—God knows I've suffered enough because of it...

But do I need love less? Have I less right to live in contentment because somewhere along the line the Almighty slipped a cog in creation?...I'm lonely! I need love like the

next man! My sort of love! Do I live in a padded cell till I
die?... [3]

It's cries like this that lead homosexuals to group together for
support and to form "Gay Alliances" and "Gay Groups" and to
have "Gay Pride Week" and gay parades to pressure for better
understanding and treatment. But it is also cries like this that
present the hard problems: What's a homosexual to do?
What's right and wrong? What should be our attitude? What
should we think?

Clearing Up the Myths
Maybe in the thinking department we ought to quickly set
aside four myths and add two cautions before we get down to
the big questions of right and wrong.

Myth 1: Homosexuality is confined to men. Not so. Homosexuality among women, though seemingly less common than
among men, is called lesbianism. We are not as apt to be aware
of lesbians, however, because our culture allows women to hug
and kiss in public but it does not allow men to do so.

*Myth 2: Homosexuals are sissified, "fruity," feminine types
of males.* The stereotype of the young homosexual is the gay
boy swishing down the school corridor with the walk and airs
of a girl. He may be gay. He may not be. True, some homosexuals are like that; they do have the traits we associate with
girls. But homosexuals are not confined to these types. Homosexuals can be found among football players, clergymen, and
master sergeants. Body build and facial image give no clue
here. You can't tell a homosexual by looking at him.

*Myth 3: Homosexuals are encountered only in certain call-
ings.* This usually means that homosexuals are found only in the
arts and in the theater. There is no doubt that they form a majority in the fashion industry and in the entertainment industry
as writers, dancers, directors, and actors. The terrible deaths
from AIDS on Broadway and in Hollywood underscore that. But
homosexuals are found in every walk of life as everyone else
and are contributing and responsible members of society.

Myth 4: Homosexuals are bad people. Speaking of their entire lives, not just of their homosexuality, yes and no, probably in the same proportion as of the rest of the population.

Caution 1: The labels "gay" and "homosexual" are adjectives, not nouns. Someone is a gay or homosexual person. If someone says, "I am gay," that locks him in, giving the impression that he is gay in everything and that there's a gay arithmetic or a gay geography or a gay weather forecast. No, the person has a homosexual or gay sexual orientation or tendency, but this does not erase the fact that he lives and acts and operates in a regular, real world as a regular, real person. And besides—it is important to grasp this—gayness, unfortunately always seems to imply sex organ activity but that is only one form of expression. Homosexuality manifests itself in a number of ways other than sexual activity and we shouldn't fail to highlight that fact. To say "I am gay" or "I am homosexual" tends to equate this condition with a person's whole personality and that's not a fair or good thing for homosexuals or heterosexuals to do.

Caution 2: Some guys are fake, or psuedo-homosexuals. Some guys are so far out and so rebellious that the only way they can really show anger and hurt someone else is to join themselves to any group they think is outrageous. So they may join a gang like "Hell's Angels" or an outlandish homosexual group. If they do, they may be less gay than rebellious. They may talk themselves in thinking they're gay when they're only delinquent.

While we're on the myths and cautions trail, we should mention some from the other side. That is, homosexuals have their own myths that are wrong and misleading.

Myth 1: Homosexuality is normal. There are societies that try to get equal rights and considerations and privileges for homosexuals, and well they should. We should support that. Discrimination against people who have no choice about their color, race, or sexual bent is hardly Christian. But some groups go too far and declare that homosexuality ought even to be considered a normal way of life, or as they might say, an "alternate lifestyle." They receive support from the general atmosphere today which says there are no fixed standards or absolutes. I don't agree that homosexual activity is merely a normal alternate lifestyle.

Our Tradition

In our tradition, homosexuality is seen as a departure from what we find in the Bible. In Genesis, we find that God made man and woman as complementary. This means that they are like hand-and-glove in every way. One fits in with the other. The way man and woman are inside and outside show they go together, even, as we say, the very arrangement of the sexual organs, perfectly designed to fit together so "that they are no longer two but one flesh." And this unity reflects the inner unity of God. There is, in a word, a whole "spousal significance" to male and female. That fancy phrase means that it is written into the very nature of man and women to be united, to be one, to be a normal pattern of mind-body togetherness. There is a basic relatedness here, a special relationship that is a natural give-and-take, a life-giving relationship especially with its direction to having children.[4]

Granted that homosexual persons are often generous and giving of themselves, they simply cannot express this complementary meaning, this natural unity, this two-in one pattern, this life-transmission capacity in having sex with another man. There is a built-in disorder in using the sexual organs in this way. This doesn't mean that the person himself or herself is "disordered" in the sense that they are evil or wicked. What it does mean is that the person has a condition that inclines him or her to an out-of-normal pattern.

Put it this way. A person, for whatever reason, whether through nature or upbringing, may be kleptomaniac, one who steals compulsively. He may be a marvelous and fun person in every way, but he has this tendency, this bent, this orientation, this disorder. You don't label him as a total mess or misfit. No, you should say the truth. Joe is a great guy, but in this area he's got a problem. He's not in the normal pattern. In this sense, homosexuality is not in the normal pattern. It's a tendency, an inclination (not the whole personality) that we can admit is off-center. Of course the person can't help this tendency, or orientation, and so there is no fault for just being a homosexual. Indeed the church considers homosexuals' sexual identity "central to their faith-lives and that one component of this sexual identity, their orientation, can be used as a 'building block' rather than a stumbling block in their search for unity and harmony.... The homosexual orientation is in no way a sinful condition but is simply the starting point for one's unique response to Christ's call to perfection."[5] What would be objectively wrong would be homosexual acts. As Rev. Robert Nugent, who writes a great deal on the issue, says:

People came to understand the distinction between behavior and orientation...that it is still possible to arrive at a free and mature decision to forego all sexual-genital activity entirely for a variety of reasons. There are, in other words, people who are fully comfortable with the identities "homosexual" and "celibate."[6]

And that leads us to the second myth.

Myth 2: Because of their sexual orientation, homosexuals should have unrestrained sexual activity. This would receive support, of course, from all those people who think this is true of anybody whatsoever. This is the message, as we saw, that the media gives. Have sex all you want, how you want, and when you want, and even now with AIDS, do the same but make it "safe" sex.

This attitude is reflected in the newspaper account above about the gay Castro area of San Francisco:

The late 1970s and early 1980s were a period of anything-goes sexual liberation for San Francisco's gay community. On some nights, thousands of men, many seminude or wearing costumes, women's clothing or heavily studded leather outerwear, overflowed onto the community's sidewalks, some taunting heterosexual couples who had ventured into their neighborhoods as "breeders."

It was not uncommon for some men to have sexual acts with 20 or 30 partners in a single evening at bath houses that featured "orgy rooms" and other facilities designed to encourage multiple sexual acts.[7]

Of course, AIDS has chilled all that. But what about those 20 or 30 sexual contacts a night? That's not all immoral for any-

one, gay or straight, and it not only demeans sex's God-given
impulse to giveness and care, but surely it's got to be a deep
symptom of a deeper problem. For instance, how lonely how
hurt, how desperate must such people be? A well-known writer,
Rev. Henri Nouwen, visited the area and caught the mood
quickly. He writes:

> As I walked with my friend on the streets of the Castro
> district, we saw countless men walking up and down the
> sidewalks just looking at each other, gazing in store win-
> dows or standing on corners in small groups, going in and
> out of bars, theaters, video shops, and restaurants. It
> seemed as if everyone was waiting for something that
> would bring him a sense of being deeply loved, fully ac-
> cepted, and truly at home. But in many eyes there was
> deep suffering, anguish, and loneliness, because what they
> most seek seems almost elusive. Many have not been able
> to find a lasting home or relationship, and, now with
> AIDS great fear overshadows all the disillusionment.[8]

Anyway, the point is that homosexuals are bound to the same
moral standards as everyone else—chaste living outside of
marriage—and their sexual leaning does not give them license
to unrestrained sex, if for no other reason than they'll not find
what they're looking for that way, any more than other people
will.[9]

Guidelines and Challenges

Well, then, how shall we act? Are there any guidelines? Yes,
we can share some that would apply to you if you ever think
you are gay or to others in general who in fact might be.

1) *If you think you might be gay or have a friend who thinks
so, you must seek advice.* You should talk it over with a trusted
adult. There may be no homosexuality at all. It may be only a
stage of development. But you'll never know unless you ask, so if
you ever have doubts, please do.

2) *For real homosexuals, the prospects for adjusting to regular
or heterosexual directions are apt to be better than are assumed
or publicized,* and for gays to resist, as some do, the possibility

of a change is to short-change themselves. Counsellor Ruth T. Barnhouse claims that it is really well known and easy to verify that 30 percent of homosexuals who come to psychotherapy for any reason can be changed. So the idea of change should not automatically be ruled out. However, along these lines, if a boy is convinced that he really is gay, it would still be wise for him to wait a bit—maybe till mid-twenties—before "coming out of the closet" and admitting publicly his homosexuality. The reason is that if he (or she) does come out too soon while his sexual identity is still fluid and in formation, he might lock himself into an unfinished pattern and cut off further development. You usually have to experience adult living before you can accept with confidence a permanent homosexual identity.

3) Even though it is hard, gays are challenged to be chaste, to restrain their sexual impulses. The church urges them to take responsibility for their growth toward chastity and self-control. They can even find help in an organization called Courage, founded by Rev. John Harvey (who is both a theologian and psychologist), to help them live a life of prayer, self-discipline, and close non-sexual friendships. There is also an organization called New Ways Ministry that provides support and, yes, even protection from the unfair scorn of the present culture.

Models for Right Living
In fact, they might think of Aelred. Who's he? Well, for one thing, he's a saint. He was an abbot, the head of a monastery. He lived in medieval times and was quite famous then. He advised other abbots and bishops and corresponded with popes and kings. He was a writer on spiritual topics. He was gay. Like Mary Magdalene he fooled around with sex when he was younger and like St. Augustine who had sex with a woman before he converted. Aelred formed a strong attachment to and affection for one particular man, but he renounced all this and became a monk. When I say he renounced all this I do not mean that he lied and said that sex was awful (it was not; it was great) or that the man he had sex with was a monster. Nothing

of the sort. He knew it was good, but also that it was misdirected. So he disciplined himself, fasting and taking cold baths, but still he remained what he was, a chaste homosexual. In due time, even within the monastery, he felt a strong sexual attraction (with no sexual actions) to two fellow monks. He wasn't ashamed of the feelings. That's the way he was, so why should he? Instead he praised the good feeling and proceded to write beautifully on homosexual friendship (without sex organ contact) and left us a legacy of how gays can live well and happy in the Lord. In our terms, he was not gay. He was a gay person and his homosexuality was spread out in creative ways. In short, he learned to love and accept himself, acknowledging the person he was. He learned to befriend himself as this particular homosexual person created and loved by God. And that's an important step for any homosexual to follow.

In our own times, even some few priests, faithful and true to the gospel and fully committed to a chaste life of sexual behavior, have come out openly to admit that they are homosexual in orientation. They realized that this might shock some people but they were willing to risk it. They simply wanted to take a stand and say to all (including you), "Look, a person can be homosexual in orientation and still chaste in behavior, and therefore, as you can see, be a very faithful member of and even a minister in the church." They have done this and urged others to do likewise for a very important reason: image. You see, they want to counterpoint some of the really bad and widespread images that some gays admit they have brought on themselves. Images, for example, of some gays running around in outlandish and weird costumes and using exaggerated mannerisms (you see this sometimes on TV coverage of their rallies); images of gays who, like so many others, are heavy into consumerism, the "good life," since they don't have families to support and therefore come across as self-centered, not concerned about the poor and needy; images of their fixation on the body or sleazy sex and homosexual pornography, which in its way makes objects or things of people just as (as we shall see) heterosexual pornography does; finally, the image of gays having sexual activity all the time with as many other gays as possible (as we read in the article on the Castro gay area in San Francisco).

These images are widespread and generally (and rightly) they turn heterosexual people off. So better models are needed, models of homosexual maturity, responsibility, and holiness. And that, by the way, might be the God-given calling of any boy who finally does determine that he is gay: to live out and tell a genuinely religious story and demonstrate a caring, holy life for those desperately looking for models of how, as a gay person, to be like Jesus.

4) Gays must use extra caution and should have extra motivation to be chaste since they are still the prime carriers and receivers of AIDS. Often homosexuals who are sexually active practice sodomy, inserting the penis into the rectum of another. The large intestine of the rectum was meant to expel waste, not take in anything. Inserting anything (such as the penis), according to the experts on AIDS, often involves breaking the rectal tissues and so lets the dangerous virus into the bloodstream. One study has even shown that the virus may, even without any break, be able to directly infect the cells in the large intestine or rectum. So even the deadly disease should force gays (and non-gays too for that matter) into rethinking their use of sex and to concentrate where we all should: on the many ways and levels, emotional and spiritual, they can build lasting and faithful relationships.

5) Your attitude must reflect that of Jesus, who said that we are to love one another as he has loved us, and he included everybody. If there's a kid in school that the other guys call "queer" or "fag" or "homo," for you to join in the name calling would be sinful. If the kid really is gay, he will need all the help and understanding he can get. He is probably already suffering enough from loneliness and prejudice; you should not add to it. If he's generally a decent guy, he can be friends with you and you with him without any sexual overtones. The church itself, in its official letter on homosexuality, denounces outright "violent malice in speech or in action" directed against gay persons and says that they too share in the inner "dignity of each

person which must always be respected." The church realizes
that individuals are not to blame for their sexual tendencies
and so, while it doesn't approve of gay sexual acts, it reserves
judgment to the Lord. And when you come right down to it, although the ideal of a man-woman marriage relationship or
perfect chastity is not always attainable for some gays—
although all are bound to try for chastity—still an honest relationship with another member of the same sex is better than
isolation and loneliness, a permanent and loyal commitment is
better than "one night stands," and faithfulness is always better (and safer) than playing the field.[10]

Anyway, it always pays, in any circumstance, to look beyond
appearances and try to see a person's "inside," what makes him
tick, who he really is, not just what he shows on the outside. I
think of the Catholic chaplain at St. Francis Memorial Hospital in San Francisco, Giles Valcovich, who certainly adheres to
the Catholic church's stand against homosexual activity, but
also admits to a "great awakening" in working with AIDS patients for the past five years. He says:

It was a revelation to me...how much they hated being os-
tracized, being categorized as if they were all atheists...
God is very important in their lives and it only intensifies
their hurt when they are tabbed as non-religious people.
To consider that God is perhaps a bit more real to them
than for people who are thought to be God-fearing has
changed my whole outlook. I just don't generalize any
more. The last thing you want to be is judgmental or condemnatory—you've got to just take an individual where
he or she is and go from there.

This remark reminds me of the movie *Mask*. A young man is trying to live a normal life but because of a disfigured face he ran
into the problem of being accepted. The doctors who examined
him warned him and his mother that he didn't have very long
to live. The principal of the local high school tried to side-
track him into a "special school." The students avoided him.
The parents of a blind girl he met and fell in love with prevented him from communicating with their daughter. When a camp

counsellor first met him, he told him to take off his mask—but it was his real face. When you watch the movie, you can feel the prejudices but you also begin to learn, as his mother learned, that the boy has a real deep inner beauty and anyone who looks beyond the appearance discovers this too. And not only discovers it, but is made better for it. Every time you try to see Jesus in others, you are made better for it. And so is the world, gay or straight.

QUESTIONS FOR REFLECTION AND DISCUSSION

1. What is the difference between homosexual orientation and homosexual activity?

2. The Orthodox Church, Orthodox Judaism, the Catholic Church, the Church of England and the Christian fundamentalist churches all pronounce homosexual activity wrong. Why? Do you think it is? Why?

3. What is your gut reaction to Nicholas Black's statement about his body being homosexual?

4. "The labels 'gay' and 'homosexual' are adjectives, not nouns." How do you understand this? What is its significance?

5. Do you agree that homosexuals are bound to the same moral standards, concerning sexual activity, as everyone else? Why? Why not?

On "Dynasty" when Alexis and whoever it is that week go into the bedroom, they're portraying sex as so carefree and so casual. And it's not so casual. It's supposed to be a caring thing.

17-year-old Girl

17
BIRTH CONTROL

Because birth control is such a common topic and your school probably deals directly or indirectly with the subject at one time or another, let me give you some information. Birth control, or contraception, as you recall from the first few chapters, involves any means or method that prevents the sperm from reaching and fertilizing the egg, thereby preventing conception. The word itself means "against conception." There are some contraceptives for the male but most are for the female. They fall into two categories: those that put a mechanical or chemical barrier between sperm and egg, and those that prevent the egg from appearing or developing at all. Some of the common types of contraceptive methods are listed here.

1) The Diaphragm. This appliance covers the cervix, the entrance to the uterus. It is made of soft rubber or similar material and has the shape of a hollow cup. It fits snugly into the vagina and blocks the entrance to the uterus. As a plug in a bathtub prevents water from getting into the drain, so the diaphragm prevents the sperm from getting into the womb.

2) Creams or jellies. There are certain creams or jellies that contain strong chemical agents that can kill or immobilize the sperm. In addition, some of these creams or jellies form a foam over the entrance to the womb and so prevent the sperm from getting in. This cream or jelly can come in a suppository form, that is, in the form of a small, narrow "popsicle" that melts with body temperature in the vagina and so releases its chemicals.

3) *The Intrauterine Device (IUD)*. This is a metalic foreign object (often a metal object looking like a figure 7 with a coil on it) introduced into the woman's uterus which, once the egg has been fertilized, prevents it from getting attached to the uterine wall. No one knows for sure why it does this but it does. It is important to note, however, that since the egg is already fertilized before the IUD can work, the IUD is not a "contraceptive," but actually causes an early abortion.

4) *Vaginal Sponge*. This is a small sponge that is placed in the vagina and contains a spermicide, a chemical to kill the sperm. So it functions two ways: preventing the sperm from entering the uterine area and, if any do get by, to kill them with a chemical.

5) *The Pill*. This is the famous pill, really a series of pills over a period of time, that introduces an artificial chemical into the woman. When a woman is pregnant she manufactures a natural chemical, or hormone, that tells the body not to make any more eggs since she has one that is currently developing. (That's why a pregnant woman does not get pregnant simultaneously). Now scientists have developed this same hormone artificially. When a woman takes this hormone in pill form it goes into the body and tells it a "lie." It says, "I am pregnant so don't make any more eggs." And it doesn't.

But this birth control pill, which seems to be the most frequently used source for girls, has its dangers. It does not, of course, prevent the spread of AIDS or any other STD and it has been shown to have many side effects. These include blood problems, hypertension, and diabetes. For many teens, it causes nausea. As one eminent doctor put it:

If you give girls the pill before they are totally physically mature, they risk, first, interference with their normal growth; second, because it affects the pituitary, they are more likely to develop diabetes; third, they may never develop regular periods. It should never be given to anyone under 17. And because of the risk of cancer of the cervix, it is probably better not to give it to anyone under 25.[1]

6) *Tubal Ligation and Vasectomy.* These are surgical procedures. For the female, the doctor will tie a surgical thread around the fallopian tubes so that the egg can't pass through them to meet the sperm. For the male, it means snipping the tube that carries his sperm so that it runs into a dead end. These are most often permanent, non-reversible operations.

7) *The Condom.* The condom is a rubber or latex sheath, like a rolled-up balloon, which the male rolls down over his erect penis. During intercourse, when the sperm spurts out, it is caught in the condom (which is thrown away) and so the sperm does not enter the vagina. More of this later. Condoms for females have recently been developed also.

Safe and Sane

8) *Abstinence.* This and the following, though listed last, are by no means least. Abstinence is obviously a very effective means of not having babies. It works every time, while none of the above methods are 100 percent foolproof. In our society, abstinence has a bad name because the myth is that somehow every red-blooded American, male or female, married or single, must be engaged in sex much of every day. The truth is, however, that even in marriage there are periods, sometimes long ones, of abstinence. When traveling on a business trip a husband is faithful to his wife as she is to him. At times of illness and when near childbirth there are considerable periods of abstinence. In an old Jewish tradition, the couple voluntarily gives up sexual intercourse so that they may be recharged as it were and approach each other again in a fresh way. Some people, whether in religious life or not, might abstain from sex for the sake of a higher cause, like, recall, the non-Christian Gandhi. But, as I said, abstinence, in a culture based on consuming, is not honored as an ideal.

Here is a full-page newspaper ad by a pharmaceutical company regarding birth control pills and abstinence. Here are the opening lines:

It's good for you. It's bad for you. It causes cancer. It makes you more fertile. It makes you less fertile. You should get off it. All the conflicting information floating around about the Pill is enough to make you contemplate abstinence. We recommend a far less drastic measure....

Of course, they're selling pills, but notice the put-down of abstinence: "...enough to make you contemplate abstinence." Good grief, what a fate! No wonder, out of the goodness of their hearts (and pocketbooks), they hasten to add, "We recommend a far less drastic measure...." But keep an open mind on abstinence.

9) *Natural Family Planning.* Natural family planning is based on the simple principle that a woman is fertile (able to become pregnant) for only a certain period each month, while a man's fertility is continuous. The fertile time is when a woman has a ripe egg ready to be released from an ovary into the fallopian tube, or when it already has been released and has traveled down the tube into the uterus.

You remember that during the women's monthly period, her womb lining, along with the unfertilized egg, has broken down and gone out with the blood flow. After this, the lining needs to repair itself, and during this time no egg will be released because the womb isn't ready yet to receive it. Four days after this "break down" (menstruation) and if no mucus is present, sexual intercourse will not result in pregnancy.

With proper instruction, a woman can determine her fertile days by certain bodily signs, including a slight rise in temperature, mucous discharges from the vagina and changes in the cervix (the mouth of the womb). From these signs she can tell whether she has ovulated and an egg is present, whether she is fertile or not. Properly used, this method is reliable, safe from physical side effects and in harmony with nature. It also is a witness against the widespread mentality that believes contraceptives should be given to everyone, including (and perhaps especially) teenagers.

Before medical science developed natural family planning, married couples often used "rhythm" to try to avoid pregnancy. This was a calendar method for determining when the woman was fertile, but was not accurate for many women whose monthly periods were irregular. However, when properly understood and used, natural family planning is as effective in preventing pregnancy as the pill—and more effective than the IUD, the condom, or the diaphragm.

Right and Wrong

What about such birth control methods? What's right and wrong about them? Let's take the married couple first. The married couple have stood in front of the public and made an open commitment and declaration of love; to stay together for life and roll with life's punches together. Their love is sealed by sex, the way it should be. Sexual love, or sexual intercourse, summarizes and promotes the love they already have and have made into a binding commitment. The question is, may such a married couple use artificial birth control? The general answer according to the Catholic church is no. Not to leave sex open to life is less than ideal—and children are a wonderful gift, generally speaking.

Still, sometimes there are pressures that honestly tell a couple that another child at this time would be a hardship.[2] Not that they don't love children, but other circumstances, such as health, finances, emotional upset, or whatever, may lead a husband and wife to delay for a time or altogether having children or another child. This has to be a sincere and prayerful (not selfish) decision, of course, for the issue at hand is serious. So what can they do? They can refrain from sex (abstinence) or they can confine sexual love to the days of the month when the wife is infertile (natural family planning). There are cases, however, when these efforts fail and the couple may resort to using some means of artificial birth control. They realize this is not the best or most ideal way to prevent pregnancy, but again, their decision is made in a context of mutual caring and commitment and in the service of their marriage, family life, and the community.

That's vastly different from the unmarried couples who use birth control. For starters, as we saw, unmarried couples should not have sex to begin with, and certainly no teenager should. Yes, as we saw before, if they're going to have sex, better to use birth control than transfer disease and bring an unwanted baby into the world, but the issue, you recall, is deeper than that. There is no public commitment for one thing, no awareness that their love must always go beyond them and be a part of the larger community. Or the unmarried couple may be taking the sexual pleasure without the responsibility of mutual caring; or, even if there is caring, without the courage of the full commitment that a public marriage displays. Sexual intercourse without marriage is always less than it should be.

The use of contraceptives, in this instance, though practical, also makes each partner "safe" from the total public commitment that the full dignity of the other person demands. Sex without marriage, as we shall see later, emotionally sets the couple up to choose abortion if the birth control method they're using fails and, in any case, always carries with it unspoken questions of trust, permanency, and the quality of the relationship. These are the questions that must be spoken. Trust, permanency and the quality of our relationships, after all, are what commitment is all about.

QUESTIONS FOR REFLECTION AND DISCUSSION
1. The Natural Family Planning methods of limiting births is quite effective. What do you know about this method? How safe is it? Why is it not more commonly used?
2. What are the dangers, if any, of the Pill? the condom?
3. The use of contraceptives between an unmarried couple, although practical, makes each partner safe from total public commitment that the dignity of the other person demands. Comment.

I couldn't believe I was lying on that table and was actually asking them to kill my baby... But I did it. I did it and it's over. Sometimes I have to keep telling myself that it's over.
Premed Student

18
ABORTION

"How did you become interested in music?" That was the question posed to the conductor of the Hamilton (Canada) Philharmonic Symphony Orchestra, Boris Brott. He hesitated a moment and replied:

> You know, this may sound strange, but music has been a part of me since before birth. As a young man, I was mystified by this unusual ability I had, to play certain pieces sight unseen. I'd be conducting a score for the first time and, suddenly, the cello line would jump out at me; I'd know the flow of the piece even before I turned the page of the score. One day, I mentioned this to my mother, a professional cellist. I thought she'd be intrigued because it was always the cello line that was so distinct in my mind. She was, but when she heard what the pieces were, the mystery quickly solved itself. All the scores I knew sight unseen were ones she had played while she was pregnant with me.

And that true story is why abortion is wrong.

What Boris Brott said was right on target. Children in the womb are real babies, alive, intelligent, and can remember and be influenced by sights and sounds and their mothers' emotions and feelings. In a hospital in Long Branch, New Jersey, for example, there is a course called "Infant Stimulation" that shows parents that babies in the womb have developed senses and consciousness before birth and that regular stimulation programs, as studies have shown (at Brown University), can produce IQ gains of 27 to 30 points over unborn babies not in the program. The studies and the program also show that unborn babies do not like rock music—sorry about that—but prefer the three classic B's: Bach, Beethoven, and Brahms.

So the babies in the womb are feeling, remembering, aware beings, and what happens to them in those nine months mightily affect them. Therefore the mother (especially) and the father—their feelings, attitudes, values—do have a profound effect on the child. The baby in the womb can scientifically sense gentleness, softness, and caring, and reacts to heat and cold and sounds and light. Unborn babies can sense their mothers' attitudes and how they're feeling at the moment. They can remember and learn. Why, a group of scientists even taught 16 unborn babies to respond to a vibrating sensation by kicking! There have also been studies that show that unborn babies can get agitated even if the mother thinks of smoking (which is very harmful to the child—reduces the oxygen supply) and so they sense and react to it. They get very anxious and upset because they never know when Mommy will smoke again. Another study shows how unborn babies actually move in rhythm to the mother's speech.[1]

The Miracle of Life's Beginning

None of this should be news. More and more doctors treat the unborn babies as patients (and call them that). They can operate on the unborn baby, can put electrodes on the mother's womb and watch the baby on the TV monitor, and watch the baby moving, sucking a thumb, smiling, turning around, and all the rest. They can, if need be in an emergency, remove a premature baby from the mother's womb and put the baby in an artificial womb. As we said, these are the facts and maybe the best thing you can do is look at that remarkable book, or see the TV presentation on *Nova* (Public Television), *A Child Is Born*. It's a breakthrough in photography. Lennart Nilsson has developed a way to photograph the baby inside the mother's womb. What a fantastic sight! Here's some of the things it shows:

In the first hours after fertilization the mother's and father's genes and chromosomes are exchanged. This egg-sperm union is very much alive.

At the end of the third week the nervous system begins to form.

At 4 weeks the embryo (as it's called) now has a body with a head, a trunk, and a tail; the primitive heart began beating on the eighteenth day.

By 6-7 weeks the baby is making body movements. At this period the baby is called a "fetus," which is the Latin word for "little baby."

At 8 weeks the developing child can make a tiny fist, get the hiccups, suck a thumb, sleep and wake up.

At 8 or 9 weeks the face looks more "human" to us with eyelids, snub nose, and beginning ear.

Here, let me quote the book:

At eleven weeks old [2 inches long], the eyes are closed...the face is already assumed a baby's profile, with a large, rounded forehead, a tiny snub nose, and a definite chin. Muscles are already at work under the skin, and their movements become gradually more coordinated by the developing nervous system. The lips open and close, the forehead wrinkles, the brows rise and the head turns.

At 18 weeks, the baby has already formed fingers and toes and is active and kicks and punches and the mother can feel the baby's movements.

The baby, of course, can now hear and can hear a good deal (as we have seen from the experience of the musicians) and can remember. As the book says of the four-month-old baby in the womb, he or she can "probably hear the woman's voice, the rumblings of her stomach and the sounds she makes eating and drinking. We also know that it hears sounds outside her body. The cries of brothers and sisters, talk, radio, TV, music, traffic—the fetus hears all this and gets used to the noise."

There's all the photographs of the five and a half-month baby scratching its forehead and one of a four and a half-month baby sucking its thumb.

And, from here on in, it's all a matter of refinement and the ongoing development of a real, human child, who, science shows us, is as much alive and human inside the womb as outside.

The Great Turnabout

So why would anyone want to kill the child? Why would people pass laws allowing it? It wasn't always that way. In the United States, as early as 1795 the courts said that in a will, the ordinary meaning of the word "children" included the child in the womb. In 1798, the courts held that unborn children "were entitled to all the privileges of other persons." In 1927 the courts ruled that an unborn child could inherit money left to all of the deceased's grandchildren at the time he died. In 1969 the U.S. Court of Appeals verified that an unborn child can receive Social Security benefits.

The church has been consistent from the very beginning too in saying that the unborn child is a real human being and has a right to life. I mention "from the very beginning" because some people try to pass along the untruth that it was only in the nineteenth century that the church prohibited abortion. Not so. Abortion was condemned from the first century. These are those old, strange churchy names I won't bore you with: names like Tertullian and Basil and first-century church documents with those odd names of the *Didache* ("the teaching") and the *Epistle of Barnabas*. They all forbade abortion. And, besides, the whole message of the gospel would tell us abortion is wrong anyway. The Jewish and Christian tradition was always defending the most defenseless: the stranger, the poor, the widowed, the orphan. Even slaves were to be dealt with as brothers and sisters in the Lord. And who is more defenseless than the child in the womb? Defending the unborn was entirely consistent with all of this teaching.

So strong was the tradition in law and in the church not to kill the unprotected child in the womb that in 1963 a Planned Parenthood pamphlet stated outright, "An abortion kills the life of a baby after it has begun. It is dangerous to your life and health."

Of the three—the law, the church, and Planned Parenthood—two have made a complete change. Planned Parenthood has for the past decades promoted and provided for abortions, and in January 1973 the United States Supreme Court ruled in effect that as a part of her right of privacy a woman has a right to an abortion of a fetus up to six months old. This right has been interpreted to mean that she can have an abortion without having to give any reason. It's all up to her. After the baby reaches a stage where it could live outside of her body—by six or seven months—the woman still could get an abortion if she and her doctor agreed that her physical or mental health might be hurt by her continuing pregnancy. That "mental health" covers a lot of ground. So, again, it's really all up to her. The unborn child, the father of the child, the woman's parents or relatives, the community itself has no effective legal way of stopping that demand. It is ultimately the woman's decision alone based on very serious reasons or very silly reasons or no reasons at all that will decide whether an unborn baby will live or die.[2]

And how strange they should do an about-face just at the very time when science was showing more and more that there is a living, active, remembering, intelligent baby inside the womb! And, as far as the law goes, we now know—and it is admitted by all sides of the question—that the polls at that time showed that the vast majority of Americans did *not* want such a law (as was first claimed) and so the Supreme Court judges made that decision without public support. Since the Supreme Court did legalize abortion, more than 21 million lives have been destroyed in the womb and about one-quarter of these were performed on teenagers.

Why Kill the Miracle?

Why would people ever think of, much less actively promote, the killing of the unborn child? Here are some of their reasons. I list these reasons here with some responses (even though it makes for heavy reading—sorry about that—but stick with it) because I have found that in almost every book or article I've read that people usually get only one side of the argument. Since you seldom hear another side, I wanted to give that too.

1) Pregnancy can sometimes be a health problem to a woman and if it is, she should abort. Thus, abortion here is said to be a "medical decision" based on clinical judgment by a woman and her doctor. But the facts are very much different. Surveys have shown that *in less than one percent of abortions today in America is there any threat to the health of the mother.* A woman hardly talks to her own doctor. She goes to an abortion clinic. Abortion is no more a "medical" procedure than filling your tooth. No, the majority of abortions are not done for grave medical reasons. They are done primarily for convenience, even though, understandably, that convenience may be sought out of fear or anxiety or a host of other motives.

2) Many women die from illegal abortions. Planned Parenthood and newspapers like *The New York Times* maintain that 5,000 to 10,000 women die from such illegal abortions, so let's make abortion legal. Such figures were deliberately made up; when the real facts were revealed, the certified published report was that there were some 133 such deaths a year. Even from a numbers point of view, that's a large and tragic tradeoff for the 10,000 unborn children who are now destroyed for every mother who previously died. Moreover, while it is true that death rates for mothers and newborn infants have fallen since abortion became legal in 1973, the fact is that they were falling at a steeper rate *before* that time.

3) It was claimed that the public supported legalized abortion. As we saw, at the time of the Supreme Court de. ʌion, it was exactly the opposite and *continues to be so.* To this day, less than one-fourth of the public supports abortion on demand, which is the abortion of a developing child at any stage of pregnancy for any reason whatever, even if the mother just "feels" like it. A poll released in January 1988, on the fifteenth anniversary of the Supreme Court's ruling, shows that public doubt about abortion still persists. As the report indicates, only

a minority of the public, only 39 percent, support a right to abortion for "any woman who wants one," which is essentially the current state of the law, while 49 percent limited their support to particular circumstances, such as a pregnancy resulting from rape or one that endangers the mother's life. Even those who support abortion rights, the report says, are uneasy about abortion and believe that too many women are having abortions.[4]

The pollster Louis Harris in his 1987 book *Inside America* says that "by 56% to 40%, most Americans feel that to perform an abortion is the equivalent of murder, because the life of the fetus has been eliminated. By 68% to 27%, a bigger majority also holds that no one's life should be taken without the permission of the individual, and an unborn baby cannot give or refuse permission. And a 60% to 37% majority believes a fetus should have rights, just like all other human beings."[5] Most polls indicate a rejection of abortion without the husband's consent and in abortion clinics. In short, to this day the public consistently rejects abortion on demand.

4) For some radical women, the cry is "I have a right to my body and I can do what I want with it!" But that "begs the question," which means that that is the very issue at hand: She may have a right to *her* body, but science clearly shows that there is *another*, completely whole, functioning independent body, the baby's—whose only dependency on the mother is that she let him or her live. (Remember, we saw that the baby even has its own independent blood stream.) The mother doesn't have a right to that body, no matter how closely it is joined to her. And, as common sense tells you, she doesn't really have an absolute right to her own body anyway, and can't do as she pleases any more than you and I can. She can't, for example, drape her body over a fire exit door to block others. Why? For the same reason she can't (or shouldn't) destroy the baby: There are others to consider, their safety, their lives. The baby, too, is an "other."

5) Planned Parenthood claims that people who are against abortion promote having babies but then they have no concern for such babies *after* birth. At least abortion cleans up the prob-

lems all around. "They don't care about life after birth" is the Planned Parenthood slogan. But the strong, mathematical fact is that those who oppose abortion have set up centers to help pregnant women and their children; there are more than 2,100 of them all over this country. All of them offer counselling and many offer housing, medical care, maternity clothes, baby clothes, cribs, nutrition classes, and help with job skills. For example, Rebecca Younger of Long Beach, California, was asking women entering an abortion clinic to reconsider when one of them said to her, "I'm only 21. I have two kids at home that I can't support. If I deliver this child, will you take it?" Mrs. Younger, the mother of four, said yes. That was the start of New Life Beginnings, which now provides counselling and operates a 16-bed maternity house.

Tom Bresler of Chicago sold his business to open three centers that help pregnant women.

Maureen Shields of Oak Lawn, Illinois, got her fellow parishioners to help the local hospital to contribute maternity clothes, furniture, and medical and psychological help.

Mom's House in Johnstown, Pennsylvania, provides long-term after-birth care.

A Connecticut newspaper man, Chris Bell, has opened homes in New York and New Jersey for young mothers who intend to keep their babies.

The Nazareth Life Center in Garrison, New York, helps pregnant unmarried women who plan to give up their babies for adoption.

And practically every Catholic diocese has homes and resources for mothers-to-be who are in any kind of difficulty, especially unmarried mothers. And not only Catholics, of course, but others who also are concerned about the life of the unborn child, such as Lutherans for Life, Methodists for Life, Presbyterians for Life, and the Choose Life Society, a Jewish pro-life organization.

Those who advocate abortion have nothing like this. Not only that, but Right to Life people are highly active in community and charitable programs, clinics, hospitals, youth work, and programs like Meals on Wheels. Nor do all pro-lifers, contrary to more false accusations, want to save babies from abortion, on the one hand, but are all in favor of the death penalty on the other. The fact is that a high proportion of pro-life activists oppose the death penalty as well as abortion—some 57 percent in contrast to the average 30 percent across the country. So, to be in favor of protecting the human life of the unborn implies a great deal of concern and care after the baby is born.

Choice: Choosing What?

6) Some are in favor of abortion because it gives the woman a "choice." That's why they call themselves pro-choice. That's a clever slogan, for if there is one thing that we have been trained to accept it is that the holiest word in our language is "choice." That implies I'm free. No one is going to impose his or her morality on me. I can do what I want. As if choice in itself were some kind of sacred state. It doesn't matter what you choose so long as you choose. In the pro-choice view, the very idea of choice itself is what is important. But you can see that that is nonsense. There are different values, and one actually is better than another. To justify everything because it's your "choice" and therefore untouchable is like saying that Hitler was "pro-choice," never mind that he chose to have 6 million Jews killed. How can we say he was wrong? He was only exercising his choice. In abortion, being pro-choice is only telling the woman she can choose to kill. It doesn't ask the baby and it doesn't even challenge the morality of what she's choosing. No, there has to be more to the argument than merely saying it's OK because it's my choice.

7) Some have said in effect, so what, it (the fetus) is just a blob. It's like having your appendix removed. The answer to that is found in *A Child Is Born.*

When you look at those pictures, you know you are killing the most defenseless of all. So in order to get the courage to do this, you change the language. You begin to use "thing" and "object," instead of personal and human words. This disguises the real issue. Instead of unborn child, people like those in Planned

Parenthood will use words like "fetus" or "fecal tissue" or "the uterine contents" or "the products of conception." These phrases sound so much more clinical, detached, objective. It's like saying, "Ouch. I didn't crack my skull; I merely fractured the cranium." See how the second sentence is impersonal? In the same way, to say "kill the unborn baby" or even "kill the fetus" is a bit too personal (and conscience pricking). So you change the language to "terminating the pregnancy." But no matter how much people try to cram that language down our throats (and use it in the literature they give you), the basic instinct of every man and woman is to know deep in their hearts that they're really talking about a real, living, human child. Listen. "Mary, thank God, survived the car crash, but they're afraid she'll lose the baby." "Cindy knew the baby she was carrying wasn't Tom's." "My baby seems to kick every time I sit down." "I'm going to have a baby!"

QUESTIONS FOR REFLECTION AND DISCUSSION
1. View the videotape *The Silent Scream* and discuss it.
2. Discuss abortion in the light of Lennart Nilson's book, *A Child Is Born*.
3. What do you think of the pro-abortion arguments? The pro-life arguments?
4. What is the link between contraception and abortion?
5. A high school girl from Virginia says that they always have abortion to back up pregnancy mistakes, giving testimony to the fact that abortion is not just something among the very poor and deprived but is an upper middle class, white solution to unwanted pregnancies. Discuss.

As we often speak of preventing abortion, we must speak of our concern for the mother of the unborn child. Cardinal John J. O'Connor of New York

19
CONFUSION AND COMPASSION

Beyond all the reasons we've mentioned in the preceding chapter against abortion, for some there is a confusion born of misinformation (such as we've just seen) and a confusion born of fears. For some unmarried teenagers—maybe you know some of them—as well as for some married women, the first sign of a pregnancy can throw them into panic. A teenager may not know to whom to turn. She may be afraid to tell her parents or even the boyfriend. Her whole future is threatened: her life, her education, the hurt to her parents. She may see one of the ads for abortion clinics, or "Pregnancy Termination Centers" as some of them are called. Or her friends may direct her to one. All she knows is that she wants to get back to normal, to keep her life going. Under all this pressure it's easy to understand why she would turn to abortion. The same might be true for a married woman who's already raised her family and now finds she's pregnant again. Or one who's health and finances are poor. There are many reasons that might prompt an abortion. Not all understand what it's all about or perhaps even feel that there's any particular moral issue at stake. Therefore, it must be as easy (and right) to be sympathetic and compassionate with them as it is hard to blame them or accuse them of sin. Which is why Cardinal O'Connor of New York has said:

No discussion about abortion can be considered adequate

which does not come to grips with what can be a dilemma for a single or married woman faced with an unplanned pregnancy, and frequently from enormous pressure from every side to solve her dilemma by abortion. As often as we speak of preventing abortion, we must speak of our concern for the mother of the unborn child who is searching for understanding, acceptance and assistance.
So we must rather help such people to heal their feelings and move ahead in life. Yet, at the same time, knowing our own moral vision, we must bear witness to the principle of being "pro-life" in the best and most effective and convincing way we can.

You see, like so much else, what you think about abortion comes from what you think about life in general, your values, what human relationships are all about. And about God. And so when you come right down to it, your stand on abortion is really about whether you think there is some meaning to life, some meaning built into the universe (by God), or whether the only meaning there is is the one you impose. Think about this in terms of abortion. If whether the child (the fetus) lives is totally up to the woman, then you're saying that the child in the womb has no rights (no inalienable rights such as the Constitution provides for all), has no inner, built-in worth or meaning. No, the only worth that the child in the womb has is that conferred by the mother. If she wants it and puts thumbs up, then the child is declared to have worth and it will live. If she doesn't want it for whatever reason or no reason and puts thumbs down, then the child in the womb is declared worthless and it will die. You see, in this abortion system, the child has no worth of itself, just by being who he or she is. The worth is conferred by another. Otherwise, if the child has an already built-in worth, just by being, just by being made in the image and likeness of God, then you could not kill it. So that is why those in favor of abortion have to declare: "Every child is worthless unless I give it worth by my decision to let it live or die." And we could never agree to that.

The horrible irony of this is apparent, as some have pointed out, when one woman with a sick baby in her womb decides to have an abortion while another woman in the hospital room next door, with a baby in the womb the same age and with the same sickness, decides to keep the baby. Then the doctors call the baby-in-the-womb their "patient," treat it like the living person it is, and do all they can to bring the child to birth.

Other Attitudes
Such strange contradictions are why the issue of abortion is debated even among feminists. On the one side there is NOW, the National Organization of Women which is pro-abortion or, as they like to sanitize it, pro-choice (the baby, remember, has no "choice"). They are angrily against the church and have vowed to buck it at every turn. There is Planned Parenthood which is also against the church, or at least against its anti-abortion policies, and have decided to zero in on the bishops and make them the fall guys. Then, on the other side, there is the FFLA, the Feminists for Life of America who contend that abortion threatens not only the baby but actually women as well. Abortion, they say, makes women conform to a world controlled by men, instead of making the world conform to the needs of pregnant women.

Still, in all these disagreements, I want to return to what I said before. As sharply as I have drawn the lines, I want to urge you to always make a distinction between a person's opinions and the person himself or herself. You should listen to them, to their views and arguments. You are entitled to disagree, and disagree you should. You are entitled to be impatient with insincerity and easy slogans (and so is the other side). But for those who sincerely don't see our view and who play fair in the search for the truth, give them respect. Don't be quick with either condemnation or labels. Some of these people deal with the most deprived and underprivileged segments of society and they know these unwed mothers will often live in poverty and their babies will have a life of poverty and want and likely enter the world on instant welfare. So they feel sorry for the girl and counsel abortion as the best answer all the way around.

While we can understand their compassion, we must pronounce it confusion. We must still protest that abortion is a short-term response. Like handing out condoms, it all becomes too simple and easy. What's worse, in the long run, abortion soon becomes a cheap and routine way of handling the problem of an unwanted child and, as recent studies have shown, an accepted way of practicing birth control. But these approaches never get at the root of problems. Some girls from underprivileged homes or social levels *want* the baby. They know how to prevent birth, but they want something to call their own, to love them back in a world where they often receive little love or attention. The root is that these girls need better homes, better opportunities for schooling, employment, acceptance, and above all, self-esteem. That's hard work, but that's where the long-term answer is.

The Seamless Garment

In the meantime, while the disagreement is going on, the church continues to uphold the sanctity of all life. Why? Because it has a sense that once you start the killing and give reasons to justify it, then where will it stop? That is why our bishops speak of a "seamless garment." That figure of speech refers to Jesus' robe which, you recall, was stripped off him by the soldiers at his crucifixion and then they rolled dice to see who would get it. They couldn't tear it apart because it was woven into one piece. It was a seamless garment. So our bishops say that respecting life goes all up and down the spectrum, from before birth to old age. It's of one piece, a "seamless garment." That is why, for example, they are against the death penalty. Although people in polls will vary in opinion about this, the official stand of the Catholic church is summed up by Rev. Robert Drinan:

> The Catholic bishops continue to insist that the seamless garment of life includes opposition to abortion, nuclear arms and the death penalty... .Amnesty International, the Catholic bishops, the National Council of Churches, and many other humanitarian groups around the world will continue to teach that the death penalty cannot be justified by any valid scientific, moral, religious or legal evidence.[1]

Nat Henthoff, a civil libertarian, shows the necessity of a seamless garment approach to respecting all life by mentioning how already at least 500 newborn infants—notice: *already born*—have been killed mainly because they were handicapped.[2] Then there are those who abort the baby, who, although completely healthy, is the "wrong sex." The couple, let us say, wants a boy and if the fetus is a girl, they kill it. Then there is the case of multiple pregnancies where a woman has two or three or four or more perfectly healthy fetuses in her womb and has some of them killed. Sometimes there's a hard situation where none of the unborn babies will survive unless some of them are killed and you can understand this is a very troubling situation to wrestle with. But there are cases where a woman has healthy twins in her womb and these twins could easily come to birth but she has one killed because she doesn't want to raise two children! That's frightening. George Annas, a professor of law and health at Boston University, expresses these doubts which are the doubts of us all who see abortion becoming more and more a convenience rather than a necessity. As the newspaper article reported it:

> Mr. Annas and others ask where, if at all, individuals should draw the line. If a person finds it morally acceptable for a doctor to reduce quadruplets to twins, why is that different from reducing twins to a single fetus—or choosing to abort a single fetus? And should doctors agree to selectively abort fetuses solely on the basis of sex?[3]

And, furthermore, to show you how the media can indeed make and change values, one in five college students surveyed accepted the idea of abortion for sex selection! And the birth control mentality easily lends itself to abortion. If a couple, especially an unmarried couple, is having sex and using birth control because they really don't want the responsibility of a child, then if she does get pregnant (and it happens), the strong tendency is to have an abortion. As Kristin Luker writes, there is the emergence "of a heretofore unsuspected but universal relationship between the availability of contraception and the use of abortion." One doctor, a former medical director of International

Planned Parenthood has written, "As people turn to contraception, there will be a rise, not a fall, in the abortion rate." Another doctor-researcher also in favor of abortion has concluded, "There is overwhelming evidence that, contrary to what you might expect, the availability of contraception leads to an increase in the abortion rate." Why not? If the mind is determined to prevent children, then it will follow that determination all the way.

Listen to this taken-for-granted solution from this high school student from T.C. Williams High School in Alexandria, Virginia, describing the general attitude of her peers: "There's a feeling that it's okay for us to have sex because we're educated and know what's going on. We're not going to get pregnant and burden society with unwanted children. We're going to college and have a future. If we do slip up, *we'll get an abortion*" (italics mine). Jean Hunter, the director of the family-life program in that school (and an expert on adolescent sexuality), comments, "Many parents agree to pretend that their kids are not sexually active and in return the kids pretend for parents' sake that they aren't. When these kids get pregnant and take *the usual middle-class solution—abortion*—they end up counselling themselves without the support of parents"[4] (italics mine). So, as predicted, what is serious has become routine, casual, and acceptable. And this should not be for the boy or girl who respects life on all levels.

Reactions

I won't go into all the ways the over two million annual abortions are performed in our country; it's too brutal to mention. Nor will I mention having an abortion is not a minor operation like cutting out an ingrown toenail, and that after the third month it's especially dangerous, and that women do die from legal abortions. In 1975, for example, four women died from illegal abortions but 27 from legal ones. Harder on the woman or girl is the spiritual aftermath, the realization that they lost a child, going against every natural instinct that they have to bear and nurture life. There is untold mental anguish and suffering for many after an abortion and you don't hear about that. So much so that thousands of girls and women are trying to cope with anger and guilt over what they've done or what they were led to do. There's even an international organization called WEBA, Women Exploited By Abortion, that provides healing and counselling for women who have had an abortion. As Dr. Diamond says:

> In this country, the press, media and even professional journals will not admit there are often significant physical and emotional complications following abortion. You have to read European medical journals...to discover that 18 to 20 percent of women having abortions in those countries suffer serious psychological problems including suicidal tendencies, preoccupation with death, withdrawal and despair that require medical attention...studies in these countries also show that 12 percent of women who have aborted in the first trimester (first three months) suffer severe physical problems, with the percentage rising to 30 percent in the second and third trimesters.

In line with this, the WEBA reports that the most often repeated statement the hear is "I didn't really want the abortion, but I didn't have any choice." Too bad they didn't know they did. And now I'm telling you, so do you.[5]

As we close this chapter, what you want to hear about is, so what's a girl to do? What if I ever do get someone pregnant? What alternatives do we have? For a high school boy or girl, this is most agonizing and we must sympathize with the dilemma. A girl knows her whole life's suddenly changed. Her career, her college plans perhaps are about to go down the tube. And the same for the boy. Who will pay for all this? What a burden the whole mess is. No wonder the temptation to an abortion is strong, especially when your friends and sometimes your family tell you this is the way to go. But one answer must be clear: For one who believes in God, for the one who knows there is life there in the womb and human life at that, abortion must never be an option.

The options are keeping the baby or adoption. Keeping the

baby is less desirable. A high school girl (or boy) is too young, too immature to raise a child and continue school, or worse, drop out of school and have the parents (who have already paid their dues) raise the baby. I know it's hard, but adoption is the best bet. And it's a little easier to make this choice if you shift your focus away from the girl and yourself to the baby. What's good for him or her? How will he or she have the best chance of being raised in a loving, stable home with the advantages two good married parents can give? How can I make another couple happy? Every parish has a good referral for you. Every diocese has a home where you can continue your education, receive expert medical care, and put the baby up for adoption. There are even wonderful families who will willingly and lovingly take a girl into their own homes for the duration of the pregnancy.

Talk to your parents. I know that if this ever happened, you would be scared to death to tell them. You don't want to hurt them. You don't want to disappoint them. They might yell. They might disown you and throw you out of the house. But, then, again, they may not. After the initial shock, I have always found parents very supportive, very caring. Still, if you can't at first talk to them, go to your parish priest or some adult friend who can direct you to people who specialize in helping teens in their choices about a baby. Or call one of the toll-free hotline numbers listed at the back of this book.

The last word is to you as the boy. Abortion wounds the males too. Remember, every aborted child has a father somewhere. Think of that: Every aborted child has a father somewhere. But, in this case, it's a father who has failed to be a husband or at least a support for the woman. It's a father who has not provided for or supported the child. It's a father who had not admitted publicly or stated publicly, "I think this girlfriend of mine some years ago aborted our baby, but I'll never know for sure." It's a father therefore who has not repented and so it's a father who has failed—failed himself, his girlfriend, his unborn baby. So there is a great spiritual risk in having sex outside of marriage and its responsibilities. Therefore, you have to ask yourself, would you really want to risk giving a girl you say you love a disease, an unwanted pregnancy, an agonizing decision, guilt and false hopes since, as a teenager, you will not and cannot marry her? The answer has to be no, and the other side of that answer is to make the decision to put your energy into self-control, into the challenge of finding answers to one of the world's favorite love poems, "How Do I Love Thee? Let Me Count the Ways." The truth is that there are many, many ways besides sexual intercourse.

QUESTIONS FOR REFLECTION AND DISCUSSION
1. "...the only worth that the child in the womb has is that conferred by the mother." How do you understand this statement?
2. What is the "seamless garment" argument?
3. How might you respond to a girl who says, "I really don't want an abortion, but I don't have any choice"?
4. "Abortion wounds the males too." Do you agree or disagree with the reasons given for this statement? Why?

If a guy sleeps around, he's a stud. If a girl sleeps around, she's a slut.
                                            17-year-old Girl

20
THE DARK SIDE

In Psalm 139 the writer sings out what should always be our thoughts about sex and our bodies, "Truly you have formed my inmost being; you knit me in my mother's womb. I give you thanks that I am wonderfully made; wonderful are your works." Have you ever given thanks to God that you are a boy (as a girl should for being a girl), that you have a body, that you are your body? A boy should feel this way. He should be comfortable with his body and enjoy it. He likes to eat and sleep and go to the bathroom. He enjoys having sexual organs and the hair growing around them. He is pleased every time he has an erection and more so if he has a wet dream. He can stand naked in front of a mirror and be happy at what he sees as he can be happy seeing the bodies of others, male and female. He can enjoy the feeling of his legs and thighs and buttocks. He is happy with his body that can dance so wildly, ride a skateboard, lean into the wind as he rides his Honda, soak in the sun at the beach, and taste hot pizza. He rejoices that he can maneuver his body in sports, bend it low in worship, and give it to the service of others. He likes looking at females and falling in love every third week. A lot to be thankful for!

That's the way you should feel. There's nothing wrong with sex, with being a sexual person, of having a body that enjoys stroking, touching, and feeling. Sex is good, but it is a powerful good. Remember, we said sex is like Niagara Falls: beautiful,

---

roaring, magnificent, awesome and when its great power is carefully channeled into turbines it can generate electricity for hundreds of thousands of homes. But if you let Niagara Falls run loose and don't channel it properly, it will drown hundreds of thousands of homes. Sex is like that. When channeled, it produces light and life. When allowed to run wild, it produces dark and death. Think, for example, of all those out-of-wedlock children who are born into welfare or of those with AIDS or addictions. Think of all those death-dealing diseases. Think of all those abandoned pregnant girls. And think of pornography, a dark thing if there ever was one.

Pornography is hard to define, although we all know what it is in our hearts. But we might say that it is the kind of sex that shows the use or hurt or humiliation or domination of others in such ways as to arouse sexual pleasure. And there's the heart of the matter: porn uses people and makes them objects, especially women. Moreover, it has been shown that for some reason porn very, very easily slips into violence and violence is often shown in connection with it; and also that porn often destroys the lives of the people who pose for it. Remember Linda Lovelace who made one of the first mass porno films, *Deep Throat*, and how she testified she was drugged and abused and forced to do things she didn't want to do? Remember the TV special we mentioned earlier, "Death of a Porno Queen" about a 16-year-old girl "who wanted to be somebody," got pulled into the porno movie business, and wound up killing herself?[1] Think of the children involved in the illegal porn business. Pornography is not a "victimless crime." The porn business, as a matter of fact, is an eight-billion-dollar business, heavily run by organized crime.

I think teenagers like you page through the skin magazines mostly out of curiosity, but that adults do it to get sexually aroused. Probably most teenagers feel that there's no harm for models to pose for nude pictures since they do it willingly and get paid for it.[2] But still there are dangers.[3] Let me list some:

1) *More and more, violence is associated with porn.* The record jackets, some of the music videos (as we saw earlier), the

movies, and magazines show a great amount of violence connected with sex, and violence against women. The danger is, I think, that if you see this often enough, you're going to start thinking that violence and force automatically go along with sexual activity. A disturbing number of child molesters, rapists, and murderers admit to using porn to stimulate themselves before seeking out victims. You guys especially have been programmed by the media to think of the ideal man as cool but powerful, right? Your heroes are Rambo and Clint Eastwood. A "real" man gets what he wants, even if he has to use force. I wouldn't want you to grow up thinking that. But it's possible. In 1984 the President's Commission on pornography was concerned with actual or simulated violence associated with sex scenes and said that an individual's exposure to this "causes an increase in the likelihood of aggression" and may bring "significant attitudinal changes," including the belief that rape victims enjoy being forced into sexual activity.

Moreover, such porn may make you think that your basic relationship to females is dominance. You will not learn to see them as equal partners in life, love, and marriage. You will see them as objects to be enjoyed like toys. Porno therefore is sexist. You'll start coming off like Archie Bunker reminding Edith that she "don't know nothin'." Worse, you will be less likely to develop your tender, gentle, and caring side if you think you have to play some role that you picked up from the movies. In a word, one of the things that disturbs me about porn is that it keeps guys in self-destructive roles.

2) Porn mutilates your woman image. That sounds gruesome but what I mean is this. Like all males, you have a natural, healthy desire for a girl, to know and relate to and love her. But if you keep looking at those skin magazines and watching cable porno, slowly but surely your natural desire for a girl is turned into a desire for a certain kind of girl, the girl in the photo. You're going to get faked into thinking that only those who look like those hyper models are really attractive. Only girls who are, say, blond and have large breasts and a great figure with half-closed eyes and half-open mouth (actually it took the photographer about 50 shots to finally get that picture right) are *real* girls, the kind you want. Really? How about if all the girls only yearned after the Rambo type? How would you come off? You see, it distorts your ideal image and can cause you to "type cast" all girls into that kind of woman you see in the magazines. And you may pass by a wonderful girl whose beauty is lasting and true because it's also in her character.

Pornography Distorts

   3) Porn distorts the divine intention when God gave us sex. Porn tells us that sex is public, commercial, bought and sold like anything else, and divorced from any degree of affection, love, commitment, or marriage. That's why they say that "porn is the sex of the lonely" and for those who cannot show their feelings or make commitments. It's easy to look and drool over and get aroused over a sex film and maybe even wind up masturbating. But it's all turned inward. It's all self-stimulation. It's all too easy. Building a relationship with a real, live human being is hard work. Communicating and sharing are hard work. The girl in the photo or on the film is, after all, only a piece of paper or celluloid or tape and there's no relationship to her. She's not a real human being to you. She's an image that excites, that's all. Porn makes it too easy to settle for the self-stimulation provided by an image, rather than venture out to a relationship with a real, live human being. That is why porn is really anti-sex. It keeps commitment and the hard work of relating at a safe distance. That's safe sex, all right, but so safe it will keep you forever infantile.

   Actually, you know, there are strict laws against most pornography but they are not enforced, and most likely laws will never do away with it not only because there's so much money involved with it, but also because it's so popular and will continue to be as more and more people have broken relationships or broken homes or are unwanted. I think of those sad stories of those kids your age who wind up in New York City from all over the country; how Father Ritter's Covenant House tries to save them from the pimps, but still how so many kids, alone and homeless, get pulled into the porno and prostitution business (selling sex for money). For the kids who act in these flicks it's a source of money (and often too, of violence and force for them; a good number commit suicide), and for those who buy or watch their films it's an outlet from their loneliness and lack of friendships.

There's another interesting sideline to porn that some have pointed out. Porn is popular because it feeds one's surpressed fantasies of need. You see, in so many of these porn movies and magazines that the man is passive and the woman fusses over and fondles him. That's telling us that many men are really not happy with the role they're "supposed" to play, the role of dominating, taking charge, and being in control and running things. The fantasies of porn give them a chance to get out of that role and for once be helpless and stroked and cared for and catered to—like a child, like a little boy. I think there's a message here: If you try to cultivate your caring and sharing side and let yourself be ministered to, you won't need the fantasies of porno. I think too that for a bunch of guys who normally don't have that many friends, seeing an X-rated movie together is an excuse to bring them together. And if there's anyone in the crowd who has any doubts that he may have homosexual feelings, watching a porn movie with the guys reassures him and says, "Wow, I may be hanging out with the guys, but we all have the hots for girls. I'm all right. I'm a red-blooded, normal, regular American guy!"

Anyway, it's not that you are going to avoid some pornography—or even want to—or that passingly it will harm you. But if it's a pastime, it will, and for all the reasons mentioned above. I think you can do something about it, about keeping your mind from getting warped. Practice, for instance, seeing people as whole, just as you like to be seen. People are not their bank accounts or their cars or their clothes or their breast size or body measurements. They are not commodities or objects. They are people, complete people, and try to see them that way. Porno focuses on an external part of a person and that's a terrible putdown, like seeing only a girl's bank account and marrying her for her money. Then, too, as the moral person that you are, as a boy with values, don't buy the porno videos or magazines—even *Playboy* on the pretense that it has some good intellectual articles! Your money finances and encourages this abuse of people.

Rape

Rape is another darkness. Rape, as you know, is forcing one's penis into any opening of another's body against his or her will. Many times rape is accompanied by threats of violence and even death. Normally you think of rape as something done by a complete stranger and this is often the case. But also the reality is that more often the victim knows her attacker. Rapes by acquaintances and especially by dates make up almost half of the reported cases (and Lord knows how many of the unreported ones). This is popularly called "date rape."[4] In 1984 one rape crisis center reported that 75 percent of the victims knew their attackers and 35 percent of the victims were between the ages of 13 and 18. A three-year study and survey of over 7,000 students at 35 colleges showed that one in every eight women was the victim of rape and forty-seven percent of these rapes were by casual dates or boyfriends. You see, most boys don't consider it rape if they force sexual intercourse with a date, but it is and they can be prosecuted for it. The reason the boy doesn't think so is because he didn't actually use hard violence, "just forced her a little." But if he pressured her in any way at all, he is liable and legally guilty of rape. Or the girls at the time don't think there is rape because many of them simply don't recognize that they are being pressured by the boy's actions or even by his words. Besides, the girl is only a teenager and may think she's "in love," and since, like you, she has seen those 20,000 sexual scenes on TV each year, she thinks that this is the way it ought to be, or what's expected of her, or that's the only way she can keep the boy interested in her, even though she really doesn't want sex and tells the boy so.

And the boy-rapist? He usually makes excuses like these: (1) She's to blame. She started it and got me all excited. (2) She secretly wanted it. (3) I knew she wanted it as much as I did and no girl can be raped unless she wants it. (4) Maybe I forced her a little but she was really into it; in other words, she said no but really meant yes. (5) She drove me wild and I couldn't control my hormones. (If her father suddenly opened the car door, he'd suddenly discover the fastest control in the world.) None of these excuses are valid, nor do they cancel out the rape, the boy's liability, nor, I might add, the emotional damage done to the girl. Rape by a date is especially hard on her because it calls into doubt every sense of trust and good judgment. She judged this boy to be a good guy, someone she'd like to go out with, someone trustworthy, and it turned out he wasn't. So now the questions plague her: How could I have been so wrong? Can I ever trust another male? Can I ever trust anyone again? The damage has been done and she will be hard to heal.

Again, it goes back to the images you're both receiving. A boy thinks he is supposed to press hard to have sex with a girl and that, anyway, she secretly wants it. After all, the word is that the guys are expected to be "macho," aggressive, and in control and besides, the girls expect them to be in charge and are pleased with a "real" guy who knows what he wants and goes after it. On the other hand, the girls are expected to be "feminine," passive, and pleasers. Or the boys feel that if a girl did in fact have sex once with someone else, she ought to be available to every boy and if she doesn't "come across" she deserves to be raped (and, besides, with her reputation, no one will believe her anyway).

Drink, Date, Danger

There are also those dangerous situations that bring trouble. A boy with poor self-image will try to boost it by "scoring"; or if a couple is making out too much a boy may be pushed over the edge and force sex. And mostly if there's alcohol involved, there's danger. In many instances of sex and in many date rape cases, alcohol is the chief instigator. What happens is that alcohol lowers a boy's inhibitions and a girl's ability to resist. In that high school in Virginia I mentioned earlier almost every kid says that students who drink a lot tend to be more sexually active—and more promiscuous—than those who do not. One party observer remarks, "I've seen couples who hardly know each other start drinking at a party and get so carried away they'll slip off somewhere and have sex. Sometimes it's really funny to see these girls who act like such prudes at school start coming on to guys after they had a few drinks." So, again, alcohol and preserving our sexual values don't mix. But, however it happens, pressured or forced intercourse is all technically rape, even if it's date rape, and is liable to prosecution. But that's the technical law. Beyond that is the real issue: Rape, at the bottom of it all, is anger, violence, self-hatred, and the selfish use of power.

Like so much else, the avoidance of rape is once more tied up with your values and the values you both understand and the limits you both set when you date. And common sense. And your self-esteem. Remember, there is no medical or mental reason in the world why a boy "has" to have sex. There is no sense in going to a lonely, isolated spot where it can happen. There is no point in exposing one to pregnancy (even one time can make a girl pregnant) or disease or shame. There is every sense in clarifying and talking over your expectations with your date and explaining your morals and your values about sex. And in any case, where in fact rape has taken place, a girl must get a medical examination at once. She will likely be ashamed or afraid to tell her parents, but she should seek the advice quickly of some trusted adult, such as a teacher or priest or aunt. Or, if they're still anxious about being known, she and/or he can call Birthright (usually listed in your telephone book) or one of the toll-free hotline numbers listed in the back of this book. The girl particularly will need help in dealing with her eventual rage and fear, and recovering her sense of worth and goodness and self-esteem, especially in cases where the rape has indeed been violent or circumstances make her feel that somehow she was at fault. A side issue, by the way, from what we said above, is that here is one more reason to avoid the more brutal sides of porn. It simply can pressure you too much and force you to relieve sexual tension in forcing sex on someone.

And speaking of that, the boy too needs healing if he's lost control and has raped someone, even if he didn't realize it was a date rape. He should seek some counsel, some trusted adult. He should pray, really pray for forgiveness, stop in at church, go to confession and be reconciled to God and eventually apologize to the girl (even if she rejects it). If it turns out she's pregnant, then even more so he'll need help to assume whatever responsibilities he is able to, however limited. The critical thing to remember is that one mistake as a boy shouldn't, by God's grace, prevent him from becoming "The Man I Want to Be."

QUESTIONS FOR REFLECTION AND DISCUSSION

1. Organized crime is heavily into the pornography business. Why?

2. Porn desensitizes. Explain.

3. "Porn is the sex of the lonely." Explain.

4. In what way is pornography "a terrible put-down" of women (or men)?

5. What is date rape? Do you think it is immoral? Criminal? Why? Why not?

21
THE MAN I WANT TO BE

Once upon a time there was this boy. He steals all the time. He sits down at a table at Burger King and while he's eating a hamburger and looking casually to his left into space, the fingers of his right hand are walking along the table and snatching a ten dollar bill (his favorite prey) under the plate of another patron. The trouble is that lately ten dollar bills have become contaminated and can cause sickness. Anyway, one day he is caught. A patron who just happens to be an off-duty cop sees this right hand walking over to his plate and grabbing his ten dollar bill. He cries out, "Hey there, kid, what are you doing? That's my money you're stealing! You're a thief!" and he grabs the kid. The kid, who was looking off to space, acts completely surprised.

"What's wrong?" he asks.

"What do you mean 'What's wrong?' You were stealing my money; that's what's wrong."

"Oh, I wasn't" replies the kid. "That was my right hand. It has nothing to do with me." And he turns and looks at his right hand and says, "Shame on you, you naughty, naughty hand! Take that! And he slaps it with his left hand.

And the cop answers, "Well, maybe you're right. But tell that hand of yours to behave. And, besides, doesn't

your hand know that ten dollar bills are contaminated?
Tell your hand that if it's going to steal them, then at
least wear a rubber glove."
"Thank you, officer. I will do that the next time. Hand,
say thank you to the nice policeman." And the hand
waves at the cop and both get up and depart.

Now if you saw and overheard that conversation you'd think
you were in Looney Tune Land. It's silly as can be. It's silly because (1) the hand is not independent of the boy; it's attached
to the arm and the arm to the body and the body to head. In
short, the whole boy is involved. He's a thief, not just his
hand. You don't arrest his hand and send it to jail. You arrest
the person, the one responsible. (2) What the hand does is
what the boy does and what the boy does is what he is. His actions tell us about him, his values, his character, his future. (3)
Putting a rubber glove over his right hand may save the hand
(and him) from contamination, but it doesn't even begin to touch
the real issues: What about the boy? Why is he stealing? Why
is he hurting people? Why can't he earn money like the rest of
the kids? Why didn't the cop see the larger issue? Did he just
give up on the kid, assuming he's a thief and will always be
one? Isn't there another way besides concentrating on handing
out rubber gloves to thieves?

That's the way it appears to me about all these condom advertisements. Everywhere you see them. On buses. In magazines. TV spots. In school. In "sex" education classes. Cheap. Cut
rate. Free. Why do you see them so much? Because, of course,
the AIDS scare has made them popular as never before, and because of this deadly disease even the U.S. Surgeon General has
said that if people won't control their sexual lives, then condoms must be used to check the spread of deadly disease. Or, as
some put it, "I don't want you to drink and drive son, but if you
do, here's a phone number to call. We'll come and get you." So:
"I don't want you to have sex, but if you do, here's a package of
condoms, son." But there are some things wrong with this.

1) Your penis, like the boy's right hand, is attached to you. It's not a "naughty, naughty" penis apart from who and what you are. It's *you* and your conduct that should be looked at. Why are *you* having sex? What does it say about you? Sure, you can cover the penis with a condom to prevent getting disease (remember, again, it is not foolproof) but you can't cover the flaw in your character that you're not being responsible to this girl.

2) The condom mentality *gives up on you!* It says that you really can't be chaste, really can't control your sexual drive with another. I don't think that's true. In fact, statistically, it's not true. The polls still show that the majority of teenagers have not had sex. Did you know that?[1] And what makes them choose that way? The answer: They have another vision of life and of themselves.

Moral Vision

Child psychologist Dr. Robert Coles makes an interesting remark that is a powerful commentary on that 1988 survey we saw earlier, which, you recall, showed that incoming freshmen put very little emphasis on developing a philosophy of life and a great deal on making money. He writes:

I think that what children in the United States desperately need is a moral purpose, and a lot of our children here aren't getting that. They're getting parents who are very concerned about getting them into the right colleges, buying the best clothes for them, giving them an opportunity to live in neighborhoods where they'll lead fine and affluent lives and where they can be given the best things, to go on interesting vacations, and all sorts of things.

That "moral purpose" is something more than consuming clothes and vacations and things like that. He contrasts this with kids in Poland. There, morning, noon, and night, for the past 40 years the government tries to get them to buy into a Communist vision of life. The government uses magazines, movies, newspapers, and especially TV, since it knows how influenced kids are by it. But:

The Polish kids I met consistently ridiculed the messages

they heard on television and radio and they scorned the textbooks they were given in school...Why couldn't the state-run government brainwash the Polish kids? Well, they and their parents shared an alternate vision that couldn't be shaken....Moral vision doesn't only come from what a culture fights against. Moral vision comes from what a people fight for, what they're willing to die for and live for.[2]

Well, there you have it. If you have a moral vision, if you stand for something, you can make your decision to be chaste. Or, put another way, you have the vision when you can say out loud to yourself and to your family and friends that you know you haven't developed enough to make the kinds of commitments and choices that go with having sex with another person. You know you need more time to grow, to get the inside of you matured and straightened out. You know there are deep psychological and spiritual effects from having sex too early. You know that everyone pressures you into being aggressive and athletic and "making it" with a girl; that's supposed to be a sign that you're masculine. But you know that's what it is, pressure: being told you're being left out, everybody's doing it, what's the matter, do you have hang-ups?

But you know there are other considerations: What about your genuine feelings of tenderness and love? What about learning how to be intimate, that is, close to and understanding of a person? You're told in so many ways to have sex and protect the penis with a wrapping, but what is there to wrap around you and a girl to protect you both from exploitation? All the sex education in the world, as survey after survey has shown, has not had a significant effect on preventing teenage pregnancies. What the adults should tell you outright is that sex for teens is a serious business with serious consequences, that you have to make hard decisions to go against the tide, the "normal" pressures of peers and the media. And the only thing that will do that is another vision, a moral vision.

A moral vision might include these considerations:

1) In a very recent survey, seventh and eighth graders say

that the greatest single influence on their intention not to have sex is that it is "against my values for me to have sex while I'm a teenager."

2) A teen services program at Atlanta's Grady Memorial Hospital found that of the girls under 16, 9 out of 10 wanted to learn how to say no.

3) Studies show (as we mentioned before) that one of the main reasons kids do or do not have sex is their self-image, how they see themselves. What and who they are and what and who they want to be and can be, these are the crucial items in conduct. In other words, those kids who saw themselves as pretty good had a supportive family and had a sense of goals, where they're going and what they might want to be; they did not have to have sex.

4) Long-term clinical studies find that there is a difference between the kids who have sex and those who don't. Those who don't are almost all college bound (that is, they have a goal), more likely to have leadership roles, have a more active social life, talk more freely with their parents, are in better physical shape, and are better able to control their impulses than the sexually active kids.

5) It is good always to remember that sex is not just your glands working but that sex changes things: your attitudes and feelings and self-image and, most of all, the girl who is involved. Sexual behavior is a matter of character and personality, among other things. It has to do with what it means to be a father (have you ever thought of that?) and what the responsibilities of being a father are.

6) Although the music and media tell you sex is OK "if you're in love," you know there's a difference between love and infatuation.

Infatuation

Adolescents by definition are rarely ready for long-term commitments. That's the way it should be because adolescence itself is not a long-term event, right? It's a fairly short passing-through time: a transition on the way to adulthood. No one expects a long-term commitment from a short-term person. And when I say this I do not mean to imply that adolescents can't be caring. That's a different story. They can be very caring and loving, generous, and at times quite heroic. I know of many of them. But that's different than commitment. In fact, our relationships generally fall into three categories: (1) uncaring and uncommitted, (2) caring and uncommitted, and (3) caring and committed.

Some teenagers I know fall into the first category, but not many of them. Most fall into categories 2 and 3. They are caring but whether uncommitted or committed they usually can't "go" anywhere with it. That is, they can't get married or afford to; they can't always deepen the relationship since they're in school or going to college, and so on, and so don't have the time. Although the caring is there, either they acknowledge they can't complete the commitment and say so right up front, or they do make a commitment but have to postpone final opportunities and arrangements. But there's that other factor, infatuation.

Infatuation sparks a lot of caring but really is not interested in commitment. And that's all right; that's the way it's supposed to be. So, what is infatuation and how does it differ from committed love? Infatuation is a hormone-induced, short-term, in-love "high." Because the chemicals are working fast and furious in your brain, you get attracted to this or that girl instantly—only to be attracted to another girl next month! The attraction, the feeling, the pulse are warm and wonderful, painful and wild. Shakespeare has fun with this when he writes of the young man writing poetry in honor of his lady love's eyebrow! Anyway, you're in love. Not really, it's infatuation. It's nature's way of introducing you to members of the opposite sex and getting you to try out how your personalities might mesh or not. It's a time of experimenting with getting along, with learning how the other thinks and feels and acts. It's practice time for the real future.

The trouble comes when adolescents mistake the short-term practice time for the long-term real thing. Most sense the difference but once in a while some don't. You probably know teen-

agers who have gotten married. They are almost guaranteed to
get divorced within a few years (and statistically most do).
Why? Not because they were insincere, not because they were
not caring. They could not, were not ready to, be committed.
They confused infatuation with love. And this confusion is
what's wrong too with the common excuse that says, "Well, no,
I don't believe in promiscuous sex, but if you're really in love, if
you're really committed, then sex is okay." The trouble is that
while most teenagers can be very caring about another, very few
are really into committed love just because of the stage of their
life. Most often they are confusing infatuation with love. Committed love, with all that it implies for long-term care and
bonding, is really very hard to come by or to promise at one's unfinished stage of life. The seal that sex implies is not present
yet, the seal that says for richer, for poorer, in sickness and in
health, for better or worse until death. That's commitment and
that usually comes another day.

Maybe I can sum it up by simply saying that real, genuine
love, the kind that is sealed with sex, takes a person for all
three tenses: past, present, and future. Anything less than all
three tenses is a fraud. Real love says, "I take your past: your
Mom and Dad, your sisters and brothers, your grandparents,
your past, your heritage, and make them mine too. I take your
present, as you are now, my beloved, my friend, my wife. I take
your future, when you get old and sick, when you lose your outside beauty, when you're happy and when you're sad, when
you're up and when you're down. I won't abandon you when you
need me most." That's love. Three tenses. Are you ready for
that?

I ran into real love one day as I was driving along a quiet
country road when I suddenly realized that I was lost. I stopped
at a small farmhouse to ask directions. I saw an elderly woman
sitting on the front porch and an elderly man who was working
around the front yard and whistling non-stop. The whistling
was loud and clear and not that great and seemed rather pur-
poseless. There was no tune I could make out, just whistling.
When I walked up to the man, I couldn't resist saying, "I see

you're fond of whistling." He said, "Oh, it's second nature to me now." Then pointing to the woman on the porch, he explained that they had been happily married for 38 years when she became blind. Coming as it did so late in life, the blindness had been a very frightening experience for her and she was still feeling a deep insecurity. The husband said, "I figured if I just kept whistling when I'm outside the house, she'll have the security of knowing I'm still with her." That impressed me. I thought as I was driving home, "You know, what that man was really doing by his constant whistling was saying to his wife, "Don't be afraid! I'm here. I will be with you always—as I have been, am, and will be."

Fake Love

Fake love says, "I take you now when you're young and fun and beautiful. I don't want your past and I certainly don't want your future and have made no provision for caring for and loving you then. I only want you *now*." And you know what that reflects, don't you? Our old friend, the media, which in turn rests on the notion that we must all consume all the time, immediately. We are a consumer society that can't wait. You should own all you can *now*, experience whatever you desire *now*, relate instantly with whomever you wish *now*. But in such consuming there is no responsibility, which is filtered away: Drink the soda without the calories, smoke the cigarette without the tar, have the sex without the baby. No, there are certain basic attitudes and values that go with having sexual relations and you have to learn what makes love mature and how you become a good and faithful lover and a good parent. What makes good marriages happy and growing? How do you develop such qualities as warmth, communication, caring, and unselfishness? These are what love is all about and you don't get these qualities in a store or instantly. They take time to be learned and cultivated. You can be a great success perhaps in avoiding pregnancies if you have "safe sex," but on the way your capacity for meaningful, loving, and trusting relationships can be lost.

Which is why...

If someone says, "If you really love me, you'll have sex with me," it is always a lie; sex is never a proof of love; sex is never a proof of being a man.

If you say, "If you don't have sex, I'll go crazy," she should say, "Go."

If you say, "Would you like to get in the back seat of the car?" she should respond "No, I'd rather sit in front with you."

If you say, "But everybody's doing it," she should reply, "Then you won't have any trouble finding someone to do it with."

And the reason is that such lies should be met with wit and truth, the truth being that there is more, much more, to human relationships than connecting sexual organs.

Her "Yes" as a Symptom

But suppose she says yes? Judging from the statistics, many (not a majority) girls do, but that should tell you something. It should tell you that, like boys, girls' sexual activity is very much related to their self-esteem. If they feel good about themselves, if they come from good homes and have goals in life, they simply do not need to have sex. But if they are unsure, if their own homes are troubled, then they are wide open to the movies and television and magazines that put pressure on them to "put out" or they won't be wanted, won't be attractive, won't "fit in" with the crowd. Supporting this are some words from a director of the Department of Psychology in a mental health hospital. She says:

> Many young teenagers are sexually active not by mature choice but because of loneliness, peer pressure or feelings of inadequacy. Many of these youngsters, overwhelmed by emotional involvements, need and wish for parental help...Just handing out contraceptives...does not solve many of the problems that these youngsters frequently encounter.

Another woman, Eunice Kennedy Shriver, writes:

> Working in the field of adolescent pregnancy for more than a decade, I have spoken to hundreds of pregnant ado-

lescents. The chief reason that teenagers become pregnant is not that they lack access to contraception, but as one 15-year-old said, "I'm pregnant because I want to be pregnant. I could have controlled it. I wanted a baby so I could love it and just make me feel good." These young women engage in sex not out of grand passion but because of emotional problems, school problems, peer pressure, and trouble at home.

(Just like the boys!)

Establishing Ties

You are old enough to understand what they are saying, which is what we have been saying all along. There's more to sex than sexual organs. Sexual activity among teens is always a symptom of a greater need, of the lack of solid principles at home, of the desire to be loved and feel important. This means that basically kids don't want to be handed condoms. They want to know what life and love are all about and how they can overcome their feelings of inferiority. Some girls who aren't loved enough at home do want a baby so someone will love them. Some are angry and rebellious and get pregnant as a way of saying to the world and to their parents, "So there! See what you can do with this!" Some, without a good self-image, feel that they must follow the media's advice and be a junior sexpot; that's the way to be popular. They are under stress, like all teenagers, to make decisions that would boggle an adult: how to spend all the money they get, whether to use drugs or alcohol, whether they should see an X-rated movie or have sex. And, believe me, the girls are under tremendous pressure to have sex—from the boys who use lines, from the popular culture that tells them that they won't amount to anything in this life unless a boy wants and "loves" them.

And, of course, the girls are hardest hit with such pressures because, besides the danger of sexually transmitted diseases, it's the girl who gets pregnant and these days she ultimately must decide even to have an abortion. Furthermore, you should know that sexual intercourse is a special health hazard to young teenage girls. Read this from a medical journal:

> A girl who begins having coitus [intercourse] before 17 (and subsequently has other sex partners) doubles her risk of developing severe cervical dysplasia and invasive cancer. In addition, if a girl becomes pregnant, she is statistically likely to have an abortion. However, the immature cervix resists dilation, often leading to cervical injury. A girl under 16 who has an abortion thus faces an increased risk of fetal loss in her future.[3]

On top of all this physical risk are the emotional ones. It is a common and well known fact that almost every boy who has had sex with a teenage girl eventually abandons her. So—you're a boy. What have you decided is to be your relationship with a girl? What are your needs? What are you acting out? Even the girl who pushes you, who wants to make out and presses you for sex, what's behind that? What are her hidden needs? You've got to make up your mind now how you want to act and what your actions will say about you and the kind of man you want to be. When you relate to a girl, of course the sexual tension and need for release is there. Don't deny that; just enjoy the fact. But always the greater need is for trust, security, the need to be recognized, wanted, and appreciated just as you are. Having sex apart from all of these long-term, challenging, and developing needs is wrong and sinful.

Abstinence

So, it's not a matter of condoms for the Christian boy. It's a matter of morals, of love, of caring, of respect, and of that "disciplined and devoted delay" which is right and proper for every teenager. And this makes good practical sense. Consider that if you are chaste and choose not to have sexual intercourse outside of marriage, then you know that you have chosen wisely because:

Abstinence avoids a bad reputation.

Abstinence relieves you of the worry about "doing it right."

Abstinence doesn't even raise the question of getting caught.

Abstinence is the only perfect, guaranteed method of birth

control. It is 100 percent effective and there are no side effects. There is no known psychological or physical harm to abstinence.

Abstinence certainly prevents the risk of pregnancy and the risk of putting the girl through terrible turmoil and decisions (though if sperm are even spread near the entrance to the vagina, they can swim up and in and so cause pregnancy).

Abstinence prevents the STDs for sure, unless you catch something from mouth saliva.

Abstinence reduces a risk most boys and girls don't know about: cervical cancer, since it seems that early sexual activity can cause this in a girl.

Abstinence allows a boy and girl to develop deeper and wider means of building a friendship and communication, of learning to share good times other than on a sex organ basis. This friendship and communication are, after all, going to be 99 percent of your married life.

Abstinence can give you both the opportunity to hold to your values and support them, to learn how to resist pressure.

Abstinence builds trust. If you can refrain from sex before marriage, chances are you'll be a faithful and loyal spouse. If you "play the field" before marriage, chances are that the pattern will remain the same and you'll never make your marriage grow.

Abstinence honors the girl, even the girl who doesn't want to be so honored.

Abstinence is what Jesus wants.

So abstinence has a lot going for it. And, besides, if you want to put the whole thing into perspective, imagine that you practice abstinence and then get married, say, at 25. Given the fact that the average male today lives till about 70 or 75 or more, that gives you a good forty-five to fifty years of having sexual intercourse. As one mother said to her teenage son in one of their discussions, maturity means self-control. People who aren't mature have no business having sex. No birth control methods are safe; a baby isn't something to fool around with. Besides, there's no rush. At the time, it may seem you've waited for a long time. If you wait until you're married maybe at age twenty-five and live to be seventy-five, you'll have fifty years for all the sex you want!

This is the same mother who told of the time her teenage son, now a junior in high school, came home with a friend and in front of herself and her husband burst out with, "Hey, Mom, we're wondering what to do with all of these feelings we have. If we're going to wait until we get married, we gotta know or else we won't make it!" Her husband nearly choked on the cookie he was eating, his friend got red in the face, and she stalled for time. With a prayer and a deep breath she told them, "First, you need to learn to control your mind. Work at not thinking in those terms. Physical exercise helps. Get too tired to even think about it, much less do something that you'll regret later. Run or work out on your weights—anything to get tired. Take cold showers." Her son said, "Okay, thanks, Mom!" and as he headed for his room with his friend he was overheard to say, "See, I told you my folks were pretty cool."[4] I don't know if your folks are "cool" like that, but this is what they would say—or would like to say—if you wanted to talk about sex with them.

Let's close this chapter with a bit from a story you may have read (or seen as a movie), *The Little Prince* by the famous pilot, Antoine de Saint-Exupéry. It's that part in the story where the Little Prince, who's been planet hopping, stumbles upon a fox. It was then that the fox appeared.

"Good morning," said the fox.

"Good morning," the little prince responded politely, although when he turned around he saw nothing.

"I am right here," the voice said, "under the apple tree."

"Who are you?" asked the little prince, and added, "You are very pretty to look at."

"I am a fox," the fox said.

"Come and play with me," proposed the little prince. "I am so unhappy."

"I cannot play with you," the fox said. "I am not tamed."

"Ah, please excuse me," said the little prince.

But, after some thought, he added:

"What does that mean—tame?"

"It's an act too often neglected," said the fox. "It means to establish ties."

"To establish ties?"

"Just that," said the fox. "To me you are still nothing more than a little boy who is just like a hundred thousand other little boys. And I have no need of you. And you, on your part, have no need of me. To you I am nothing more than a fox like a hundred thousand other foxes. But if you tame me, then we shall need each other. To me, you will be unique in all the world. To you, I shall be unique in all the world....

But if you tame me, it will be as if the sun came to shine on my life. I shall know the sound of a step that will be different from all others. Other steps send me hurrying back underneath the ground. Yours will call me, like music, out of my burrow...

"What must I do to tame you?" asked the little prince.

"You must be very patient," replied the fox. "First you will sit down at a little distance from me—like that—in the grass. I shall look at you out of the corner of my eye, and you will say nothing. Words are the source of misunderstanding. But you will sit a little closer to me, every day...."

That's the way it should be. The popular culture would tell you to immediately sit close—have sex—but the wisdom of ages and of the gospel tell you that all relationships take time. To become and remain special takes time. ("You must be very patient.") And after, and only after, when you have learned and communicated love and know who and what you really are and are ready to commit yourself to another ("tame them") can you sit close—forever. Condoms tell you nothing about that.

QUESTIONS FOR REFLECTION AND DISCUSSION

1. Dr. Coles speaks of a "moral purpose." What does he mean? Do you have a moral purpose in life? If so, where did you get it?

2. What are the pressures on you to have sex?

3. What is the difference between infatuation and love?

4. Sexual activity is often a disguise for other greater needs. Explain.

5. In his short but fine book, *Loving Each Other*, Leo Buscaglia writes, "Teenagers admit that the lack of tenderness in their lives often leads them to promiscuous behaviors. ...Human sexuality...has over the years lost its relationship to affection...Sexuality and loving intimacy are not necessarily synonymous...." (p. 141). Discuss.

22
TIME OUT 3

Here we are again. Another informal, out-in-the-open routine. Oh, yes, just so I don't disappoint you, I will inflict one of my limericks on you just to wake you up. You need it after that last section.

> There was a young man from New York
> Whose morals were lighter than cork:
> "Young chickens," said he,
> "Have no terrors for me:
> The bird that I fear is the stork!"

That's a good one after the birth control chapter. Let's see, now, any questions, comments, criticisms?...Yes, Bob. "Well, I don't I know," he frowns. "After listening to all those diseases you can get and going over that long chapter on abortion and then there's porn and rape...it all seems like such a hassle. Like it might be better to go hide in a closet somewhere or become a hermit."

I have to smile at that one, Bob. You're right. It seems like it's best to seal you all in plastic at puberty and let you out when you're ready to marry. But it's really not that bad. What makes it seem so formidable is that we've taken those tough subjects all together. When you treat them like that all in one glob, you get overwhelmed. But when you step back, you'll find there's lots to enjoy and be comfortable with. Let me put it this way. When you're a little kid and you're going out to play in the neighborhood park, you mother warns you, "Now watch crossing the street, don't talk with strangers, keep away from the water, don't fight, don't pet dogs you don't know, watch where you step, look out for the birds, don't get your clothes dirty, and be home before dinner. Now have a good time!" Man, you feel like turning around and going to bed! But actually all those things fade into the background. They're good common practical sense, most of them anyway, and they soon slip into a kind of mental signal you carry with you. But, more importantly, *within* those cautions and rules kind of floating in the background, once you get to the park, you really have a good time. You meet the guys, have a game, and just have fun. And it's neat. So it is with some real wisdom we've seen. It is wise to be careful of the STDs. Who wants to get sick or die from them? Or spread them? It is wise to think of your relationships with girls and not press them sexually. It is wise not to feed your mind with porno. And so on. But within these good sense cautions, you can have fun, great times, and genuine relationships.

Pedro? "What about being in love or the infatuation you mentioned in class. What about that again?" Well, sometimes we use different words: love, crushes, or sometimes we say infatuation. Probably the different words show our awareness that we vaguely know there's some distinctions here, even though they're not always clear in our mind. A crush or infatuation, we might say, is having a wonderful romantic or sexual feeling about that person you call someone special. Of course, this "someone special" can be a million miles away and you've never met her. Say, like a movie star. You see her every movie and her photo's on your wall. She just gets to you, sends you into tailspins. You have a crush on her. Or it can be a certain girl you know and she either returns the feelings, or, like Charlie Brown's redheaded schoolmate, doesn't even know you're alive—and cares less! And that can be painful. In any case, you can imagine all sorts of romantic things with her. She can make or break your whole day. You can date her and have fun.

But the infatuation or crush, for all of its romance and excitement and wild, wonderful feelings, has some limitations and is not the same as love. There are some differences easy to spot. (1) love lasts and infatuation is short-term. (2) Infatuation tends to catch and hold on to you even after it's all over and you discover that you two aren't really meant for each other. You know, after the excitement wears off, infatuation holds you to each other even when one or both of you in your heart know you should shift gears and move one. (3) Real love takes time. It must work through the rough times as you really get to know another person and it survives the arguments and ups and downs. Which is why love has to be tested over a long period. (4)—and this is important, even if it sounds very unglamorous— when all is said and done, love lies in your decisions, not in your feelings. Your feelings and emotions are very, very important, of course, and always will be, but, in a pinch, it's not how you feel, but what you will do and what you will decide that counts.

I mean, when the feelings are down, what will you decide? It's great to be with someone full of life and always laughing. Can you stick it out when the other's sick or has a downer? It's great to have the raving beauty on your arm, but what if she is disfigured in an accident? What will you decide? It's wonderful to be together on top of the world, but can you stay together when you're on the bottom? When you've lost your job, have to sit up with sick kids, move to another town, what will you decide? That's what's behind that story we saw of the man whistling for the sake of his blind wife. That's what's behind my principle that real love loves in all three tenses: past, present, and future. That's what's behind those old, but wise marriage vows; for better or worse, for richer or for poorer, in sickness and in health. Till death.

And I guess while we're on the subject, I should share one more thing with you. If you watch all those movies and listen to all those songs, you may think that having sex is just one big wonderful explosion, the greatest high, the biggest thrill you or your body will ever get. Sometimes it is like that, and when it is, fantastic! But sometimes it's not. Sometimes it's not. You have to learn that sex, like all things human, is uneven, to say the least. It's wonderful, but it's not always wonderful. A lot of factors can make it a just-so, routine, boring, or even a horrid experience.

You know, it's like this: Your mother's a great cook and you love what she makes. But maybe this evening for some reason she flubs it: The meat is overdone, the potatoes are soggy, and the peas are like BB's. Or else everything's super, but *you're* not. You've got a headache. You're nervous because you've got a big exam tomorrow. You're feeling punk. So although the food is great, you can't enjoy it. You see, everything in the world is like that and sex is no exception. You need to roll with the punches and take the good with the bad, and that takes time. This means that you have to have a certain level of maturity to have sex so that you can put it in a larger context of the person you love and not worry about the mistakes or bad experiences— just like Mom's one bad cooking night is put in the context of all of her years of care and love for you, no matter how this particular meal turns out.

That's why I like a word that's often used instead of "premarital sex." Many psychologists use "premature" sex. This means that you can be physically ready for sex and that your sex organs are in full operation—but you're not ready on the understanding, the acceptance, the whole-experience-of-this-person-over-a-period-of-time level; that is, in all the many moods and feelings in different phases of your life together. You expect sex to be a great time bomb each time, but the simple fact is that it's not. And that's the truth. It works best only when surrounded with a lot of caring, forgiveness, humor, and lots of place and space so that even the poor sexual times too are a part of your growing together. And it takes maturity to learn that. You mother's steak tastes good because there's years of invisible love and concern for you floating around the kitchen. Try eating the very same steak alone in a closet and see the difference. Sex is like that. You need a context, you need lots of practice to get it right—not only physically, but spiritually and emotionally, and you have to be mature enough to roll with the failures and the times of the sexual blahs. Let me quote some of those medical and psychology people again:

Young people today feel enormous pressures—their own as well as from peers—to have sexual intercourse, even though it may not be enjoyable or provide freedom from inhibition. Indeed, many girls report that they don't enjoy sex, are unable to have orgasms, and frequently feel either pressured into having sex or used sexually. Sexual experience often seems threatening to adolescent boys and girls for a number of reasons.[1]

So that's why you have to be a certain age. Teenage is too "up and down" yet. Having sex as a teenager is truly "premature"—before your maturity time—and that can be hurtful both to you and to others. Anyway, now that you know that sex too is a human thing and goes through normal ups and downs and even sometimes runs into a snag, let me stick this into the back of your head: When you're married and if you do run into trouble with sex, you and your wife won't be ashamed to seek help to get it back on the track. I hope you remember that.

At this, Mark raises his hand and, OK, I say, one more question. Mark? "Yeah," he says, "but still, you know, if you don't...you know...kind of put out, do things, how're you going to, you know, get close?" Here I pause, wondering how I'm going to get this across. And so I begin by telling Mark and the others that what he's raised is the question of intimacy. Once more, I reach into my briefcase and pull out an article.

I wasn't going to go into this, but just listen. There was a famous psychiatrist named Erik Erikson who did a lot of work on adolescence and he talked about intimacy because intimacy is important to us all and especially to adolescents. Anyway, he gave it this definition: Intimacy, he said, means openness, sharing, mutual trust—and self-abandonment and commitment. What do you think? Is that your definition of intimacy? But I want to get back to those last two items: "self-abandon" and "commitment." They're the powerful ones. By them Erikson meant that the focus of true intimacy and love can't be mainly of oneself, or one's needs or desires or drives, but on the other person. You hear that? In our discussion here, he means that intimacy fundamentally has nothing to do with sex as such. It has everything to do with whatever makes the other person— let's call her the Beloved—better, freer, responsible, and more comfortable in relating to others. And sex may—or may not—help her do this. But this article that I have from one of those scientific studies[2] says that, for many boys, that's all changed. For many boys intimacy *does* mean the same thing as having sex and very, very few think in terms of abandoning themselves in the interest of the Beloved. Very few think of intimacy primarily on the spiritual level, on the level of "what's best for the Beloved."

I see you're frowning, so let me put it this way. You see, love is centered in relationship, right? That's what love is all about: relationships. Now, there are many ways to build that relationship, many "outside" ways to express one's "inside" love. The question always is: How do I know what outside ways best express my inside love? I need a guide, a rule, a measurement. Well, the answer—the answer Erikson gives—is that the measurement for love is the Beloved. If the Beloved is the guide (not myself or my selfish desires), then we have to ask ourselves when the many ways or expressions of our love will really be loving the Beloved. For example, I'm on my way to see my girlfriend. Having some extra cash, I pass a florist, go in and buy some roses, and off I go. I get to her house and, putting the flowers behind my back, I ring the bell. She comes to the door, is (naturally) delighted to see me and, noticing I'm hiding something, asks what it is. We horse around a bit till I finally whip out the flowers and present them to her. She is thrilled and, as I hoped she would, she gives me a big kiss. Where's the love there? Is love the flowers (the "outside" expression)? Or is love the loving relationship that is only expressed by the flowers?

To show you what I mean, consider this scene four months later. Same route, same florist, same roses, same bell-ringing, same inquiry. To her question what am I hiding, I finally whip out the flowers. "Ta-daah!" But she shocks me by crying out, "Oh, no!" "Oh, no?" "Oh, no!" she repeats. "I have rose fever and they'll make me sneeze my head off! Please, take them away!" I think a minute and say, "Like fun. These flowers cost me. If you think I'm going to waste my money, you're crazy. These flowers are my love for you. So here!" And I shove them into her face.

In this second case, what do we have? We have a boy who mistakes the sign or the expression of love for love itself. We have a boy so focused on his own needs and his own feelings that that's all he cares about. He forgets that in one case the flowers did in fact point to love while in the other case they didn't. He failed to realize that it wasn't the flowers as flowers that mattered. What did matter? The Beloved! She is the measurement. She guides me. Which means that at one time I give the flowers as a sign of my love; at another time I withhold the flowers as a sign of my love. What's best for her? Got that? What's best for her? If I'm really "intimate" with her in the full and honest sense of that word, then it means that I must be open to her, share what's best with her, and take the focus off myself in commitment to her.

Well, think about it. It's the same with a kiss (when I have fever sores) or candy (if one day she develops diabetes and can't have sweets) or a red valentine (if she hates red)—I'll use or withhold these things with one guide in mind: The Beloved. What is good for her? What honors her? How will this make her better, healthier, happier? After all, the flowers, the kiss, the candy, and the red valentine are *not love itself*. When given, they're just ways to express it, but they are equally powerful ways of expressing love when, for a good reason, they are withheld.

Once more: You haven't seen your best friend for awhile. Suddenly you bump into him at the Mall. He sees you at the same time and runs over to you excitedly, "Joe! how are you!" and he thrusts out his hand to shake yours. But you have poison ivy all over your hand. So you hold it up with a shrug and smile and say, "Hi!" He doesn't get offended and say, "What kind of a friend are you? You didn't give me a handshake!" On the contrary. You're a good friend by not shaking his hand and, besides, is that where the friendship is, shaking hands so that if you don't do it, the friendship collapses? No, the friendship is a relationship that you honor by not, in this instance, using the handshake. How did you decide that? The answer: Your friend, the Beloved, he's the measurement. What's best for him?

And so it is with sex. Sex is not love. It is a powerful sign of love. Notice, a powerful sign. But not the only one. Love is essential to all of our human relationships, but sex is not any more than candy or red valentines are. It is often withheld if it is not good for or fitting for the Beloved. Think for a moment: You love your mother and father—there's no sex. You love your friends, you love a teacher, a coach, grandparents, and many others. The love is genuine and yet real sex is not involved. It doesn't fit your way of life. It is not appropriate. Nor is it appropriate to say to a girl, "If you love me, you'll have sex with me" as if they were the same thing. Picture yourself saying that to your mother or your grandmother. See how ridiculous it is?

So that's my long answer. Premature sex doesn't fit your way of life, your vocation, your calling as someone "becoming a man." You have to learn that true intimacy is moving away from yourself to the good of the Beloved, and we have already seen that real love for any teenage girl would never expose her, physically or spiritually, to hurt, disease, pregnancy, and fractured relationships. Once more, then, to be intimate is not the same as having sex. To be intimate is abandoning your horneyness, your seeking pleasure, your need to conquer and brag, your sexual pleasure. To be intimate is learning to abandon all that and learning instead to be committed to the well being of the Beloved. And maybe, too, what Jesus said begins to make sense: "Greater love than this no one has than to lay down his life for his friend."

No more? Well, maybe that's enough to think about, so we'll call it a day. But not, of course, without a limerick.

> There once was a maid with such graces
> That her curves cried aloud for embraces.
> "You look," said McGee
> "Like a million to me—
> Invested in all the right places."

Goodbye. See you next time.

PART FOUR
THE ANSWERS

No boy has ever asked me if it was OK to have sex. They want to know if it is normal not to have sex.
                                        Dr. Sol Gordon, Sex Educator

23
CONVERSATIONS, QUESTIONS, AND LINES

Here are some conversations (with some remarks attached) you might want to listen into, like having your ear glued to the door. But in this case, it's OK. In fact, you might want to put yourself or your parents into the roles and figure out what your conversations might have been like. Anyway, listen:

Fifteen-year-old Rick wants to go to an X-rated movie with the gang.

Rick: "Aw...but dad, it's not so bad. Some of the guys have gone before and they say there's nothin' to it."

Dad: "Rick, I feel that movies like that are degrading to both women and men. You know they make sex seem like something dirty. The actors must not value themselves very highly if they sell themselves for so little."

Rick: "But I promise, I'll mow the lawn every Saturday for you. I'll show you I'm old enough. All the guys are going. I'll be left out!"

Dad: "No, I won't sell my values. And this really has nothing to do with your age or how responsible you are. I don't want to separate you from your friends, but I feel very strongly about these movies. By paying to see them, you're supporting their false values. And I don't want you to grow up thinking sex is as they show it in those movies. So, you're just not going to go. We'll plan to do something else Friday evening."

Rick: "Aw, rats!"

Rick is not happy with this. But dad is firm. He can still control Rick's behavior. He doesn't criticize Rick or put down his friends or make deals. Dad sticks to just the central question and explains his values about it before laying down the ultimatum. Dad's primary goal is not to break the peer pressure on Rick, not to get Rick to be more responsible or have the lawn mowed regularly, so he passes over these unrelated and therefore minor issues, putting them in perspective. His real goal is to impart values about degrading sexuality and so this is what he centers his conversation on.

Tommy: "Dad, why is it wrong to say 'fuck you'?"

Dad: "Do you know what the word 'fuck' really means, Tom?"

Tommy: "Yes, well, I guess it has something to do with making love—doesn't it?"

Dad: "Yes, some people use that word when they mean sexual intercourse. When people say 'fuck you,' do they sound very loving?"

Tommy: "Gee, no."

Dad: "That's what's wrong. It takes something beautiful and good and makes it into something nasty, used to hurt people."

In this conversation, Dad has tried to deal with the complex issue of sexual slang, the human inclination to use intimacy to hurt those with whom they are angry.

Again, when talking about the use of sexual slang with your family, it is important to defuse the word, to take part of the mystery and secretiveness out of it by saying it yourself. Sometimes children really don't know the meaning of a particular word. This meaning should be made clear, as should your feelings about it.

Dad is playing basketball with eleven-year-old Tommy and his friend Joe. Joe bumps into Tommy.

Tom: "You fag, Joe. Watch out."

Joe: "You watch out yourself."

Dad: "Whoa, fellas, that kind of talk doesn't go over big on this team." (The boys stop playing and look a little shy.)

Dad: "Do you know what that word means, Tom?"

Tom: "Yeah, I guess it means you're gay or queer."

Dad: "What does that mean?"

Tom: "Well, homosexual, I guess."

Dad: "Do you remember when we talked about that a couple of weeks ago?"

Tom: "Yeah."

Dad: "So, Joe must be a homosexual. How did you decide that?"

Tom: (embarrassed) "Well, no, I guess I didn't mean to say that."

Dad: "Well, Tommy, we need to say what we mean. Otherwise how will we understand each other? What did you really want to say?"

Tom: "I was mad 'cause he ran into me."

Dad: "Good. It's OK to be mad. But say just that. When you're angry, say 'I'm angry.' OK? Don't hurt people with words you don't mean."

Tom: "Yeah, Dad. OK."

Sex and Commitment

Nineteen-year-old Keith has brought his girl Cindy home from college for the weekend. They had intended to sleep together in Keith's room. The conversation has already covered the parents' disapproval of the proposed sleeping arrangements. That phase closed with the parents' firm statement about what they value as standards of behavior in their house. Keith has put forward, as one of his justifications, the fact that Cindy has been using a contraceptive pill. Keith seems to feel that this makes their sexual relationship all right, with no serious consequences. Mom and dad have kept the discussion on the conversational level. They are concerned that Keith and Cindy are very casual about their sexual relationship, and they want to keep the conversation going so that they might have some chance to influence them.

Mom: "Keith, I'm concerned about how you feel about using contraceptives."

Keith: "Yeah? It's a good thing to have. We wouldn't want Cindy to get pregnant. She has to finish school, and I need to graduate and get a job before we think about that."

Mom: "Well, I'm glad you're clear on the importance of education. You seem to care enough about one another not to put an end to your plans in this way. But how do you feel about sex, then? What is the reason for it?"

Keith: "Huh?"

Dad: "She means, why have sex?"

Keith: "Because we love each other... it makes us feel great. Isn't that the way it's supposed to be?"

Dad: "Yes, it should bring you together, it should be great, but your mother and I believe there should be more to it than just that."

Keith: "More?"

Mom: "Keith, a sexual relationship is much more than just the time you spend in bed with each other. It's your whole life of commitment to each other. Your father and I feel that, for some people, the easy use of contraceptives can take away that deep commitment and make a relationship shallow and casual."

Keith: "Holy cow! I can't believe you'd want us to risk getting pregnant. And how come you have no children younger than Tommy? He's fourteen."

Dad: "Of course we don't want you to risk pregnancy. But we do want you to grow into an appreciation of the real value of a sexual relationship, not just as a way to feel good."

Mom: "You're right, Keith. Your father and I decided we just couldn't have any more children after Tommy. That was when he was out of work, and we didn't know what the future would bring. Later, we felt we were just getting too old."

Dad: "Your mother and I use natural family planning, Keith. It's a way of controlling our family size while respecting what we feel is God's will for our sexuality. At first it wasn't easy. But it really means a lot to us now. You know, I think we love each other more now than we did then."

Keith: "But what does that have to do with me and Cindy?"

Mom: "We think your love might have more chance to grow and you'd be able to develop a deeper relationship if you took your sexual expression more seriously. We feel that your contraceptive use might be preventing this, that it makes sex easy and cheap and of little value."

Keith: "Naw...I don't know...it sounds too risky to me."

Dad: "Well, think about it while you're here, in separate bedrooms. And if you want to talk more later, we're here."

Keith's parents know that they can't force Keith and Cindy to change. A hellfire-and-brimstone sermon would only force them away from any future conversation or influence. Mom and dad have stuck to their own values on the bedroom arrangement. They have set forth their beliefs about contraceptive use and have allowed Keith to see how they've lived out their values. If it's obvious to Keith that they love one another, if they let him see some of their genuine affection and depth of relationship, then he will know that this strategy works in real life, not just in flashy brochures and well-written homilies. He may not change right away, but he's been given a solid foundation block; he's been set to thinking. He's been shown a facet of Christian life that is proven successful.

Henry's dad has been divorced for five years. Henry is twenty and lives with his dad in their large house. Dad has dated several women over the years, but none have made him as happy as Ruth, whom he is seeing now. Henry likes her, too. They've spent the day cross-country skiing and the evening romantically curled up before a fire in the den while Henry worked on a term paper. Dad is now returning from driving Ruth home.

Henry: "Gee, dad, you're back awfully soon."

Dad: (laughs) "It's just three miles."

Henry: "Yeah, but I expected you to stay there a while at least, or maybe overnight."

Dad: "Oh no—no overnight."

Henry: "Why not, dad? You really love each other, don't you?"

Dad: "Yes, we do. That's why no overnight."

Henry: "Huh?"

Dad: "Love is very special to me, Henry. I know what it's like to have love and lose it, to be empty and lonely. Love was cheap and superficial for me once. I know better now."

Henry: "Yeah, but I mean, what about sex? If you love each other so much, you must want to have sex."

Dad: "Well, I guess we do. But, you know, we put a very high value on ourselves, and our sexual expression as well. We may want to get married."

Henry: "Great! But then there's no reason not to have sex. You were both married before, so it's not as though you're virgins or something like that."

Dad: "Henry, love is a commitment, and intercourse is one of the highest expressions of that commitment. We both know what it means to have a commitment fail. Ruth and I believe in marriage. We'll complete our commitment in love on the evening we complete our commitment to the community."

Henry: "But what if you find out then that you're not compatible?"

Dad: (laughing again) "Henry, your sexual expression is just that—an expression of who you are and how much you love, not the other way around. If we've found ourselves compatible in other things, then we'll be compatible sexually. What differences there are bound to be, we'll work on. That's what love means."

Henry: "Yeah, but..."

Dad: "I've got to go to bed now, kid. Why don't you go back to work on that paper, and we'll talk some more later."

Henry: "Yeah, but..." (Dad leaves.)

The Playboy philosophy notwithstanding, Henry sees his dad as a success. Dad does not mope, frown or express tension or impatience at waiting for sexual gratification until remarriage. He is happy with his choices and lets Henry know. Both are fully aware of the time of loneliness, but dad doesn't dwell on this now. He has chosen a course for life that works. He is not afraid to be transparent to his child. He doesn't need to give a theological background for his beliefs or quote Scripture. Those aren't his personal style. To let his son know his choice and see that his contentment with it is real—this is the example that teaches the value.[1]

You notice in these conversations that members of the family have been used to talking with each other and that makes it easier to talk about sex and human relationships. That's not true, unfortunately, in many homes—and sad. Sad because all the surveys show that boys (and girls) like you would far rather get their information about sex from their parents than from the street or the other kids or from all the rest of the world which is pouring garbage into their heads. But parents (and you) are embarrassed. For one thing, you're used to each other and don't even think of each other as sexual beings. Your Mom has given you so many baths and wiped off your behind so many times that all that she sees is her boy that she loves and cares for. She certainly sees you now as sexually maturing (you're showing all the signs!) but in the same way as you see your sister as sexual: You know in your mind your sister is sexually mature, but living so close together has created an emotionally neutral zone, so you're not normally attracted to her that way.

In the same way you see your parents as sexual beings (after all, you're here!) but that close-living neutral zone puts up the block in openly admitting it or discussing it. And if from the beginning your Mom or Dad hasn't said anything about sex, then it's too awkward for them when they sense you're beginning to develop. Of course, their example and their caring and their marriage is the best education in the world, but there should be time for more detailed information. But, as I said, familiarity and embarrassment keep everyone silent on this issue. Your parents, however, should see that some respected adult who has good values is available for you to ask questions of.

Of course, all this is so much harder when someone's parents are divorced or they both work outside the home or the kid is a latchkey kid—nobody home when he comes home from school. When it's an "adult free" house there's danger. Then the TV fills the gap and, as we have seen, its portrayal of sex is juvenile and cheap, and is a lousy source of sexual "education." Also, as we know, kids left alone too much are more likely to fool around with sex (and drink) just to have someone to relate to. When questioned about where they had sex, teenagers most frequent answer by far was at the adult-free home of his or her own house or the partner's. That's why some latchkey kids who feel a lack of support and nurture tend to find sex as a way of satisfying these needs. So, if you're in one of these situations, talk it over with a parent or teacher or adult and come up with creative use for your time. Anyway, we've just answered the first question: *(1) Why don't parents and teens talk about sex?* Now, to the others.

2) Are some boys more "sexed" than others?

Yes, they are. Just like some boys are more nervous than others, more alert, more sensitive, more prone to sickness or temper. So, too, a boy may have a more responsive "sexual" system. He may be an early or late developer. His interest in and response to sex depend on many factors.

3) Is sex uncontrollable? I mean, if you really have a hard-on (an erection) or you're all worked up, do you just have to masturbate or have sex with a girl?

Contrary to all you see or hear, sex is controllable and not by some button or switch in the sex organs but by the brain. Your feelings and life situations powerfully affect sexual activity. Husbands, for example, who have lost their jobs, often cannot have sex for a while; an erection will just not happen (called impotency). The reason is that the emotional and mental anxiety in the brain gets in the way of reaction in the penis. All studies continue to show that the best outside physical sex occurs where the inside feelings and emotions and love are strongly present. In other words, the state of mind in the brain has a lot to do with control. If you don't believe me, picture this. You're up in your bedroom having just come out of the shower. For some reason you get an erection like a baseball bat and you're just starting to touch yourself when your mother calls out, "Johnny, I'm bringing up your laundry, OK?" and you hear her footsteps getting near your door. Wow, everything changes right? Your brain throws a quick S.O.S. to the sex organs. How quickly you deflate, as you put on your underpants or throw a towel around yourself! But if this were strictly a physical thing, like a bullet on its way, then you couldn't stop any more than you could stop the bullet from the gun. So sex is not just a sex-organ thing. It's wrapped up with the brain, with emotions, with feelings, and they are in control. That's why I told you that if you're getting all excited, start counting backwards from 100, skipping every multiple of 7. By the time you figure it out and distract your mind, you'll have less trouble with the sex urge. That is why I also said that your overall attitudes are important, like Henry's dad in the conversation above. His philosophy, his values, his mind-set are a great help to him to control his physical sex. So it is with you. You are not the slave of the penis; you are the master of your brain.

4) Can a girl get pregnant without actually having intercourse?

Yes, she can. As we indicated earlier, if sperm is spilled even near her vagina it is possible for the sperm to swim into it and toward an egg if one has been released.

5) How long do sperm live?
Up to about three days.

6) What is sterility?
Sterility is the condition where either the man or the woman cannot produce children. There's something wrong with the egg or the sperm or some other physical condition.

7) Are there foods or drugs that will increase (or decrease) the sex drive?
There is no evidence that certain foods pep up or slow down the sex drive. Nor do most drugs, although a few street drugs do have an effect. For example, marijuana may heighten sexual sensation for its users, but it also may dry the vaginal mucosa (the natural lubricant in a girl's vagina), cause panic attacks, and hinder concentration on anything, including sex. As for cocaine, it can jazz some guys up sexually, but you should know that chronic use will often have the effect of preventing his having an erection and even an orgasm. So keep away from drugs for more reasons than one. Alcohol acts as a depressant. Far from increasing sexual feeling and performance, it dulls the sensations and reactions. The only thing alcohol does do is to lower a boy's or girl's inhibitions so they will have sex more readily. That's why, as we saw, drinking and sex so often go together.

8) What is incest?
Incest is having sexual intercourse with a family member, a relative.

9) Can a girl get pregnant the first time she has intercourse?
Absolutely.

10) Am I abnormal if I have thoughts about sex with people I know, such as in my family?

No, that can happen sometimes and it usually is a passing thing. If it happens all the time for a long time, you should ask someone for help.

11) Am I abnormal if I get sexually excited when I play with the dog or when my little sister or niece sits on my lap or I wrestle with my brother?
No to all three. That's normal enough and don't let it bother you.

12) Do normal husband and wives need to have sex every two or three days or once a week?
The fact is, in spite of what you hear, there is no such thing as a normal number of times. Some married couples enjoy sex frequently, others once a week or once a month. The point is not to count. The point is that sexual intercourse, whenever it happens, should be a mutually committed, loving, and satisfying experience.

13) What is oral sex?
Oral sex is using the mouth and applying it to the sexual organs. One may insert his penis into another's mouth and have it masturbated that way or he will put his mouth to a girl's vagina and use his lips and tongue as a mini-penis. This is not ever right to do for the unmarried on the principal that they should not be using sex without responsibility anyway. And be warned again that STDs are also transmitted through the mouth. (And remember this is spreading fast.)

14) Can a girl get pregnant if she has sex standing up, or the boy pulls out his penis before the sperm comes out?
Yes to both questions. A few drops of sperm are always there even before the sperm-spurting (orgasm) and therefore they can make a girl pregnant.

15) What about those four-letter words?
When I was teaching, I used to have the kids write the

words on the blackboard (amid all kinds of giggles) and then repeat them over and over again. After a while, the words and the exercise became boring. And that was the point. Obscene words lose their meaning after a while and get boring. Most guys use the four-letter words to show they're big shots and I guess there's no harm in that occasionally. But I worry about the boy (and increasingly the girls) who can't say one sentence without using them. It's a sign they're stuck in a stage, like a teenager who's still making little-boy bathroom jokes. That's OK at 7 but a bit retarded at 15. So using the four-letter words is bad taste, to say the least, and after you've learned to shock everyone, the words should be dropped. You can be who you are without them. Have you ever noticed, by the way, that all of the four-letter "dirty" words refer to the parts of the body below the belt? Which means that someone has done a job on you, that they are not really happy with sex, the sexual parts of the body. They can't handle it and so they cover up their embarrassment with vulgar words. But if you really believe you're made to the image and likeness of God and that the body is good and sex is good, then how could you ever use words that degrade them? It's like calling your mother names in public. This whole discussion reminds me of the story of a son's college roommate who was spending Thanksgiving dinner with his family. Accidentally he overturned his soda. Forgetting that he was in the presence of his friend's family, he let out a string of curse words. The grandmother, very much shocked, said to him, "You *eat* with that mouth?"

16) What should I do if I (or my friend) was sexually abused when I was younger, or even recently?

The sexual abuse of minors, that is, of boys and girls who are teenagers and younger (as far back as three or four years old) is a growing problem. More and more cases are being reported. In 1976 there were, for example, some 1,900 cases reported; in 1977, some 4,300 cases; and in 1982 some 23,000 cases. Adults who fool around sexually with little children or teenagers may have severe problems. Often they are immature people or people who have low self-esteem, and have so many problems they can't cope with that they find it reassuring to have power over someone smaller than themselves, such as children, by sexually abusing them. Many of these adults themselves were sexually used as children and so have the pattern taped in their brains—and maybe there's a hundred other reasons. The real clinker is that often such adults are usually known and trusted by the children and teens they wind up abusing! So such adults could be a relative, a parent, a neighbor, or a family acquaintance. That's why they're so successful. They use several natural come-ons, such as the natural affection the child has for the person. Or such people may use the disguise of those the child trusts—a police officer, a firefighter, or a member of the clergy. Or the adult may use candy or toys as a bribe, or even threats, fear, or games. Some even will pretend there is an emergency: your father (or mother) is sick, so come with me to the hospital. Some will lure teenagers with the promise of fame and fortune, appearing on TV or in ads, or induce them with magic or sorcery or satanic rituals. And others turn to our old enemy discussed in Chapter 20, pornography.

There was a documentary on Public Television called"Breaking Silence." It points up the importance of one thing: If you have ever been sexually abused by an adult (even your parent), you must tell someone. That's important, as the program points out, since you may be so affected as to replay the very same thing on someone else when you grow up—and that would be tragic. Or you may feel so ashamed that you bury it deep within yourself and feel guilty and anxious all your life long. And that's no good either. So if by chance there has ever been anything like this in your life, seek out a trusted adult and tell him or her.[2]

17) What about people "living together"? Is it all right for unmarried people to live together?

No. It's not all right. It's not decent. It's not, when you come right down to it, real love, and this is where living together fails.

A) No matter how hard they try not to, the girl often gets pregnant. Yes, twenty years ago they thought contraceptives would solve such a problem but today, with 1 million IUDs, 100 billion birth control pills and 18 million abortions later, it hasn't worked. No matter how you look at it, sex is a reproductive act. So when pregnancy occurs unmarried couples either are not prepared to take care of the baby or, worse, they have it killed.

B) *Without the pledge and public bond of marriage, one or the other is unsure of the relationship.* There is no commitment and there is much anxiety as to where each other stands. Uncommitted sex, even for (and especially for) the male, is a barrier to building relationships. From life's most intimate relationship, you can't just walk away without a great deal of pain, and yet merely living together tries to say you can.

C) *Sexual relationships dismiss the fact that the couple is morally involved with lots of people who have a right to have that involvement openly acknowledged;* namely, their parents, brothers and sisters, other family members and friends; living together fails to celebrate this official relatedness publicly. It pretends that the two of them are unconnected to the rest of the world.

D) *There are no legal obligations in living together,* no bonded mutual responsibility beyond the couple's own (unreliable) feelings and that is sad.

E) *The statistics show that live-ins are less likely to marry and, if they do, less likely to have lasting marriages.* A report of a recent study from the National Bureau of Economic Research at Cambridge, Massachusetts, begins: "Couples who lived together before marriage have nearly an 80 percent higher divorce rate than those who did not and they seem to have less regard for the institution...."[3] Living in, it seems, is not a good preparation for the "real thing." "Try Before You Buy" doesn't work in human relationships. Live-in couples don't even stay together that long: 8 to 10 months on the average.

On the other hand, the advantage of marriage is that it pulls a person out of his or her own individuality (the temptation is always there, you know, to be self-centered) toward another, and says it "out loud" for all to hear. That's why marriage is a public, openly celebrated ceremony. From this newly formed bonding of marriage, the couple creates a base to move beyond themselves to serve the world and the Kingdom of God. But the outside-of-marriage joining of the live-in couple stays within itself. It keeps the uniting with another person private and uncelebrated. It lets the couple play the marriage game without taking the risk—stated loudly and clearly—for the other. And the other, as a result, is never sure of commitment and that rankles, for sooner or later the average person desperately wants the dignity, the sense, that he or she is worth an open commitment for the outside world to know about, applaud, witness, and support.

18) Does the semen mix with urine when I have a wet dream?
No, whenever the seed fluid ejects in an orgasm, there's a valve that automatically closes off the bladder that contains the urine so that the two don't mix.

19) What is puberty?
Puberty is all those physical, emotional, and sexual changes that occur as one develops into a man or woman. Someone who is going through puberty is leaving the body and ways of a child and moving into adulthood.

20) Can a boy use up all his sperm?
No, since it is continually being reproduced in the testicles.

21) The other boys make fun of me because I"m fat and my chest looks like I have breasts. Is there something wrong with me?
Likely not. Breast enlargement is very common among adolescent boys. It's a temporary condition.

22) How do mothers have twins?
There are identical and non-identical twins. The non-identical twins mean that for some reason there were two eggs in the mother's womb and so sperm entered and each egg was fertilized at the same time. The children are born, but as non-

identical twins since they came from two separate eggs. Identical twins, however, come from the very same egg and sperm, which for some reason breaks off within the first few days into two separate individuals. They'll be much alike since the very same genetic material went into their making.

23) What is a miscarriage?

When a tiny baby in the womb is not for some reason very strong, it may die within the mother's womb, usually during the first three months of pregnancy. Then the womb expels the tiny fetus. We don't always know for sure what causes miscarriages.

24) What is a hysterectomy?

It is an operation to remove the womb if it has become unhealthy. After the surgery a woman cannot bear a child.

25) Some of the guys ask what I "got" on my date with my girlfriend. I "got" nothing. We just had a good time and we talked. What should I tell them?

Well, this is the old macho pressure, isn't it? They want to know if you "scored," if you had sex with her. Notice the "thing" word: Did you score, as in, did you hit a homerun? To them, your date is not a person to be loved and respected, but a prize to be won. Anyway (1) recognize how dumb the question is, and (2) tell them the truth even if they (unsure of themselves) try to save face by saying you don't have what it takes. That's right. You have what it (love) gives.

26) Why are some babies boys and some girls?

The sex the baby will turn out to be depends on the father's sperm. He carries a X or a Y chromosome. When united with the ovum, the X will produce a girl and the Y a boy. Recently scientists think they have found a gene called TDF; this triggers which chromosome gets used.

27) What is a Caesarean Section?

A Caesarean Section is when the doctor makes an incision in

the woman's abdomen and uterus and removes the baby through this incision (which the doctor sews back up) because for some reason the baby can't be born safely the regular way through the vagina or birth canal. It's called Caesarean because that's the way Julius Caesar was supposed to have been born.

28) What's stillbirth?
Stillbirth means the baby is born dead. These days this is very rare.

29) What's a hernia?
This means that part of the intestines bulge through a weak spot in the wall of the abdomen and if it happens in the lower part it can cause pain in the sexual area. Surgery is called for to correct this.

Pressure and Response

Well, 29 questions are enough. Let's now take a look at some lines and the responses to them. This is important because one of the chief concerns of the average girl is how to say no to sexual advances from a boy diplomatically. And not only the average girl, but even those who have had sex and babies—almost all wished they had had some way of refusing without making the boy mad at them. Teenage girls, like teenage boys, haven't yet acquired the skills to be assertive. If the girl is insecure, if she doesn't get much love at home, if she's flattered by a boy's attention and doesn't want to lose him, then she's more apt to cave in, even though in her heart she wants to say no. She needs help in saying no and among her helpers should be her parents and her friends.

But the most important helper of all is *you.* To pressure a girl to have sex, as we said before, pressures her into possible pregnancy, possible abortion, possible school drop out, and possible STD. Can you be a Christian boy and trade off all that because you can't (won't) control yourself or your need to feel big or score? If you have your values straight before you date, if you have made up your mind to save sex for the commitment of marriage, then you have brought to the girl the greatest gift of all: respect for her and for her wishes and the time just to be herself, to grow, to get ready for the future. But for those boys who do not have these values, and so hand a girl a line, here is something she can hand back to them:

He: If you really love me, you would prove it.
She: If you really love me, you wouldn't ask me to prove it.

He: Don't you want to make my day?
She: Don't you want to make my life?

He: It will help you to get to know me better.
She: I'm afraid I'm learning all I need to know about you right now.

He: Are you frigid?
She: No, just smart.

He: When a guy starts, it's too painful to stop.
She: Well, then, go on without me. I can wait till you're done.

He: But it will break off.
She: I'll call the doctor to sew it back on.

He: Do you want me to break up with you?
She: No. I'll do it for you.

He: I want to prove to you I'm a real man.
She: You can do that by showing me respect.

He: Everybody's doing it.
She: I thought you loved me because I'm not just "everybody."
Or: Then you won't have trouble finding someone else.

He: I have this urge.
She: I have this dream.

He: Is it against your religion?
She: Yes.

Remember what we mentioned earlier: 70 percent of the boys polled said it was all right to lie to a girl to get her to have sex. So we know we're dealing with a line. The girl is entitled to hand one back (and should) and her best line is always the truth. "Sex works best in the committed relationship of marriage." Case closed.

QUESTIONS FOR REFLECTION AND DISCUSSION

1. What is Erikson's idea of intimacy? How does it differ from yours?
2. What is the measurement for love? What does this mean in practical terms?
3. Comment on this: "Sex is not love. It is a powerful sign of love."
4. It seems teenagers and parents don't converse about sex much at all. Why do you think this is the case?
5. Write down or ask any questions you're interested in that did not appear on the list of questions and answers in this chapter. Discuss it.
6. In the boy-girl conversations, do you appreciate (agree with, understand) the girl's responses? Which, if any, do you disagree with?

Golda, do you love me?

Tevye, from Fiddler on the Roof

24
MARRIAGE

Dolores Curran, a committed woman who's a national figure and has devoted her life to researching and writing on family life, was on a TV talk show recently to discuss her book *Traits of a Healthy Family*. At least she thought she had been invited to talk about her book. But the talk show host just went on at length with the litany of what's wrong with families, saying that things are so bad that many couples won't get married today; they're so afraid. They just live together. And there's the divorce and abuse, and so on. Finally, Curran grew exasperated and got a word in edgewise to the talk show host, "Why would anyone want to get married after listening to you? You haven't said one positive thing about marriage and family in the past twenty minutes!"

She was right. Pointing out the good things about marriage and family life is not "newsworthy," not the stuff the media people want. They don't want to hear about it and they don't promote it. As a result, young people—even teens like yourself—have a negative view of marriage. "Who wants to get married with so many divorces?" Or "Why bring children into a world which is choking on pollution and where you can't walk the streets at night?" So people shy away from marriage and try all kinds of "lifestyles."

Anyway, if the fear of future divorce and a polluted world are reasons why some teens think they don't want to get married, some others have different reasons from their past for not getting married. And that's interesting because it underscores a lesson we've been seeing. Those people with a past are the bachelors—those males and females in their late 20s and 30s and older who are afraid of marriage. In fact, "scary" is the word they use. And someone wrote a report on them appropriately called "Why Wed?"[1] Well, what was found to be scary to them? Believe it or not: commitment! Why? Because these eligible bachelors have played the field and had sex with so many partners, they wound up eventually seeing people as so many "disposable" objects. And how can anybody be committed to something that comes and goes? And how can anyone even trust himself to be committed when he himself is also a part of the "come-and-go"?

Well, you ask, what made them that way? The answer is our popular consumer culture that they bought into, the one that promotes "Looking out for Number One" and "Doing your own thing," which includes having and consuming sex whenever one feels like it. If someone buys into that, especially starting as a teenager, then he or she forgoes the practice, the training, the slow but valuable learning process of really reaching out to another at deeper levels. (Which is what teenage chastity is really all about!) With unmarried sex there's no encouragement, no incentive to be committed to another. In a word, there's no inducement to learn the process of loving another. Listen to the author of the article:

Unwed men and women in their 30s both talk of carrying around a lot of emotional baggage, a lot of anger and wistfulness from past love affairs, and what they seem to be saying is that it can be incredibly daunting to shuck that load and fall in love again. So they withdraw from one another. [As a result] in case no one's noticed, it has become less common for single people in their 30s to move in together. Remember when we were all going to make marriages that were better than our parents' by getting to know each other really well before the wedding? That idea seems to have fizzled, perhaps because millions have discovered that living together takes as much hard work as the real thing.... [One] man reported that things were more "complicated" because good sex was no longer a reliable indication that he and a woman were clicking.... He said, "...As you grow older, you're a lot smarter and you're looking for different things than when you were young and almost trying to get burned by sex."

But now he's burned and so are many like him. They'll move into old age alone because fundamentally they never learned to love. All they can do is shrug their shoulders and ask, "Why wed?"

The Good News

So, what do we have? Some teens are afraid of the future and some bachelors are burdened with the past. But what about others? They, I am happy to report, have made a new discovery of an old treasure: marriage that can and will work. A reaction has set in and a new confidence about marriage has surfaced. So that's why I'm not surprised today to find in a popular national magazine a lead story entitled, "How to Stay Married"![2] Nor am I surprised that the lead caption of the story reads this way:

> The age of the disposable marriage is over. Instead of divorcing when times get tough, couples are working hard at keeping their unions intact, and they are finding that the rewards of matrimony are often worth the effort.

And that's why current research shows that the old traditional family values are still very much desired today: kinship, trust, support, responsibility, and religion. And, besides, people are tired of temporary unions and they've been enormously hurt by divorce, mistrust, living together, and "lifestyles" that, at the end, leave them empty and alone. So commitment and responsibility are the old "new" words today and they're good ones. Survey after survey still shows that most people want to be married and after a fifteen-year rise, the divorce rate has not only leveled off, but is dropping. As the *Newsweek* article remarks:

The landscape is littered with victims of the divorce epidemic: ex-wives raising their children alone, former husbands trying to start new lives and still be good fathers to kids they see only on specified days, and the children themselves, often torn between two warring parents. In a recently completed 10-year study of 60 divorced, middle-class families in northern California, psychologist Judith Wallerstein found that only 10 percent of the ex-spouses said they had succeeded in improving their lives. Divorce, Wallerstein says, "has been a wrenching experience for every family I've ever seen."

High on Marriage
So counsellors are reporting today that once their clients used to say, "I want a divorce. How do I get out of this marriage?" They hear today more and more the question, "I want to stay in this marriage, but it's under stress. How do I fix it?"

Studies continue to show what characteristics in fact not only "fix it" but make for a lasting and happy marriage. For one thing, as we mentioned in the first chapter, the most successful marriages are those where the couple recognize (not deny) the differences between them and learn to live with them; for instance, one is a nighttime person and the other is a daytime person. How do you work out your routine and social life? Another key to a successful marriage is that you're married to your best friend, that is, even if you weren't married, this person would be your best friend. So friendship, not some vague, romantic feeling of "love," is important. One recent study showed that the most admired qualities in spouses were: integrity, caring, sensitivity, a sense of humor—and commitment—. The commitment was not just to each other, but, more importantly, to the very institution of marriage itself. Such a commitment says, "We so believe in marriage that we'll work through anything to preserve it."

Are you listening? Where's the mention of sex? Nowhere! Which, of course, is not to say it is unimportant. Not at all. But it is to say what we mentioned in a previous chapter: When it comes to human relationships, sex is number nine out of a list of ten in importance. So again, you see the danger of getting sexually involved before marriage? It saps too much energy that should be going into practicing the qualities of being a good lover, a good spouse, a basically decent, good, reliable, committed person who can stick with someone "in good times and in bad, till death do you part."

How much like *Christian* marriage this sounds, at least with a qualification or two. Marriage as an intimate partnership, an exclusive and permanent relationship, an openness to life, love, and children and the basic unit of society—all these are traditional Christian teachings. Plus the conviction that God is its author and that the love and commitment of marriage are so much a reflection of the kind of love God has for us in Jesus that they form a sacrament. That is to say, when we look at the committed marriage, we can see *through* it as well to a steadfast, faithful, and loving God to whom it points.

Two in One
So, if you get married, and you probably will, realize that in your love you can be sign to others of God's love for them. Also, don't be afraid. You're in that time of history when people are realizing once more how satisfying married life can be. Sure, it has its hardships as in all states of life, but there's nothing like it. In fact, I saw recently that there is genuine scientific evidence that couples who are married for a long time do really begin to look alike! Some thought, since they did live together so long, that they unconsciously began to dress alike and comb their hair alike and that sort of thing. But others pointed out that, no, the changes were deeper than that; they found this out: The couples lived together so long and had grown so sensitive to each other's needs that even in their faces (as well as in their hearts) they began to mimic each other's feelings and pain and joy so that the face muscles conformed to one another and that accounts for the looking alike! That's beautiful and that is, I think, what the Bible also means when it says that a man and woman in love become "two in one flesh."

But of course the other meaning of "two in one flesh" is sexual intercourse. Here in marriage it finds its fulfillment. For one thing, as someone once said, you're still both there when you wake up in the morning. That is, it's not a hit and miss affair. In other words (you may recall) there's the deep satisfaction that all three tenses are operating: husband and wife have pledged to accept each other's past, present, and future. Likewise, there will be two parents in the event of a child. So, secure in the knowledge of each other's love, not just for now but for always, not just in good times, but in bad ones too, the married couple are free to enjoy sex, have fun with it, and use it as a way to make love grow. And that's why, in case you don't know it (I wish married couples would share more here) many married couples rightly have a sense of God's presence in such pleasures of sex.

I recall one man who made up a little prayer in anticipation of his marriage. He wrote, "And when we meet breast to breast, O God, may it be upon Thine own." This means he understood that the sexual union of husband and wife necessarily included the presence of the God who gave them the gift of sex. I like, too, the wife who mentioned that in all their years of marriage, whenever she and her husband had intercourse, he always said a prayer. What was that prayer? As they lay together in bed in a state of anticipation he simply said on behalf of them both, "For what we are about to receive, may the Lord make us truly thankful." And that's the way it should be. A good, blessed, joyful God-given time in bed for husband and wife because the boundaries, the pledge of acceptance and responsibility are there. For, you see, here sex is a kind of sacrament. A powerful outward sign that gives a mighty hint of the deep kind of union God has with us.[3]

Well, if I could say that fear of failure plus not realizing God's involvement in the sexual union of husband and wife were enemies of marriage—and we just saw that the fear is happily diminishing—I could say that, for you, another enemy might be more of a problem. And that is careerism. This means that you or your future wife might be so caught up in the glamorous, fast-lane corporate life, so caught up in the consumerism that you won't learn to "establish ties." One of the most chilling articles I read appeared in *The New York Times Magazine* (April 5, 1987) about the attitudes and values of young college graduates in our country. The article, significantly, is entitled "Alone Together." The author presents the results of his nationwide interviews with young adults between the ages of twenty-two and twenty-six. He found them the TV's sitcom dream: self-preoccupied, career-minded, and firmly self-reliant and independent.

One young accountant described his peers this way: "Here's how we think: Get to this point, move on. Get to that point, move on. Acquire, acquire. Career, career. We're all afraid to slow down for fear of missing out on something. That extends to your social life as well. You go out on a date and you're thinking, 'Hell, is there someone better for me?' I know how terrible that sounds, but it seems to be my problem. Most of my peers are in the same position." A lawyer remarks, "Finding a man is not a top priority. I want to travel. I want to do well at the firm. I want to establish myself in the community." Another says no to marriage: "I want to be really well-off financially, and I don't want that struggle to interfere with marriage. I want to be able to enjoy myself right away. And I never want to look back and think that if I hadn't gotten married I could have accomplished more."

The Relentless Life
What you hear throughout the article is the intense, almost religious, drive to establish a career, acquire the good life, get material things and consume. And you sense—or should sense—that there is something radically wrong here, something seriously hurtful in the making, something off-center about such expectations and drives. And it is this: By having such an intense drive to get yourself the best and live "the good life" and do what's best for yourself you are not preparing yourself for that other-centeredness, the compromises and the necessary sacrifices that any good marriage requires. It's as basic as that. To de-

vote oneself so relentlessly to the acquiring style of life, to such a self-focused approach to life, is bound to sabotage the kind of self-forgetful love that successful marriage and family life demand (not to mention just plain human relationships).

And there's another zinger to fast lane, consumer-bent careerism: Frequently when two such career-hyper people do in fact marry, they become victims of ISD. What's that? Inhibited Sexual Desire, a lack of interest in sex. You might smile at that one and say, "No way, not me!" But so did those super young men and women protest when they were teenagers. But the simple fact is, there is only so much energy in the human being and if all of it is going into the career and into acquiring and consuming, there's not much left for that beautiful relationship of sexual love with one's marriage partner. So common is it that ISD is called the "plague of the 1980s." As one article describes the people so afflicted, ISD

> ...can be caused by performance anxieties—brought on, to some extent, by the images of sexual athleticism relentlessly purveyed in the movies and on television. [Ah ha, you see once more the negative impact of the media?] Both men and women worry that they are not up to those largely mythical standards.... busy two-career couples make up the largest contingent of ISD patients.... [A co-director of Northwestern University's Adult Sexuality Program is seeing so many turned-off young professional couples that she calls ISD "the new Yuppie Disease."[4]

All right, I want to pause here for a moment to ask: Now do you see why I harped so much in pages past on our lifestyles, values, and what the media can do to us? And the importance of chastity as a means of putting your energy into building true relationships? Think back a minute and look at the connections, the slow build-up, step-by-step to what? To being "alone together"! Here's the whole message in a nutshell:

1) Society tells us that not only life but a successful life consists in consuming.

2) Therefore the media in turn through non-stop advertising,

glamorized lifestyles and showing us super-rich role models, encourages us to buy and consume as marks of our "success."

3) We get caught early in this philosophy (mostly through the TV) so that by high school we agree that we will dump toxic waste into public sewers for money.

4) And we're off to college, not to develop a meaningful philosophy of life, but rather as a means to make money and lots of it.

5) After college we will religiously and relentlessly dedicate our lives to our careers so we can finally make that fantastic money we desire, in order to consume.

6) And this dedication to consuming and money will become so important in themselves and take so much effort that we simply won't have time for others or time to develop deep and lasting relationships with them, so that even when I go out with a girl we will be "alone together."

7) And if by chance I do marry her, I may be afflicted with ISD because there's no energy left, not even for sex! It all went into making money.

8) And so I will have "arrived," become successful, for the goal seems to be that the one who dies with the most things consumed wins.

When I put it so bluntly this way, then you should catch the message. It seems you have to be careful of such conditioning that leads you to pace yourself so tirelessly in the pursuit of wealth, position, and career that you can't take time "to make love grow." And this might be your problem and increasingly the girl's as well. So you might do well to think about not just your career, but your larger, loving life and how important it is for you to take the time to build relationships. You see, it's the old Scrooge theme all over again in modern dress, isn't it? Ebeneezer's life was a failure because, though rich in money and career, he was poor in human contact and relationships, while Bob Crachitt was the opposite: poor in career and money but rich in wife, children, and the bond that united them. Ebeneezer, you recall, even lost his one true love because his "career" came first. He became a rich bachelor, period. Watch out for the Scrooge in you. It can be lonely at the top. Careerism can deny you the adventure of marriage. And even when you're with somebody you'll wind up being "alone together."

So it's all tied together. Once you start consuming even people through premature sex, once you learn to "collect" girls like so many acquired victories, once you turn the energy away from the patient and careful building of relationships toward your own selfish needs, then you're on the way from step 1 to 8. Jesus has a different agenda; what can I tell you? "Man does not live by bread alone, but by every word that comes from the mouth of God" is what he said, quoting his ancestral Bible. And what are those words God gave? Words like: "Blessed are those who hunger and thirst for righteousness...Blessed are the merciful...the pure of heart...the peacemakers." And he warned about the thorns of life—the riches and pleasures—that choke off decency, sensitivity, and compassion for others. So you want to be the World's Greatest Lover? Listen to Jesus.

QUESTIONS FOR REFLECTION AND DISCUSSION

1. Are you afraid to get married and bring kids into the world? Why? Why not?
2. Is marriage becoming more "in" today? Why? Why not?
3. Having lots of sex before marriage makes it better, like"try before you buy." What do you think of this? Do you agree? Discuss the very last paragraph of this book, a man's letter on no sex before marriage.
4. Define "careerism" and why it's hard on marriage. What priorities would you and your bride-to-be set before you get married?
5. "Success" is defined differently by the media and Jesus. Pick out any magazines at home or off the newsstand and check all the advertisements. What's the bottom-line message of all of them?
6. Describe the qualities you believe are needed for a good marriage.

Others have renounced marriage because of the kingdom of heaven.

Matthew 19:12

25
VIRGINITY AND CELIBACY

Virginity. That's a word guaranteed to bring a laugh and some strong reactions. You want proof? Then think for a moment of your (honest) reaction if someone wrote about you on the school wall, "Bobby is a virgin!" Honest, now, how would you feel and what would you say? Would you protest, "I am not!" loud and clear to the whole school? Is there a suggestion here that you're gay? You're unmasculine? You see how the culture can be tough on you? All in the name of freedom to be yourself, you must wear the right jeans and listen to the right records and have the right hair style—or else you're not in. You're really not being yourself, of course, but whatever the media or the "role model" figures command and pressure you to be. Don't feel bad. Calvin Klein and others like him spend millions of dollars in (sexy) advertising just to get you to wear their jeans. How can a single person fight against all that money and all those enticing ads in the magazines and on TV?

Pressure
Still, it's healthy to realize that you *are* being pressured. And there's the same pressure with this virginity thing. Since the media dictates that all boys must be macho and that one of the surest signs of being macho is having sex all over the place and making it with the school's most popular girl—then what an insult it is for someone to accuse a boy of not ever having sex. So

strong is this prejudice (for that's what it is) that one counsellor who spends all his life teaching teens about sex, remarks that, in the past, boys would come to him in a panic and ask if there was something wrong if they wanted sex. Nowadays, he reports, the boys come in anguish to ask if there is something wrong with them if they hadn't already had sex—and don't care to have it. So you can see being called a virgin in this climate is like being called a wimp. You don't have what it takes.

But "having what it takes" should be normal for the teenage boy in the sense that it takes no character and no strength or no morals at all to have sex. But it takes character, self-esteem, respect, and a firm moral stand not to have sex. Being a virgin, therefore, is the most natural and most normal state for you. The trouble is that virginity is seen in its negative sense: A virgin is someone who has not had sexual intercourse. But virginity is not something negative; it is something positive. It is the absence of the intimate one-to-one commitment in order that a person may be free to give himself to a wider commitment. The virgin, then, is one who scatters his love over a wide area. He lives for service to his family, his community, his church, and his education (not just school learning but life-learning as well). Not obligated to the sexual commitment to one particular person, he is open to growth and service *precisely at the time of his life when he most needs both.*

And that exactly is the normal, healthy state of any teenage boy (and girl). Virginity (as someone will remind you in the next chapter) is not freedom *from* but rather freedom *for.* Freedom to grow, for one thing, to get educated, to learn about life, to become financially secure, to develop character, to become a man. Teenage sex, as we have seen so often, is anything but freedom. It is slavery and bondage: bondage to fear (of pregnancy or disease), to dreadful decisions (adoption, abortion), to exploitation. As one author warned:

Having sex has a way of taking over a teenage relationship. It can put a lot of personal and social pressure on one or both the partners. Once a couple enters into a sexual relationship, the uncertainty and worry begin: "Is it me or is it the sex?" "Will it last?" "What would my parents think?" or "What if she gets pregnant?" And then there is sexual jealousy to deal with, and it can be a heavy burden because each is expected to cleave exclusively to each other at the state of their lives when they want to explore the edge of the envelope. It's perfectly natural to be attracted to a lot of different people, but most teens can't handle their sexual partner showing even a friendly interest in another person.

Many teenagers find that after they began having sex everything went sour in the relationship. Becoming involved in a one-on-one relationship kept them in a Noah's Ark mode. Being a couple put a damper on hanging out with other people and having time to do what they want to do. Teenage girls complain about having less time for girlfriends, studying, being involved in school activities, and going places with their families; they feel cut off from the rest of their world. Some say dating isn't fun anymore, because going to the movies or dances gets shortchanged. "He doesn't want to do anything anymore but go someplace and have sex." Boys say that pressure to be committed to the girl—by her, his friends, her friends—forces them to continue a relationship they would rather end, or makes them feel more obligated to the girl than they would like to be. Said Gene, age 17, "You can get stuck. Everybody knows you're a couple and if you try to break it up with her so you can date someone else, everyone gets on your case."[1]

Virginity: No Apology

So, for these and many other reasons, teenage virginity needs no apology. It should be the normal, healthy condition of any growing boy in order that he *may* grow. Virginity gives space and time to become what you should become. It's a great gift. Those clowns who write on walls or tease about virginity are the unhealthy, abnormal ones. Trying to pressure you to be "sexually active" or "experienced" like themselves is like pressuring you to smoke pot: a dead-end excuse to make themselves feel justified for what they're doing as they slowly but surely become less and less free. And there's no one as un-free as an OD'd student, a pregnant girl, or an unwed father. Virginity is freedom.

Celibacy

While we're at it, we might mention that when virginity is freely adopted as a lifestyle for adults, we call this celibacy. Again, the special note is the same: it is a chosen freedom for wider service. Like Jesus and like St. Paul. And like priests, brothers, and sisters. They, who are sexual beings, are celibate because it gives them freedom to donate themselves more fully to the community. They can be free to move around and go where needed. They are in a sense "married" to the community. By being "Father" and "Sister" and "Brother," they are father and sister and brother to all. Because no individual person has claim on them, everyone has; they can readily give themselves to all. Their celibacy is their freedom to move in where others need care and help. They use their sexuality for the sake of the gospel and give their hearts in many ways. Because they gave their hearts fully to the One, they can love the many.

I'd like to share with you what celibacy means by introducing you to a dumb kid who became a saint, Barney Casey, the son of a Wisconsin farmer. Because of the many hours he had to work on the farm, Barney was 17 years old when he finished eighth grade. Well, after working as a logger, a prison guard, and a trolley car motorman, Barney decided one day he wanted to be a priest. So he went to the seminary but flunked out, too slow to keep up with the studies. So, encouraged by another priest, he entered the Capuchin seminary (a religious order like the Franciscans or Jesuits) and there he had his name changed (as is the custom) to Francis Solanus. Still he couldn't crack the books and catch the subject matter. His superiors didn't know what to do with him. They knew he wasn't smart enough to be a priest, yet, there was something about him, some holiness that they recognized.

So they decided on a compromise: ordain Francis a priest but on the condition that he would never preach formal sermons or hear confessions. So he was ordained and at the different places in New York and Milwaukee he was given the "peasant" jobs of doorkeeper and collecting money as offerings for Masses. But something happened. In these humble tasks, Father Solanus touched people deep in their hearts. People found him a wonderful listener and very, very kind and compassionate. He would often meet with people from seven o'clock in the morning until ten o'clock at night. And many people whom Father Solanus touched reported healings, conversions, and reconciliations. Now in all his years as a priest, Father Solanus never held a position higher than a doorkeeper—but after his death in 1937 at the age of 87, more than 20,000 people filed past his coffin before his burial. That's celibacy.

Of course, you should remember that the first pope, Peter, was married. And so are your father and mother and lots of other people. And this means that each person has his or her own calling and each serves in his or her own way. Being married or celibate are not "better" or "worse," but two special and different gifts for the sake of serving others. And that's always the bottom line, isn't it? As a Christian I must always reach out to others in loving care and service. For the truth is that what life is all about is written in that sentence and makes up the two-in-one commandment Jesus gave us: "You shall love the Lord your God with your whole soul, your whole mind and your whole heart and you shall love your neighbor as yourself. On these two commandments depends the whole law and the prophets as well."

QUESTIONS FOR REFLECTION AND DISCUSSION

1. "Losing it"—becoming a non-virgin—is a pressure. Why?

2. "Premature " sex is a good adjective for sex before marriage, especially teenagers. What's so premature about it? If you're ready, you're ready. Comment.

3. Virginity is normal. Do you agree. Why? Why not? Do you believe it is desirable? Why? Why not?

4. Celibacy is not denying or downgrading sexuality. It is using it totally for the sake of others. Discuss how this works in the life of Mother Teresa.

People don't care any more. People have no
shame. It's all in the movies. It's all in the mu-
sic...what was the name of that song? "This Girl's
a Slut"? No, not that one. "Treat Her Like a Pros-
titute"? No, no, not that one. "Rose's Cherry"?
No. Oh, I hated that song—it's all about what
he's going to do to her. "Go See the Doctor"?
Yeah, that's the one. All this time we're talking
about sex, and nobody has brought up love.

Teen Conversation

26
ELIMINATING THE WINDOWS

Caesar's Boardwalk Regency is the name of a gambling casino
in Atlantic City, New Jersey. Recently it spent seven million
dollars to redo its interior in order to "create an atmosphere
that relaxes the morality of people" (that's how *The Wall
Street Journal* put it). The new lobby is lined with Italian mar-
ble, the music is soft, and—get this—very deliberately all
windows are eliminated! Why? So that people would not relate to time or other places or other people. By blocking out
other sources and considerations (such as the poor people a few
blocks away) the casino makes you forget them and so pulls you
into its gambling games and machines. You see, the trick is not
what the casino shows you; it's what it doesn't.

And that's the problem we have with three groups of peers
(your equals who influence you): the TV, the school, and your
friends. It's not what they tell or show you. It's what they
don't. Let me demonstrate.

1) Our friend again, television. TV Guide[1] has as its feature headline, "Is Sex Getting Bolder?" The answer inside is that yes it is (surprise!). In spite of AIDS and teenage pregnancies, TV is showing more and more explicit sex and will continue to stimulate young people into using it before they're responsible. Why? The usual answer as you can guess by now: money. As the article puts it, "The willingness of the networks to test the limits of viewer's tolerance is not unrelated, of course, to the quest for ratings." So, what do they show you? The example in the article is "Miami Vice" where the vice cop, Sonny Crockett, has a passionate, explicit sex scene with another actress, Melanie Griffith, a sex scene that was intercut with the graphic murder of a prostitute. That's what you see: two unmarried people, TV role models, having sexual intercourse, on a popular program that most teens watch.

What don't you see? What did the absent "windows" eliminate? Several things: You don't see any results like pregnancy, disease, or plain hurt feelings. For another, there's the connection with violence again, that intercut murder scene. For another, these are actors and there's a whole crew of people watching and filming this scene, so it's make believe. For another, Don Johnson who plays Sonny Crockett was once married to the actress in the scene, Melanie Griffith, so even though they are shown having sex, they do not love each other. They have divorced in real life. So, again, we do not have love joined to sex or sex as committed love's expression. We just have sex, period, by two actors making believe. But by "closing the windows" and eliminating all else and just showing you a filmed sex scene you're not getting all this background, the full picture of real human life and human relationships and consequences. You're seeing a provocative lie, closed off from truth.

2) There's the school. All the schools (like your own) are putting in sex ed programs because of the high incidence of teen pregnancies: A baby is born every two minutes to U.S. teenagers and almost 40 percent of them have abortions. That's truly a horrible situation and you have to say to yourself that you never want to be part of that. Anyway, some schools have established "health" clinics where the students can get birth control pills and condoms and abortion referrals and have an abortion without their parents' knowledge or consent. Catholic bishops have strongly condemned such "health" clinics, and sex education courses that leave out any moral considerations.[2] Why? The usual thing you hear is that the bishops are not "with it," that they ought to catch up to the twentieth century. But the point is that here at least they are smack into the twentieth century with hard facts and good reasons for their opposition. Here are some of them:

First, the most basic reason to be against those health clinics is that they don't work! There is little documentation to show that they work and much more growing documentation showing that they don't. By not working I mean that they cause an increase of pregnancies, not a decrease. As some researchers said, "Although more and more teens are practicing contraception and doing so consistently and early, premarital pregnancies continue to rise."[3] Another set of researchers say, "No significant association can be found between taking a sex education course and subsequently becoming premaritally pregnant before age 20."[4] Another author states, "Those who had taken sex education courses that were considered 'comprehensive' by Planned Parenthood—that is, courses that included contraceptive instruction—were also nearly twice as likely to have had intercourse as those who had taken no courses considered as 'noncomprehensive.'[5] Another says, "Like past programs...school-based health clinics fail to simultaneously reduce pregnancy, sexual activity, abortion, and venereal disease among our young people."[6] Finally, there was a powerful article in *The Wall Street Journal*, written by the director of an independent research institute, whose opening paragraph goes like this:

More than a million teen-agers—most of them unmarried—become pregnant each year, and the number is rising. The belief is widespread that the number will be reduced by opening more "family planning" clinics and making them accessible to teens. However, research a colleague and I have done suggests otherwise.

As the number and proportion of teen-age family planning clients increased, we observe a corresponding increase
in teen-age pregnancy and abortion rate. The original
problems appear to have grown worse.[7]

So I mention all these people just to show you that the bishops
are not a bunch of grumpy old men who are out of it. They are simply listening to the scientists and passing on their findings:
"Health" clinics simply don't do the job, and in fact they undo it.

Second, you notice that I put the phrase "health" clinic in
quotations marks. That's because people often try to get them
into schools under the general theme of "Well, let's have these
clinics to help the kids keep well." And you assume that you
can go there with a hangnail or a toothache or pinched nerve.
You can. But, though they begin with such health items their
real aim is to move into family planning services.That's why in
most clinics, no matter what you go in there for, you're likely to
be asked if you are sexually active or plan to be so soon and, if
so, you'll be encouraged to use contraceptives.[8] So the bishops
are against this dishonesty.

Third, such "health" clinics, dominated by Planned Parenthood, give advice for abortions as a back-up for failed contraception, and we've seen how wrong that is. And they give it
frequently, so frequently in fact that the teen abortion rate has
gone up greatly and continues to do so. The increased reliance on
abortion as a form of birth control is well established; furthermore, "according to the 1986 Planned Parenthood service report,
216,366 pregnancy diagnoses were done by their organizations;
91,065 abortions were done by Planned Parenthood services,
while 94,404 of these cases were referred for an abortion. Thus,
over 85% of the pregnancy-positive cases seen by Planned Parenthood result in abortion. The income generated from abortion
procedures is substantial, which may amplify the pressure to
rely on abortion as a means of birth control."[9]

Fourth, the very presence of such "health" or family planning clinics in school takes a sexually active lifestyle for granted among the students and creates a climate that may make the
chaste teenager feel "out of it," not with the mainstream—and

we all know how severe peer pressure is. The bishops believe, as do many others, that what is missing from all this is any hope or belief that teenagers can control themselves or be chaste. What is eliminated, what you don't see, is the reality that schools do in fact carry authority and share in the parents' role.

Values and Sex
Finally and perhaps most seriously, the schools and their clinics cannot talk to you about right and wrong, the very area that needs examining! Talk about eliminating windows! All a teacher is allowed to say about any sexual question is that some feel one way, some another, but it's up to you to make up your own mind. The teacher may not offer any moral judgment, which is ridiculous and leaves you nowhere. As William Raspberry said so well:

> Suppose [parents] learned that their adolescent sons had a public school unit on shoplifting. Suppose that the teacher described in full detail the mechanics of shoplifting and also spent some time about its legal penalties, all without offering any moral judgment as to whether shoplifting was right or wrong. Now suppose that the final segment of the unit dealt with techniques for avoiding the consequences of shoplifting. ("I leave it to you to decide whether shoplifting is something you want to do or not. But if you do decide to shoplift, there are some ways to avoid detection. This method is 94 percent effective, while this one is 89 percent safe.") Would [the parents] consider this a good thing? Yet, this is the usual conclusion in any sex ed course.

But the point is: What are the values surrounding sex? Just knowing about it, how it works or how to prevent children is just not enough to make us happy and good human beings. "Results show that knowledge, as measured by sex education courses and self-reported birth control knowledge, has no effect on the chances that a black or white female will experience an out-of-wedlock birth as a teenager. However, when adolescents and their parents hold values that stress responsibility, the adolescents' chances of experiencing an out-of-wedlock childbirth are lower."[10] So it is a question of values, values that you need to be told honestly and forthrightly.

What you need to be told is something like this, and I have never known a young man (or woman) like yourself to be insulted, since most adolescents are quite realistic: "You should not ever have sex as an adolescent since you are different from adults and that difference is everywhere: for example, we have a separate legal system for you and you cannot vote. And the reason is that by nature children and adolescents are less responsible than adults. And that's not a put-down; it is simply true. We cannot expect a child who still forgets his lunch money to cope with birth control." As one person put it, telling a teenager that it's OK to play with sex is like telling a four year old that it's OK to play with fire if he is very careful and stands way back.

What is needed, then, for you and for other teens, is not contraceptives, but a loving, accepting, and forgiving family that's rooted in religious faith and a deep sense of right and wrong.

Peer Pressure

3) *Your immediate peers, your friends, and schoolmates.* They too, without always meaning to, can push you into actions that you might not ordinarily do yourself. That's what we call pressure, peer pressure. For example, the majority of teenagers know that shoplifting is wrong, but only 6 percent would tell about their friends doing it. (How about you?) Again, 62 percent know that alcohol is bad for them but they drink anyway out of peer pressure. So you see it's not always easy to make your own decisions and you certainly want to be "in" with the crowd. You want to be accepted, for when your peers accept you they're telling you you're OK and everybody needs to hear that. However, sometimes this need for acceptance conflicts with your need to be true to yourself. It's a struggle. Let's say you wind up going along with the group who's really mocking a kid and making him close to tears and you feel bad about that—but it's hard to step out of it, isn't it? The group might turn on you. You are pressured to wear the "right" clothes so you'll be a part of

things. Sometimes, things really go far and some kids do serious harm because they were dared or egged on or didn't want to be called chicken.

Inside, the real you knows what's right and wrong, but peer pressure is tough and it can lead you to things you really don't want to do. The trouble is that it gets to be a vicious circle for the more you follow the peer pressure, the less self-esteem and assurance you have and the more you have to be a follower. Still, somewhere along the line you must make decisions that are best for you.

And this is especially true when it comes to sex. There are simply too many consequences, as we have repeatedly seen, for you to listen to your peers alone: the TV, the school, or your friends. You must make your own values and follow them. Like Laura Wilder who wrote *Little House on the Prairie* while still a young woman. Her publisher wanted her to change her ideals and her style or else he would not publish her book. She badly wanted the fame and the money, but finally refused. It was only decades later that her books were published. Laura had made a decision based on her personal values, despite the sacrifices involved. She refused to compromise her values. Or John Drew, basketball star (Atlantic Hawks, Utah Jazz) whose life was almost ruined by cocaine. But he admitted his problem and went for treatment but his hardest task, he says, was his peers. When he came out of treatment, his peers wanted to "celebrate" with drugs and, as he said, "I was so scared, I started shaking. I went right to the phone and called an A.A. contact in the city. He helped me through it." And he wound up doing one of the hardest things he ever did. He called his friends in the drug scene and told them he never wanted to see them again.

Adding Windows

But remember, in *your* struggle to be strong, you're not alone. There are always people who will add windows and open them wide so you can get the wider view of life, love, and sex. Molly Kelly is one. She's from Pennsylvania and she goes all over the country and even into Canada and she speaks to teenagers like

yourself and she gets standing ovations from the kids! What
are they clapping about and what is she telling them? Simply
put, she is telling them that "chastity is the way to go"—
chastity, the control of the sex urge, the saving of sex for marriage. She admits it's an old word you don't hear too much these
days, but it's a word kids really want to hear. And in using that
word, she gets a kick out of some adults' reaction:

Some adults have commented, "Chastity! What an
old-fashioned word! Do you really say that?" Some still
think that chastity only refers to Sonny and Cher's
daughter! Others, realizing it to be a virtue, comment, "I
guess you never get into the public schools with a message
like that!"

Such a comment could lead us to believe that the virtues of honesty, integrity, leadership and truth must also
be banned from public schools. Isn't the coveted American
Legion Medal awarded for such virtues? Why then should
chastity be excluded? One woman thought chastity was a
perfume....

Still, for all of its misunderstanding and underuse, chastity, she
repeats, is a word the kids really want to hear. And Molly's
high on chastity "because I'm high on teens." She refuses to assume what others assume, "that you're sexually out of control."
She respects you too much to believe that. Moreover, as Molly
points out, "chastity is the only solution that is in full tune
with physical, mental, spiritual, and social health. It is 100
percent effective, costs nothing, has no harmful side effects, and
it puts our young people in control of their lives." That's putting
the windows back in.

Another window opener is Ingrid Trobisch who reminds teens
like you that your destiny is in your hands. She likes to recall
something an African father said to his teenage son, "A real
man learns how to control his sexual energy." I like her reminder that chastity is *the decision to be free.* It offers freedom
from exploitation, fear of pregnancy or disease, freedom from
fatherless children, and from guilt and pain. It means freedom
to plan one's own future, to channel one's energies, to choose

one's life partner, to develop one's character. That's freedom.

Or there's "Dear Abby." One column that caused a great deal of response was about a 17-year-old girl who wrote that she wanted to say no to sex with her boyfriend, who gave her the line that if she didn't the relationship would break up. She struggled and finally said no, but felt hurt. Here are some responses from the males themselves:

I am a 20-year old male who reinforces your advice to keep saying no until you feel you are ready. I've been dating the same girl for two years. She was a virgin when we started to date and she still is.... I appreciated what a prize she was after I had dated the easy girls.... I am now willing to wait until after we're married. Sex can cheapen a relationship, not make it more valuable.

I'm a 20-year-old male university student.... You are not weird for wanting a relationship with a guy without having sex. There are plenty of attractive, available guys who don't really care about scoring. Trust me. I know, I'm one of them.

I am a 22-year-old male college senior. I am also a virgin. You are not weird; you are unusual. But the best always is. Be true to yourself. Some men still appreciate the obvious goodness you possess. And lastly, it does not take experience to know that having sex is not a substitute for making love.

These are the kind of letters that should be normal for you to write now and until you are married.

And besides, open the window to more facts:

1) *It is still true that most teenagers do as a matter of fact practice chastity.* That's not what you hear. The impression is that all the kids are doing it, and those who do get all the publicity. But a Harris poll says not so.

2) *Those teenagers who attend religious services frequently are less likely to be sexually active.* That's always been true. Why? Because they're tuned into higher values. Getting back one more time to that report on that Virginia high school:

Gary Alward says flat out that he doesn't believe in sex

before marriage. He and his tall, attractive, blond girl-friend, Katherine Reilly, have been dating each other exclusively for almost three years. Gary says his belief in abstinence comes from his Baptist faith. Katherine, a Catholic, says, "I just don't feel ready for sex now. One of the reasons that Gary and I have such a good relationship is that he doesn't pressure me." Family-life teacher Jean Hunter says that adults have to help more kids to realize what Katherine and Gary have discovered: It's difficult but possible to have a meaningful, intimate relationship without sex." [11]

Now that's a good witness. There are still really more virgins, the report adds, male and female, in our high schools than generally assumed.

3) Eighty-six percent of kids live with their own biological parents. You would get the impression that every kid in America has divorced parents. There's a lot of divorce but a lot of these are multiple divorces and lots don't have kids.

4) Most of all, recent surveys consistently show that three-fourths of all teenagers and parents, here and abroad, feel quite close to each other and report getting along very well. That's different from the media's impression that all teens and parents are in a state of constant warfare.

So, this is a more realistic picture. It's not the stuff that newspapers and television zeroes in on. It's like the only house in your town to make the 6 o'clock news is the one that burns down. So the kids that make the media are the ones in trouble. But that's not all of reality. All of reality, the reality that is not eliminated by having no windows to see through, shows us that teens like you are basically good, from good families, and that with values from parents and God, chastity is, can be, should be, a normal part of your life.

QUESTIONS FOR REFLECTION AND DISCUSSION

1. How does the metaphor of the chapter title apply to sexual activity?

2. Why are our bishops against "health" and sex clinics in the public schools? Find in the press their reasons and discuss them. (See, for example, the newspaper, *Our Sunday Visitor*, December 20, 1987).

3. What do you think of sex ed classes in school?

4. How do you form and how do you maintain your values against society?

5. What did you think of those male responses in this chapter from Dear Abbey?

Jesus grew in wisdom, age, and grace.   Luke 2:40

27
A WORD FROM OUR SPONSORS

Here's some final words from the three sponsors of this book. The first is from a teenage couple who represent a lot of kids, and whose voices for chastity are becoming louder and louder. In this case, the voices are singing. The Latin teenage couple, Titiana and Johnny, look sexy and their singing is smooth as can be and the song's got a beat you can really dance to. It's hot music—but with a "cool" message. When they start to sing they look for all the world like they have sex in mind, but the message is abstinence. They're a hit teen couple singing a hit song in South America and Mexico called "When We're Together" ("I don't want us to regret/Having lived an encounter./You'll see I'm right/When I say 'no.' ") and they've followed it up with another hit song, "Wait." Now they're singing their songs in North America, singing for people like you because they want to spread the truth: sex is tied in with commitment and responsibility and "wait" till you're ready for both.

So real love, they're saying, is upbeat and caring and takes on responsibility. By the same token, as we have seen, it's easy to spot by contrast what love isn't:

It isn't love when it's easier to touch than to talk; when kisses are easier than communication; when you're sexual partners but not friends.

It isn't love when you want sex but refuse to take responsibility for what might happen from pregnancy or disease.

It isn't love when you use the feelings and the body of

another person to make yourself look like a winner and then treat that person as a trophy, a thing that you've won, a game that you "scored" in.

It isn't love when you manipulate another person's emotions.

It isn't love when you do things that violate another's privacy and self-esteem.[1]

So, whether it's from Titiana and Johnny, or common sense, the message is all a variation of what Jesus said long ago, "You are to love one another as I have loved you." The most important word in that sentence is the shortest: as. And if you want to see "as," just look at the crucifix. Love will go that far.

Chastity: A Positive Note

Now, words from the second sponsor: me. All through this book I've tried to show that basically sex or sexuality has little to do with sex-organ sex and everything to do with us as people who use our bodies to make statements all the time, whether we realize it or not. Chastity, therefore, is the use of our bodies in the loving service of others. We have to work hard at chastity because, like poverty (struggling with material possessions so that they don't become demanding idols) and obedience (struggling with power), chastity doesn't come easy, since our selfishness frequently gets in the way. These lapses are not often deadly, but if unchecked can be. Anyway, chastity, as I hope you can see, is really a *positive* virtue. It's using our marvelous bodies like the signs (or sacraments) that they are: for life-giving growth and service to others. And behind the visible sign or symbol is love.

I make a point of this because these days chastity has a new interest because of the STDs, especially AIDS. And in this context, chastity, I fear, comes across in two negative ways. (1) Chastity is seen as a way to avoid disease. It becomes simply a prudent or wise way to avoid getting sick. (2) Chastity is seen as a means of controlling this "lousy, rebellious flesh" or body of ours that seems to want to go its own way. In either case, as I said above, chastity comes across as a negative thing, a repression. Some church people may unwittingly underscore this impression by saying, "Aha, if you only practice chastity, you won't get AIDS!" Or, "If you subdue or tame the body, you won't give in to temptation (and get AIDS)." And so, once more, chastity is seen as a lid on the body, a "spiritual condom" (if you'll pardon the figure of speech). It is prevention. It is subduing. It's good for what it doesn't do or allow.

But I don't want you to have that idea. Chastity is a *positive* thing: It is a *virtue*. That means it is a geared *for* something, not against something. Like physical fitness, it is not merely a good protection against sickness and disease, but it is geared for good health and the enjoyment of the body. You see, your body makes statements all the time and lets everybody know to what you're committed and how you're committed. It shows everyone how you relate to others.

So—you can lay on the sidewalk so everyone has to walk around you; you can loll in the Acme doorway so the little old ladies can't get in with their carts; you can smoke in the non-smoking section; you can have sexual intercourse with a girl; you can talk loud at the movies; you can overeat; you can piss in the streets; you can snatch a purse. You can do all these things. And each and every one is a statement about you. In the cases I've just given, the statements that you're making with your body are that you are self-centered and relate in a most crude and selfish way to others. You're committed to yourself and yourself alone. In a word, you're not practicing chastity.

Chastity would mean that you would be conscious that you're becoming what you're doing and that you really are trying to give your body in service to others. Chastity means that you're using your sexuality (your being-in-action as a male) with a sense of caring love. This doesn't come easy, but we have to keep on trying and practicing till we get it. That's why we call it a virtue, which means a good habit, the way we usually act: lovingly. (Again, it takes time; don't get discouraged.) So all this is a way of saying that I want you to be wary of anyone who sells chastity as an antidote to AIDS or as a whip to slap down the flesh. Chastity is not geared toward prevention or repression. As a discipline it is geared to growth, service, and love.

Jesus as Friend: Forceful and Forgiving

The final words are from the third sponsor, Jesus and his church. And those words are loud and clear and right up front, as direct as they can be, assuming you are not married: *Do not have sexual intercourse as a teenager. It is wrong. It is sinful. Don't do it.* I'm not going to apologize for those words because they're right. The only worry I have is that somebody will seize on these words and say, "Aha, there they go again! The church is against sex. The only thing the church can say is no! The church is out to stamp out sex!" And they'll forget or won't even look at all the rest of the pages in this book.

No, you know by now that the church is *for sex* and considers it God's gift, one of the greatest. But that's just the point. You don't take great gifts and use them cheaply just because you want to feel big or say you've done it and think that now you're a man.[2] On the contrary, you want to surround what is beautiful and good with as much respect and love—and preparation—as possible. That's the key: preparation, not merely on the outside, but far more important, on the inside. Like Jesus, you have to be ready on all levels: in wisdom, age, and grace.

Like me illustrate. Remember Stephen Spielberg's great movies, *Star Wars* and *The Empire Strikes Back*, and the rest? Like me, you probably saw them a million times and even have them on tape. Remember near the end of *Star Wars* when Luke Skywalker is in his fantastic spaceship in pursuit of Darth Vader? He's young, he's sharp, he's ready, and he's at the controls. But things aren't going well. He can't seem to get a fix on the enemy craft. He's all over the lot. He's not hitting anything. Darth Vader is getting away. Then he hears the voice of his Mentor, the ancient wise man, Obi Wan Kenobi, who tells him in so many words, "Luke, ease up. Let go. You're trying too hard. Let the Force take over. Let it guide you. Luke, listen to me. *Let the Force be with you!*" And when Luke makes an effort to let the Force guide his ship, he is successful.

Luke Skywalker is young, maybe a late teenager or in his

early twenties. He has a magnificent ship, he's at the controls
and he's smart. We might say he has age but as yet he lacks
wisdom and grace. He needs to learn a lot yet. He needs a guide,
a Wise One, to teach him how to use his ship, how to let another force into his life. Until he does that, he's just another "fly
boy" with a souped-up plane who may wind up crashing or
creating a lot of mess.

That's the way it is with you. Sure, you may be developing
or already be developed physically and sexually. Yes, your sex
organs are working and you can have sexual intercourse. Yes, we
might say, your magnificent "spaceship," your body, is in tip-
top shape and you're at the controls. But you need a Wise One
at your side to urge you to let the Force guide your life, to tell
you that you need to grow a lot more inside yet. Otherwise, as
we have seen, something indeed to be beautiful can turn out to
become ugly because it turns out hurtful.

Yes, the church is your Wise One and its rule of saying no to
sexual intercourse now is wise. The church is like Obi Wan Kenobi telling you, "Let the Force be with you! Let it be a part of
your life!" What force? The force of experience, of wisdom, of
love, and of maturity. And such things, as you know, take time.
Remember our Latin words: the "adolescent" is one who is growing and the "adult" is one who has grown? But if you don't allow the time for the adolescent to become adult, you can wind
up crashing into a lot of people and cause a lot of harm. Until
maturity sets in, all sex is "premature" in the real sense of the
word. It is pre-wise, pre-loving. The urge is there to merge, but
to merge in lasting love, care and commitment—all of which
take time to learn. Like Jesus, you're growing in age. Like Jesus,
you've got to wait for the other two to slowly grow inside you:
wisdom and grace.

But even Luke Skywalker made mistakes. Even so, Obi Wan
Kenobi never left his side. Jesus never leaves your side, even
when you make mistakes. In fact, you remember he told a story
about a teenage boy who left his father's house, gambled his
money, and fooled around with sex and wound up, literally, in a
pigsty (a symbol of just how far he fell). But the memories of

his father's love moved him to go back home. All the long way back, you recall, he practiced his little speech of how he was going to tell his father he was sorry for messing up. At last he got near the property. But his father, who every day and every night till it got dark went to the front porch of the old farmhouse to look for his son, this time saw him. And he did what no father in the Mideast would ever do: Forgetting his dignity, he himself ran to meet his son instead of waiting till the boy got to him to humble himself in the dust! And when the old father, all out of breath, finally did reach his wayward, his prodigal son, he wouldn't even let the boy get two words of apology out of his mouth. Why? Because he was too busy hugging and kissing him! (Luke 15:11)

Put yourself in that picture. God loves you. God loves you deeply with no strings attached. God loves you as you are. God is the Force that never leaves you no matter what. God is kind and forgiving. Respond to God in prayer. Decide now never to be "pre-mature" in using your sexuality—and hold onto these words from your final sponsor:

"Take heart, son; your sins are forgiven." (Matthew 9:2)

QUESTIONS FOR REFLECTION AND DISCUSSION
1. Chastity is a positive virtue, not a negative warning. Explain.
2. Describe "real love."
3. To what extent do the Star Wars characters help you to understand your role as a sexual being?
4. What is the reasoning behind "Before maturity sets in, all sex is 'pre-mature.' "

My command is this: Love each other as I have loved you. I no longer call you servants: Instead, I call you friends.

28
TIME OUT 4

We're at the end of the book and so we have our last get-together. Therefore, instead of our usual question and answer routine, let's just share a few final thoughts. For a long time now counsellors and psychologists have known that our behavior follows from the way we look at things. If, for example, you look at people as objects or "the enemy" or just a collection of molecules and impulses, then you'll treat them like that. Prejudice, racism, abuse, manipulation, and a whole bunch of things like that follow from this view. But if you see people (and yourself) as touched by God, made to God's image and likeness, then, of course, you'll act (or should act) differently.

You're usually brought up with some basic view about life and about people, but even if you were raised with or programmed by the media into seeing people as things, you can alter your view. You can change. This is known as conversion. I think of St. Augustine, for example, way back in the sixth century. He left us his autobiography in his famous *Confessions* (which you might read in college, or you can get in any bookstore). There he writes bluntly of his trouble with sex. He even recalls his pagan father's attitude. When he was a teenager and at the public baths one day (in the warm climate in Africa where Augustine was from, they bathed in the nude), he tells us that his father saw his enlarged sexual organs and the pubic hair beginning to grow around them and he ran home to tell Augustine's mother to cheer up, someday soon now they'll have grandchildren! Well, the joker was that Augustine did have a child—but out of wedlock. And he lived this way for a long while until the day when Jesus came into his life and he turned right around and became converted and give up his sinful life. He was baptized and eventually became one of the great saints of history.

I think of Francis of Assisi in the thirteenth century, a spoiled teenager of a rich merchant father, selfish and thinking only of his own good times, who discovered the love of Jesus to be so powerful that he left his comfortable and well-to-do life to devote himself to the poor and the spreading of the gospel. He learned to see God not only in people but in all of nature (which is why he is the patron saint of ecology!). I love that one great moment when in the town square, in full view of the whole village, Francis took off all his clothes as a symbol of leaving all that refinery and materialism behind, and walked away naked to embrace a new life. (Could you see yourself doing that? But once you fall in love with God, you find yourself doing all sorts of crazy things!)

Modern Models

I think of Dorothy Day of our own times (whose life you should also read) and her living together with a man, having a child but then changing her life around, becoming a Catholic and devoting her remarkable life to caring for the poor and bearing witness to peace. She will officially be declared a saint one day. I think of Thomas Merton, also of our own time, whose numerous paperbacks right now you can find in any drug, department, or book store, who continues to influence millions of people with his views on prayer and peace. But he too was self-centered and just out for the good times. He fathered a child he never saw. But in his twenties, as he tells us in his famous autobiography, *The Seven Storey Mountain*, he finally said yes to Jesus, became a Catholic and then a Trappist monk. I think of

Patrick and Pat Crowley from Chicago, a married couple, who did so much for married and family life.

The point is that all of these people changed their vision. They learned to see themselves and others as Jesus saw them. They discovered the unconditional love of God for them and for others.

And once they saw as Jesus saw, they had no choice but to treat people differently. They didn't waste time moaning over past sins and mistakes. No, they moved ahead and, most of all, they made a difference in their own lives and in the lives of others, just as you can.

As we close, I just want to pass on this message. If you learn to see others as Jesus sees you and them, then you can make a difference in the way you act and relate, especially to girls. All this takes time and it takes prayer, but it's worth it. And you can even "speed" up the process by going away on a retreat or a "Search" weekend. Or maybe just a little bit of different reading from what you usually read will help. I recommend, for instance, Fr. John Powell's books such as *Why Am I Afraid to Tell You Who I Am?* and *Why Am I Afraid to Love?* (Again, in most stores in paperback).

Learn too to be comfortable with who and what you are and with your sexuality; that is, you recall, with your living and acting and relating positively as a male with a male body. Like yourself and like your body (and this includes the sexual organs). And acting sexually, you know by now, is not the same as acting genitally (using your sexual organs). Acting sexually is using all that you are to bring out the best in others. And if you make a mistake, don't worry. You start all over again. Sexual weakness is not the worst sin in the world; far, far worse are greed, materialism, injustice, and breaking commitments. Or if you want some real "biggies," there's going through life never really loving and sacrificing for another and, probably just as bad, loving somebody but never getting around to telling that person.

Anyway, I think I'll end by sharing with you this letter from a man who made his decision early on to save sex till marriage.

Here's what he says:

My wife and I waited until we were married to have sex, which is unusual nowadays. But I think it was a good decision. Maybe if we'd had sex with other people or with each other before we were married, we'd have been experienced or knowledgeable. But learning about sex together made it that much more special. We didn't have to worry if either of us was as good as the other lovers either of us might have had before.

Being willing to wait until we were married, I felt I was showing my wife that it wasn't just sex that I wanted from her but real, true love and lifelong commitment. And she was showing me the same thing. We really trusted each other, and that made us feel safe enough to really let go. We didn't have to worry that if we did it wrong or it wasn't great the first time that it would be all over. And, in fact, it wasn't so great the first time. It was kind of awkward and embarrassing. But I knew and she knew that we'd both be around tomorrow. This trust and commitment made us able to grow to be better lovers than we might otherwise have been.[1]

NOTES

Introduction

1. *The New York Times*, December 4, 1987, p. B5.

2. Carol Casell, Straight *From the Heart: How to Talk to Your Teenagers About Love and Sex* (New York: Simon and Schuster, 1987), p. 82-83.

3. *The Christian Century*, September 9-16, 1987, page 747.

4. See "The Role of the Family in Sex Education" by James Walters and Lynda Henley Walters in the *Journal of Research and Development in Education* (Vol. 16, No. 2, Winter, 1983) where the authors point out, "Support for the fact that parents influence children's attitudes has been provided in a large, recent study of Canadian university students (Barret, 1980). Among those students who claimed never to have had intercourse, 52% ranked their parents as the first or second most important influence. Among coitally experienced respondents, only 30% ranked their parents as the first or second important influence." p. 11.

5. And, of course, if parents default, they are left with the dubious prospect of turning over this critical aspect of their children's lives to school-based "health" and family planning clinics (see Chapter 25, "Eliminating the Windows) and aggravating the dilemma posed by the U.S. House of Representatives Select Committee on Children, Youth and Families, "Teen Pregnancy: what is being done?" 1986): "In recent years, various groups have come up with plans for addressing the problems of teen pregnancy anew. The solutions they have proposed seem to lead along two radically different paths. One leads back to the family and acknowledgement of parental responsibility while the other leads further from the family, towards schools as the provider of guidance."

6. Richard D. Parsons, *Adolescents in Turmoil, Parents Under Stress: A Pastoral Ministry Primer* (Mahwah, N.J.: Paulist Press, 1987), p. 75. See also the journal *Adolescence* (Vol. XXII, No. 87, Fall, 1987), "Adolescent Sexuality: Values, Morality and Decision Making" by Anne McCreary Juhasz and Mary Sonnenshein-Schneider. The authors report (p. 586): "The more religious individuals were less influenced by hedonistic self-gratification through sexual intercourse and conversely, the less religious were more influenced by this factor. It is interesting to note that intimacy considerations regarding sexual intercourse is reflective of religiosity only for males."

7. Fathers are typically reluctant to openly discuss sex with their sons. See J. Kahn, "Parental Impact on Sex and Development" in *Contemporary Marriage: Special Issues in Couples Therapy,* edited D. Goldberg (Homewood, Ill.: Dorsey Press, 1985).

Chapter 1: The Mystery

1 "How Men and Women Got Together," from *American Indian Myths and Legends,* selected and edited by Richard Erdoes and Alfonso Ortiz. Copyright © 1984 by Richard Erodes and Alfonso Ortiz. Reprinted by permission of Pantheon Books, a Division of Random House, Inc.

2. I am indebted for this summary here to Dave Mace's book *The Christian Response to the Sexual Revolution* (Nashville: Abingdon Press, 1970, 10th printing, 1987).

Chapter 2: Long Live the Difference

1. Marion Diamond, "Letters to the Editor," *The New York Times,* January 29, 1987, p. A16.

2. Male and female behavior differences are indeed socially and psychologically and culturally shaped, but more and more research shows that, beneath it all, there are indeed fundamental hormonal, genetic, structural differences—in short, a basic biological difference between the sexes that influences their behavior. Thus: "The tapestry of an individual's love chronicle...is always woven of a complex mixture of social and psychological imperatives. ...Many of these are contingent on gender, or gender issues in turn have social and psychological as well as biological components...the on-going cultural context locks in the pre-existing tendencies," from Ethel S. Person, "The Passionate Quest" in "Some Differences Between Men and Women" in *The Atlantic Monthly* (March 1988). The following is from the second part of the article entitled, "Sex and Hormones" by Winifred Gallagher: "Men and women have the same half-dozen sex hormones in common, but in different concentrations. ...A person's prenatal hormonal experience appears to be an especially strong influence on later behavior...says John Bancroft, a behavioral endocrinologist at the Medical Resource Council's reproductive-biology unit in Edinburgh, Scotland....'There are behaviors likelier to occur in boys than in girls, and they are partly attributable to the effects of hormones. Testosterone is influencing not just male sexual behavior, but male behavior—things like dominance and aggression. The two are not separate.' "Parts of

the male and female human brains are structurally different because of different prenatal experiences, and there are some established differences in male and female behavior," says Dr. Crews, a professior of zoology and psychology at the University of Texas at Austin. ...June Reinsch, a psychobiologist...rejects the notion of a rigid, universal biological determination of behavior...but Reinisch says, 'The male and female brains are different structurally, and probably chemically, and that means that male and female behaviors are going to be different—overlapping, but different. In certain cognitive and perceptual areas, men and women live in slightly different universes.' ...Although [Dr. Bancroft] stresses that social influences on female sexuality are very powerful, he thinks a good bit of this variation in sex drive among women, as well as the variation between men and women, has a genetic basis....'We're just learning how to talk sensibly and efficiently about sex and the differences between the sexes...you have to dig for the biological bits, because without that perspective, people can get sold on the idea that their behavior—especially their sexual behavior—is based on only all the social stuff that's so important, instead of also reflecting a basic natural pattern. And that can lead to unrealistic expectations about what sort of behavior is feasible.'"
3. Beryl Leiff Benderly, *The Myth of Two Minds: What Gender Means and Doesn't Mean* (New York: Doubleday, 1987).

Chapter 4: What, Me Worry?
1. Ferrol Sams, *Run with the Horsemen* (New York: Penguin Books, 1984), p. 194.
2. Ibid., p. 144.

Chapter 5: Masturbation
1. Those who know the church's official stand on masturbation are also reminded that especially in the case of adolescent boys the old principle that "passion lessens responsibility" is quite applicable. Interesting to note also is spiritual guide and trappist Basil Pennington's remarks to priests in an article, "Celibacy for the Kingdom": "Even in masturbation we do need to acknowledge that there are human goods and values present. This is why it is attractive to us as humans. It is a satisfying (in a passing way), tension releasing experience. Masturbation can put us in touch with the goodness and power of our physical being, something of the wonder of the human body. Yet it has to be honestly acknowledged that such an expression of our sexuality falls

short." (*Emmanuel*, December, 1987, p. 564). Such "falling short" is especially understandable for budding adolescents. See also Charles E. Curran, "Masturbation and Objectively Grave Matter" in *A New Look at Christian Morality* (Notre Dame: Ind.: Fides Publishers, 1970) and Philip Keane, S.S., *Sexual Morality: A Catholic Perspective* (Mahwah, N.J.: Paulist Press, 1977), p. 58-70.
2. Lucienne Pickering, *Boys Talk* (London: Geofrey Chapman, 1981), p. 194.

Chapter 8: Time Out 1
1. David Feldman, *Why Do Clocks Run Clockwise and Other Imponderables* (New York: Harper & Row, 1987), p. 146.
2. Lynda Madaras, *The What's Happening to My Body Book For Boys* (New York: Newmarket Press, 1987), p. 149.

Chapter 9: Good Feeling, Feeling Good
1. In these days of sociobiology where there is a design but no designer (Richard Dawkins), this basically teleological perspective of Aristotle and Aquinas may seem naive. But as Barry Schwartz says in *The Battle for Human Nature* (New York: W.W. Norton Co., 1986) "Natural selection may have taken teleology out of nature, but people are teleological, designing creatures." p. 195.

Chapter 10: Sex: Discharge or Symbol?
1. T. Benson, *et. al.*, *The Quicksilver Years* (San Francisco: Harper & Row, 1987), p. 59.
2. Richard D. Parsons, *op. cit.*, pp. 71-73.
3. Evelyn Mills, *Why Wait Till Marriage?* (New York: Association Press, 1965).
4. Sol Gordon, Ph.D. "Your Child's Sexuality" in *Experts Advise Parents*, edited by Eileen Shiff (New York: Delacorte Press, 1987).

Chapter 11: The Urge to Merge
1. Paul Schurman, Th.D., "Male Liberation," *Pastoral Psychology* (Spring 1987), p. 192.

Chapter 12: Self-Esteem
1. I want to be sensitive to the hardships of the divorced person raising children and not add any undue guilt. Still, the sometimes harsh realism of such children's vulnerability must be acknowledged so that

proper caution can be taken. For example, John Crewdson's *By Si-lence Betrayed: Sexual Abuse of Children* quotes a pedophile: "My parents are divorced" is music to a pedophile's ears. (p. 105). See also "The Development of Adolescent Sexuality" by Catherine S. Chilman in the *Journal of Research and Development* in Education (Vol. 16, No. 2, 1983) where she reports: "During this decade [the 1970's], almost one-fifth of white children and adolescents, and one-half of black youngsters were living in homes broken by divorce. There is mounting evidence that divorce tends to have long-lasting effects on the sons and daughters of divorcing parents (Hetherington, Cox & Dox, 1976; Wallerstein & Kelly, 1980). Parents who divorce are apt to lead an active dating life. This can be very disturbing to their children and teenagers. The obvious sexuality of parents is often upsetting to adolescents who are attempting to come to terms with their own maturing sexuality." p. 19. See also "Teen Pregnancy Linked to Parents' Divorce" by Neil M. Kalter, M.D. in *Medical Aspects of Human Sexuality* (November 1987), pp. 130-131. See also, *What Every Baby Knows* by T. Berry Brazelton, M.D. (Reading, Mass.: Addison-Wesley Publishing Co., 1987), p. 93.

2. "Most sexual encounters take place in the home of the girl or her male partner. ...More and more homes are in effect zero-person households during much of the time. ...It is no more than ironic specu-lation, but one wonders to what extent the upsurge in employment among married women that has helped reduce their own fertility may have been a factor in the sexual liberation of their children" (Zelnik and Kantner, "Sexual and Contraceptive Experience of Young Un-married Women in the United States, in *Family Planning Perspec-tives*, vol. 9, No., 2, 1977, p. 60 and p. 70). "A study conducted by sociolo-gist Sandra Hofferth and psychologist Virginia Cain, found that most latchkey children are from well-educated, middle-to-upper class fami-lies living in suburban or rural areas. For these families, self-care ap-pears to be a choice, not a necessity." *Psychology Today* (December 1987), p. 12. See also Rosanna Hertz's book, *More Equal Than Others: Men and Women in Dual Careers* (Berkeley, Calif.: University of Cali-fornia Press, 1987) where the author shows that highly successful dual-career couples depend on the less privileged members of society to provide child care. See also, "Today's Troubled Men" by Herbert J. Frendenberger in *Psychology Today* (December 1987), p. 46.

3. It would take us too far afield here, but I would strongly suggest that adults take considerable time—many classes and discussions and

readings—with the students to explore friendship in all of its meaning and depths for, as one author wisely put it, "For too long now in a society obsessed with the mythology of romantic love, we have allowed the concept of friendship to be grossly devalued. Everyone, it seems, must elect to be either a stranger or lover in relation to each other. Now, brought to our senses by the grim statistics of AIDS as a fact of life and death, there is an urgent need to explore the neglected potential on non-genital relationships. Friendship is waiting in the wings to be rediscovered..." (Richard Buck, "Friendship as Holiness" in *The Way*, (January 1988), p. 28). In a kind of left-handed testimony, a divorced woman bemoans her lack of cultivation of friends, friends who now came to her support: "Friends—women whom I had carelessly neglected during the 25 years when I was absorbed in nurturing my husband and my 'traditional' marriage—suddenly appeared on the scene with encouragement, wisdom and aid...In this volatile era, lovers and even husbands come and go, but friends are forever..." (*The New York Times*, February 25, 1988, p. C11).

Chapter 13: The River's Edge

1. Script of "Hollywood's Favorite Heavy," a presentation of Manifold Productions, Inc. in association with the South Carolina Education Television Network and National Video Communications, Inc., 1987.

2. *The New York Times*, January 14, 1988, page A14. Even given perhaps the financial uncertainty of these days and the understandable anxiety about security, the report is startling.

3. The 1985 Strommen and Strommen report cited in Richard D. Parsons, *op. cit.* p. 67.

4. June 1986, p. 8. See also that same journal, July 1986, "Sexual Effects of Movie and TV Violence" by George A. Comstock, p. 96; also the *Journal of Youth and Adolescence*, "Television, Teenagers and Health" by Larry A. Tucker who reports, "From the results it appears that the health and well-being of teenage males is associated significantly with exposure to television." p. 423. For a more popular discussion of TV's effects, see "Is TV Stealing the Days of our Lives?" by James Brieg, *U.S. Catholic* (February 1988), p. 6.

5. Quoted in *Raising PG Kids in an X-Rated Society* by Tipper Gore (Nashville: Abingdon Press, 1987), p. 84.

Chapter 14: Time Out 2

1. *The New York Times*, January 20, 1988, p. D1.

2. *The New York Times*, January 21, 1988, p. C6.

3. Willard Gaylin, M.D., *Rediscovering Love* (New York: Penguin Books, 1987), p. 248.

Chapter 15: The STDs

1. Earl E. Shelp and Ronald H. Sunderland, *AIDS and the Church* (Philadelphia: Westminster Press, 1987), p. 37.

2. *Ibid.*

3. See Michael A. Fumento, "AIDS: Are Heterosexuals at Risk?" *Commentary*, Vol., 84, No. 5, (November 1987), pp. 21ff. For confirmation of this view see *The New York Times*, February 14, 1988, p. 1 and the opening lines of its report, "As the AIDS epidemic moves into its eighth year in the United States, the evidence grows ever stronger that the much-feared explosive invasion of the general population is not occurring and never will." Still, as the U.S. Surgeon General insists, heterosexuals remain at risk: "There is always danger whenever people engage in casual sex outside of the marriage relationship, even if their promiscuity is heterosexual" (*The New York Times*, February 20, 1988).

4. Shelp and Sunderland, *op. cit.*, p. 20.

5. John J. Quinn, "The AIDS Crisis: A Pastoral Response," *America*, June 28, 1986, pp. 504-506.

6. John J. O'Connor ,"The Archdiocese and AIDS," *Catholic New York* (September 19, 1985), p. 21.

7. See Julia Chiapella,"Teens and STDs: Numbers on the Rise" *Family Life Educator* Vol. 5, No. 1, (Fall 1986), p. 14. See also the journal, *Medical Aspects of Human Sexuality* (May 1987), p. 8: "Young people suffer from a fear of the possibility of AIDS and some show symptoms of anxiety—irritability, palpitations, distraction—or as depression, withdrawal and also loss of interest in school." See also, Howard M., "Postponing Sexual Involvement Among Adolescents: An Alternative to Prevention of Sexually Transmitted Diseases" in *Journal of Adolescent Health Care* (June 1985), p. 271.

8. Individual bishops may disagree as to the wisdom of mentioning condoms but allowing them in principle as a lesser evil is consistent with Catholic moral teaching and tradition. See David M. Hollenbach's article, "AIDS Education: The Moral Substance" in *America*, December 26, 1987, p. 493-494. Also see the Letters to the Editor "Catholics and Condoms" in *The Economist*, January 23-29, 1988.

9. *The Quicksilver Years, op. cit.*

10. See "Condoms may not stop AIDS," *U.S. News and World Report,* October 19, 1987, p. 83. Also, *Medical Aspects of Human Sexuality* (November 1987), p. 33: "No hard data exists on the protective value of condoms against the AIDS virus. Although studies have shown that viruses smaller than HIV penetrate latex condoms if the condoms have deteriorated from prolonged exposure to heat, light or substances such as oil-based libricants."

Chaper 16: Gay OK?
1. See Derrick Sherwin Bailey, *Homosexuality and the Western Christian Tradition* (London: Longmans, Green, 1975).
2. Bruce Vawter, *On Genesis: A New Reading* (Garden City, N.Y.: Doubleday, 1977) and Nahum M. Sarna, *Understanding Genesis: The Heritage of Biblical Israel* (New York: McGraw-Hill, 1966), pp. 146-147. James P. Hannigan in his book, *Homosexuality: The Test Case for Christian Sexual Ethics* (Mahwah, N.J.:Paulist Press, 1988) says, "While Scriptures, then, yield at most a strong presumptive bias against homosexual acts, the texts alone, as we read them today, do not settle the issue of morality of homosexual behavior and relationships beyond all question." p. 41.
3. Morris West, *The Devil's Advocate* (New York: William Morrow: 1959), pp. 237-238. See also Richard Woods, *Another Kind of Love: Homosexuality and Spirituality,* Image Books, (Garden City, N.Y.: Doubleday, 1978), p. 23.
4. Hannigan, *op. cit,.* writes: "The unity ritualized and enacted in sexual behavior is a two-in-one flesh unity, a unity that has its created basis in the physical and biological complementarity of male and female. There are various ways human beings can imitate, or play at imaging this unity, but apart from the actual basis in reality of male and female sexual union, these ways are only pretense or imaginative simulations of the real thing...Hence, whatever else may be said in favor of homosexual acts and relationships, they cannot be understood as exercises and realizations of the inter-personal, vocational meaning of sexuality." p. 102.
5. Robert Nugent,"Homosexuality and Magisterial Teaching," *The Irish Theological Quarterly* Vol. 53, No. 1, 1987, p. 73.
6. *A Challenge to Love: Gay and Lesbian Catholics in the Church,* edited by Robert Nugent (New York: Crossroad, 1987), p. 261. See also Lillian H. Robinson and Richard Dalton, M.D., "Homosexuality in Adolescence" in *Medical Aspects of Human Sexuality* (July 1986), p. 106ff.

7. *The New York Times,* July 15, 1987, p. A16.

8. Henri J.M. Nouwen, "A Glimpse of the 'Gay World' in San Francisco and the 'Fast World' in Los Angeles," *New Oxford Review,* July-August 1987, p. 5.

9. "What is at all costs to be avoided is the unfounded and demeaning assumption that the sexual behavior of homosexual persons is always and totally compulsive and therefore inculpable." "The Pastoral Care of Homosexuals," *Origins* 16, 222., p. 381.

10. "For such [homosexual] acts and relationships may very well include not merely the desire for sex but also the desire for interpersonal communion and intimacy as both sign and service of one's Christian discipleship. Such acts and relationships do not correspond to the normative ideal, but they may be, in the lives of particular homosexual couples, steps toward the ideal and toward a fuller understanding and acceptance of one's sexuality as part of one's Christian vocation. Whether these acts are positive steps toward the ideal is a matter that must be left up to the conscience of individuals in serious consultation with an able spiritual guide, whose task is not to judge sins, but to remind us that the ideal continues to call us beyond where we presently are." Hannigan, *op. cit.,* p. 149.

Chapter 17: Birth Control

1. Studies have found possible links between the use of the pill and cervical cancer. See L.A. Brinton *et al.,* "Long term use of Oral Contraceptives and Risk of Invasive Cervical Cancer," *International Journal of Cancer* 38:339, 1986.

2. See Paul VI, *Humanae Vitae* 16, in Joseph Gremillion, *The Gospel of Peace and Justice: Catholic Social Teaching Since Pope John* (Maryknoll, N.Y.: Orbis Books, 1976), p. 435. We must remember that such a decision to limit the family should never be made on purely private grounds since, of course, marriage and children and the couples' vocation precisely as a Christian married couple are social realities intimately tied into all of society, into the larger secular and religious community.

Chapter 18: Abortion

1. "As fact follows upon fact, scientists realized that...the infant in the mother's arms after birth is essentially the same infant that is in the mother's womb before birth. ...Sir William Liley, the father of intrauterine medicine...writes that 'the fetus is...in command of his own

environment and destiny.' " See "The Nursing Couplet II," *Child &
Family*, Vol. 19, no. 1, 1980, pp. 2-3; also see *The New York Times*, "Infants' Sense of Pain is Recognized, Finally," (Nov. 23, 1987) and especially Marshall Klaus and Phyllis Klaus, *The Amazing Newborn*
(Reading, Mass.: Addison-Wesley, 1985) and note in a review of it
these words: "The growing knowledge of life in utero shows that the
mother and baby are engaged in a dialogue long before birth. This
contributes to our understanding of how the fetus reacts and develops
in preparation for life following the birth process" from *Child Abuse
and Neglect: The International Journal* Vol. 11, No. 4, 1987, p. 581. See
also, Melanie J. Spence, "Prenatal Experience with Low-Frequency
Sounds Influence Neonatal Perception of Maternal Voice Sample" in
Infant Behavior and Development No. 10, 1987. See even the pro-
abortion *The New York Times* editorial "Loving Babies Before They
Are Born." (September 7, 1987).
2. See *Abortion and the Constitution: Revising Roe vs. Wade Through
the·Courts* (Washington, D.C.: Georgetown University Press, 1987). See
also *Origins*, 15:215-224 (September 19, 1985) for a very complete legal
brief and response to Roe vs. Wade by the United States Bishops.
3. Here I am indebted to James T. Burtchaell (see *Catholic Update*, October 1984); also see *Commonweal* magazine for a debate between pro-
abortion Daniel Maguire and anti-abortion Burtchaell (November 20,
1987). See also Burtchaell's book, *Rachel Weeping* (San Francisco:
Harper & Row, 1984), Kristen Luker's *Abortion and the Politics of
Motherhood* (Berkeley, Calif.: University of California Press, 1984), and
Abortion and Divorce In Western Law by Mary Ann Glendon (Cambridge, Mass.: Harvard University Press, 1988). We must also take
note, however, that within well defined moral principles, there are in
fact respected and divided opinions even among Catholics. For a bal-
anced view of these differences and how to reconcile them, see Philip
S. Kaufman, "Abortion—Catholic Pluralism and the Potential for Dialogue" (a chapter from his book, *An Immoral Immorality* [Chicago:
Meyer-Stone Books, 1988]) in *Cross Currents*, Spring, 1987, p. 76ff.
4. *The New York Times*, January 21, 1988, p. A18.
5. Louis Harris, *Inside America* (New York: Vintage Books, 1987), p. 180.

Chapter 19: Confusion and Compassion
1. Robert Drinan, S.J. "The Seamless Garment." *America* (June 15,
1987), p.·483. See also the November 1980 statement of the United
States Bishops. This statement on capital punishment "presents per-

suasive argumentation that neither the legitimate purposes of punishment nor necessity justify the imposition of the death penalty in the conditions of contemporary American Society." *Origins,* (October 17, 1985) Vol. 15, No. 18.

2. *St. Anthony Messenger* (January 1986), pp. 16-25. See also Nat Henthoff's "Sweet Land of Liberty," *Washington Post* (August 17, 1987). See also "Christopher Hitchens, "Being Radical and Profile" in *Crisis,* (January 1988), p. 14.

3. *The New York Times,* January 25, 1988, p. 1.

4. It is now admitted by all sides that abortion indeed is the normal teenage backup to failed contraception. Typical is this comment from M. Zelnick and J.F. Kantor in "Sexual Activity: Contraceptive Use and Pregnancy Among Metropolitan-Area Teenagers: 1971-1979" from *Family Planning Perspectives* (The Alan Guttenmacher Center publication, a former arm of Planned Parenthood): "But at the moment, abortion remains a major means by which young women are preventing births they do not wish to have." p. 237. It's also worth noting Denise Lardner Carmody's book, *The double cross: ordination, abortion and Catholic feminism* (New York: Crossroad, 1986) where she states the difficulties that many Catholic feminists have with the pro-abortion stance of the secular feminists; she states forthrightly that for Catholics abortion is not a "rite of passage into feminist maturity" nor "an acceptable contraceptive." p. 9.

5. See David Reardon, *Aborted Women: Silent No More* (Chicago: Loyola University Press, 1987).

Chapter 20: The Dark Side

1. See the videotape documentary, *Not a Love Story.*

2. See Meg Greenfield's column, "Disgrace for Fun and Profit" in *Newsweek,* February 8, 1988, p. 80 and also Richard Schickel's *Intimate Strangers: The Cult of Celebrity* (Garden City, N.Y.: Doubleday, 1985) for an insight into the dynamics of wrongdoings as a road to fame.

3. I am indebted to the ideas of Thomas W. Goodhue from his "Youth Update" article (*St. Anthony Messenger,* March 1987). See also Wendy Bowers, "Violent Pornography" in *The Humanist* (Jan./Feb. 1988), pp. 22-23.

4. See *Boston Campus Calendar,* October, 1987 "Date Rape Can Damage Both Body and Soul"; see also Gloria J. Fischer, "College Students Attitudes Toward Forcible Date Rape: Cognitive Predicators" in *Ar-*

chives of Sexual Behavior (Vol. 15, No. 6, 1986). There she writes: "Research on both high school students (Giarusso, *et al.*, 1979) and college students (Mahoney, 1983) showed that an alarming minority of students believe date rape is not rape or is not definitely unacceptable behavior, at least under certain circumstances." p. 457.

Chapter 21: The Man I Want to Be

1. See Sol Gordon's *Raising A Child Conservatively in a Sexually Permissive World* (New York: Simon and Schuster, 1983) where he quotes the Johns Hopkins study that 1 out of 5 teenage girls has had intercourse by 16 (which means 80% haven't) and the Educational Communication outfit from Lake Forest, Illinois who surveyed the "Who's Who Among High School Students" and found that 76% of them had no sexual intercourse, a finding consistent with higher intelligence and goal oriented students (p. 89 and p. 102) and (Gordon's) assertion on page 147: "Most teenagers under 17 have not had sexual intercourse." See also Zelnik and Kanter, *op. cit.*, who cite that approximately half of all female teens remained virgins through their teen years.

2. *U.S. Catholic*, (August 1987), p. 26. What is disturbing is precisely this lack of moral vision and connection.

3. *Medical Aspects of Human Sexuality* (May 1987), p. 8.

4. Linda Frederick,"Talking to Your Child about Sex" in *Marriage* magazine.

Chapter 22: Time Out 3

1. *Medical Aspects of Human Sexuality* (January 1986), p. 68.

2. In a study of adolescents' view of intimacy, the authors were trying to see if young people followed Erikson's paradigm of intimacy defined as openness, sharing, mutual trust and self-abandon and commitment. They did not. What the authors found instead was that intimacy for adolescents translated as sexual involvement as the first form of intimacy with trust/faith, openness and love following. "Most often cited by males was physical/sexual interaction, while females cited openness. ...Adolescents tended to include physical/sexual interaction as a distinguishing component while Erikson did not and relatively few reported self-abandon and commitment as discriminating components." From Bruce Roscoe, Donna Kennedy and Tony Pope, "Adolescents' Views of Intimacy: Distinguishing Intimate From Nonintimate Relationships" in *Adolescence* Vol. XXII, No. 87 (Fall 1987), pp. 511-515. Clearly there is a need for moral education and vision and

more appreciation of male-female differences. See Lillian B. Rubin, *Intimate Strangers* (New York, Harper & Row, 1983).

Chapter 23: Conversations, Questions and Lines

1. Reprinted from *Parents Talk Love* by Susan K. Sullivan and Matthew A. Kawiak © 1985 by the authors. Used by permission of Paulist Press.

2. An excellent book on the subject: John Crewdson, *By Silence Betrayed: Sexual Abuse of Children in America* (Boston: Little Brown & Co., 1987).

3. *The New York Times*, December 7, 1987. See also David A. Scott, "Living Together: Education for Marriage?" in *The Journal of Pastoral Counselling* (Spring-Summer, 1983), p. 47ff.

Chapter 24: Marriage

1. Trip Gabriel (contributing editor to *Rolling Stone*), *The New York Times Magazine*, November 15, 1987.

2. *Newsweek* (August 24, 1987). See also "The New Marriage Therapy" by Martha Weinman Lear in *The New York Times Magazine* (March 6, 1988) p. 63. Her opening paragraph reads: "How love's sweet song has changed. Just a decade ago it was marked by bold discordancies and feisty lyrics: alternate life styles, swinging, open marriage. All those are gone now, and the new lyrics sound remarkably old: constancy, stability, tradition."

3. See David Mace, *op. cit.*, p. 109.

4. See Lillian B. Rubin, *Intimate Strangers, op. cit.*

Chapter 25: Virginity and Celibacy

1. Carol Cassell, *op. cit.*, p. 109.

Chapter 26: Eliminating the Windows

1. August 1987.

2. See Robert Lockwood, "Why the Church Opposes School-Based Clinics" and in that same issue an interview with Bishop McHugh, *Our Sunday Visitor* (December 20, 1987). See also the statement of the Massachusetts Bishops "Sex Education: Information or Formation?" *Origins*, p. 510-511.

3. M. Zelnik and J.F. Kantor, "Sexual Activity, Contraceptive Use and Pregnancy Among Metropolitan-Area Teenagers: 1971-1979," *Family Planning Perspectives*, Vol. 12, No. 5, 1980, p. 230.

4. W. Marsiglio, and F.L. Mott, "The Impact of Sex Education on Sexu-

al Activity, Contraceptive Use, and Premarital Pregnancy Among American Teenagers," *Family Planning Perspectives*, Vol. 18, No. 4, 1986, p. 151. See also the summary remarks to the article, "Supporting Teenagers' Use of Contraceptives: a Comparison of Clinic Services" by Roberta Heceg-Baron, which say, "A program to provide family planning clinic patients with special services designed to improve their ability to practice contraception effectively produced neither of these expected effects." *Family Planning Perspectives*, Vol. 18, No. 2, (March/April 1986); that same issue also has the headline: "Select Committee says U.S. Teenage Pregnancy Programs are neither effective nor comprehensive." (p. 85). The clinic minded people readily admit the ineffectiveness of the clinics and that teenage pregnancies continue to rise, but insist that's because (a) more girls are "sexually active" and at an earlier age and (b) the clinics are not comprehensive enough and that such services and sex education should be made earlier and earlier. They ignore that there are larger spiritual issues and motivations.

5. M. Schwartz, "Planned Parenthood Poll Finds Teens Reject School Clinics," *Family Protection Report* (Feb. 1987), p. 5.

6. B. Mosbacker, "Teen Pregnancy and School-Based Health Clinics," (Washington, D.C.: Family Research Council of America, Inc., 1986.)

7. October 11, 1986, p. 26. We should note that several school-based clinics are often discussed as "successful," for example, the St. Paul (Minnesota) Clinic, the Chicago Program, the Muskegon (Michigan) Program, the Kansas City program, and the Baltimore program. Usually the figures of lowered birthrates are misleading and do not take into account that the figures are those given by the school staff (with no follow-up studies), enrollment drop and, most of all, no accounting of abortions and miscarriages, etc. And in the much touted Baltimore program it must be noted that over 30% of the females interviewed dropped out between the first and last surveys and, again, abortion was not mentioned even though almost 33% of all abortions done in Maryland are done on teenagers. (See "Adolescent Pregnancy: Problems and Solutions" prepared by Babette M. Pachence, M.D., Mercer County, N.J., 1987).

8. See J. Dryfoos, "School-Based Health Clinics: A New Approach to Preventing Adolescent Pregnancy?" *Family Planning Perspectives*, Vol. 17, No. 2, 1985, p. 70. Also he says, (page 72): "High rates of childbearing among students is often cited as the rationale to initiate onsite health clinics, yet school-based clinics generally are presented as

comprehensive, multiservice units that emphasize physical examination and treatment of minor illnesses. Nevertheless, in most clinics, new patients (whether male or female) are asked at their initial visit if they are sexually active. If they are or plan to be soon, they are encouraged to practice contraception."

9. Babette M. Pachence, M.D., *op. cit.*, p. 5.

10. S.L. Hanson, *et al.*, "The Role of Responsibility and Knowledge in Reducing Teenage Out-of-Wedlock Childbearing." *Journal of Marriage and the Family*, Vol. 49, 1987, p. 241.

11. Patrick Welsh,"Sex and Today's Teen-Ager," *The Washington Post* (November 29, 1987), p. L3.

Chapter 27: A Word from Our Sponsors
1. Modified from Joan Ohanneson, "Christian Sexuality: Body and Soul Together" ("Youth Update," St. Anthony Messenger Press, 1984).

2. As the psychologists say, teenage boys often use sex as a form of "self-enhancement." See Juhasz and Sonnenshein-Schneider, *op. cit.*

Chapter 28: Time Out 4
1. Lynda Madaras, *op. cit.*, p. 233.

Select Bibliography

For Teens
Ameiss, Bill and Grover. *Lord of Life, Lord of Me.* St. Louis: Concordia.

Auer, Jim. *For Teens Only: Straight Talk About Parents, Life, Love.* Liguori, Missouri: Liguori Publications, 1985. Small booklet with a big message.

Auer, Jim. *Sorting It Out With God.* Liguori, Missouri: Liguori Publications, 1982. Another booklet that's good.

Buscaglia, Leo E. *Loving Each Other: The Challenge of Human Relationships.* New York: Fawcett Columbine, 1986. Read this one by all means.

Cooney, Nancy Hennessy. *Sex, Sexuality and You.* Des Moines, Iowa: Wm. C. Brown, 1980. Small book well done.

Cosby, Bill. *Fatherhood.* New York: Berkley, 1986. You ought to read this one.

Greene, Bob. *Good Morning, Merry Sunshine.* New York: Penguin Books, 1985. A father's diary of his newborn daughter. Wonderful.

Nilsson, Lennart. *A Child Is Born.* New York: Delacorte, 1965.

Reichert, Richard. *Sexuality & Dating.* Winona, Minnesota: St. Mary's Press, 1981.

Short, Ray E. *Sex, Dating, & Love: Seventy-Seven Questions Most Often Asked.* Minneapolis: Augsburg, 1984. 77 questions and answers. Direct and good.

For Parents and Teachers
There are three background books that I especially recommend, books that give a broader context to the whole issue of American life, human relationships and sexuality. The first is the highly acclaimed *Habits of the Heart: Individualism and Commitment in American Life*

---

by Robert Bellah, *et al.* (University of California Press, 1985). The second is *Embodied Love: Sacramental Spirituality and Sexual Intimacy* by Charles A. Gallagher, George A. Maloney, Mary F. Rosseau and Paul F. Wilczak (Crossroad, New York, 1985) which is a wonderful guide to marriage, sex and spirituality which will help immensely in seeing how they all go together. Finally, there is *Loving Each Other: The Challenge of Human Relationships* by Leo E. Buscaglia (Fawcett Columbine, NY, 1984). This is one of those books that can be passed around to every member of the family with profit. As I said, these are helpful and wise background books. Now, for some particular recommendations:

Bettelheim, Bruno. *A Good Enough Parent: A Book on Child Rearing.* New York: Alfred A. Knopf, 1987. One of the best books around on parenting.

Cooke, Bernard. *Sacraments and Sacramentality.* Mystic, Connecticut: Twenty-Third Publications, 1983. Chapter 7 explains why marriage is the "basic sacrament."

Etheredge, Joan Horan. *Sharing Sexual Values: A Parent's Approach.* Liguori, Missouri: Liguori Publications, 1986. Small pamphlet and excellent.

Fore, William F. *Television and Religion.* Minneapolis: Augsburg, 1987. An excellent look at this pervasive medium and its effects on religious values. You might also read Neil Postman's acclaimed book, *Amusing Ourselves to Death.*

Gore, Tipper. *Raising PG Kids in an X-Rated Society.* Nashville: Abingdon, 1987. Strong stuff but interesting.

Mace, David R. *The Christian Response to the Sexual Revolution.* Updated edition. Nashville: Abingdon, 1970. A good, brief, historical overview of the influences on the church's thoughts and teaching about human sexuality.

Persons, Richard D. *Adolescents in Turmoil, Parents Under Stress: A Pastoral Ministry Primer.* Mahwah, New Jersey: Paulist Press, 1987. Although directed to those who counsel and guide adolescents, this book is valuable for parents.

Shelp, Earl E. and Ronald H. Sunderland. *AIDS and the Church*. Philadelphia: Westminster, 1987. A small, helpful book on a timely topic.

Strommen, M.P. and A. I. Strommen. *Five Cries of Parents*. San Francisco: Harper & Row, 1983. Interesting and helpful.

Sullivan, Susan K. and Matthew A. Kawiak. *Parents Talk Love*. Mahwah, New Jersey: Paulist Press, 1985. One of the best for parents.

van Bemmel, John and Laurie. *We Celebrate Our Marriage*. Mystic, Connecticut: Twenty-Third Publications, 1986. A brief book of reflections and prayers on various aspects of married life.

Whitehead, Evelyn and James D. *Christian Life Patterns: The Psychological Challenges and Religious Invitations of Adult Life*. Garden City, New York: Doubleday, 1979. Really fine for parents to give them a wider perspective of their own journey and, as a consequence, of their children's.

Deeper Stuff
Benson, Peter, *et. al. The Quicksilver Years*. San Francisco: Harper & Row, 1987. Teen development.

Crewdson, John. *By Silence Betrayed: Sexual Abuse of Children in America*. Boston: Little Brown and Co., 1987.

Crooks, Robert and Karla Bauer. *Our Sexuality*. 3rd edition. Menlo Park, California: Benjamin Cummings Publishing, 1980. A widely used textbook, very complete and informative but takes a liberal attitude towards premarital sex.

Dominian, Jack. *The Growth of Love and Sex*. Grand Rapids: Wm. B. Eerdmans, 1982.

Genovesi, Vincent J., S.J. *In Pursuit of Love*. Wilmington: Michael Glazier, 1987. Moral Theology.

Kelsey, Morton and Barbara. *Sacrament of Sexuality*. Warwick, New York: Amity House, 1986.

Moore, Sebastian. *Let This Mind Be in You.* Minneapolis: Winston Press, 1985. Hard but rewarding reading on spirituality and relationships.

Soboson, Jeffrey G. *Christian Commitment and Prophetic Living.* Mystic, Connecticut: Twenty-Third Publications, 1986. A fine treatment of living a committed life.

Vernny, Thomas, M.D. with John Kelly. *The Secret Life of the Unborn Child.* New York: Delta Books, 1981.

GLOSSARY

Abortion - The premature termination of pregnancy. Voluntary abortion is one done at the request of the mother; spontaneous abortion, called a miscarriage, is a natural termination of pregnancy due to some abnormal development of the fetus.

Abstinence - Voluntarily refraining from sexual intercourse.

Adolescence - The period of time during which the boy and girl leave the undeveloped state of childhood and assume the physical, mental and spiritual tools to live an adult life.

Adultery - Sexual relations between two people one or both of whom are married to someone else.

Amniocentesis - A procedure whereby a sample of fluid surrounding the fetus is drawn and analyzed to detect possible birth defects.

Androgen - A substance that influences the growth and sex drive in the male and produces masculine secondary characteristics (e.g. voice, hair, growth, etc.).

Anus - The opening between the buttocks at the lower end of the large intestine, from which waste matter is expelled.

Birth control - Prevention of birth of any method, including contraception, sterilization, or abortion.

Bisexual - One equally attracted to males and females and may have sex with both.

Breech birth - The birth position of the baby feet or bottom first, instead of the usual headfirst position.

Buttocks - The part of the body you sit down on. The "backside," "behind," "ass."

Caesarean section - A surgical incision (cutting through the abdomen into the uterus) to deliver the baby when normal delivery is difficult.

Castration - The removal of the testicles in males or the ovaries in females.

Cervix - The narrow neck or entrance into the uterus (womb).

Chastity - Accepting and controlling the sex drive in and out of marriage. The proper use of sex.

Chromosome - The thread-like material in the egg and sperm that contain the genes.

Circumcision - Cutting away the loose skin, called the foreskin, around the tip of the male penis.

Climax - See Orgasm.

Clitoris - A small penis-like sensitive organ of the female located within the vagina and the seat of sexual stimulation.

Coitus - Another name for sexual intercourse.

Conceive - To begin a new life in the womb.

Condom - A rubber or latex sheath (like a rubber balloon) that is rolled down over the erect penis in order to serve as a protection against catching disease and preventing birth by catching the seed fluid before it gets into the vagina.

Contraception - Various methods that prevent contraception (contra=against, ception=conceive).

Contraceptives - Any means to prevent birth by keeping the sperm and egg from meeting: drugs, condoms, devices, pills, etc.

Cunnilingus - Applying one's mouth or tongue to the genitals in order to sexually stimulate the female. (One form of oral sex).

Douche - The cleansing of the vagina with a stream of liquid solution or water.

Ejaculation - The discharge of the seed fluid, or semen, from the penis. Having a male orgasm.

Embryo - The new life in the mother's womb up to eight weeks.

Erection - The enlargement and stiffening of the penis as its tissues fill with blood; a "hard-on."

Erotic - Sexually stimulating.

Estrogen - A hormone that affects the female cycle and secondary sex characteristics (breast development, hair, growth, etc.).

Fallopian tube - The tube through which the egg passes on its way to the uterus.

Fellatio - Applying the mouth to the penis to sexually stimulate the male (another form or oral sex).

Fertilization - The entrance of the male sperm into the female egg.

Fetus - A name given the unborn baby from the third month in the mother's womb till birth.

Foreplay - The touches, kisses, etc. before intercourse to get each other ready.

Fornication - Sexual intercourse between an unmarried man and an umarried woman.

Foreskin - The skin covering the glans or tip of the penis; often cut away through circumcision.

Gene - The unit of heredity.

Genitalia - The external sex organs.

Gigolo - A male whore; one who has sex for fun or money.

Glans - The very tip or head of the penis.

Heterosexual - One who is sexually attracted to and/or active with persons of the opposite sex.

Homosexual - One who is sexually attracted to and/or active with persons of the same sex.

Hysterectomy - Surgical removal of the uterus.

Illegitimate - Refers to a child born of parents who are not married. Another term is bastard.

Impotence - The inability of the male to have or maintain an erection during sexual intercourse.

Intercourse, sexual - The insertion of the male penis into the female vagina.

Lesbian - A female homosexual.

Masturbation - Stimulating one's sexual organs, often to the point of orgasm.

Menopause - The end of the ovulation and menstruation cycle in women, usually between the ages of 45 and 55. Also called a change of life or climacteric.

Menstruation - The monthly flow of blood from the uterus, usually occurring every 28-30 days; the monthly period, having a period.

Nocturnal emission - The involuntary discharge of the extra, stored-up semen at night during sleep, sometimes in connection with a "sexy" dream. Also called a wet dream.

Oral sex - See Cunnilingus and Fellatio.

Orgasm - The peak of sexual excitement; for the male it is the spurting out of the semen from the penis; for the female, an overall body glow and relaxation.

Ovaries - The two female sex glands in which eggs are formed.

Ovulation - The release of a ripe egg into the Fallopian tube.

Ovum - The female egg (plura: ova).

Penis - The male, finger-like sex organ through which semen is discharged and urine is passed.

Pituitary gland - The "master" gland in the brain's "control tower" that controls the functions of all the other (ductless) glands, especially the sex glands.

Placenta - Sometimes called the afterbirth. This is the sponge-like organ that connects the fetus to the lining of the mother's uterus by means of the umbilical cord and it serves to exchange air, food and waste matter from the mother to the fetus.

Procreation - Literally "to create for" God; to beget children as a delegate for God.

Prophylactic - Another term for the condom.

Prostitute - One who has sex for money.

Puberty - The start of adolescence.

Pubic hair - The course hair that grows around the sexual organs usually in a triangular patch.

Rape - Forcible sexual intercourse against another's consent.

Rectum - See Anus.

Safe period - The interval in the female menstrual cycle when no ripe egg is present in the system and therefore she is unable to become pregnant.

Scrotum - The thick sac of skin between the male's legs containing the testicles.

Semen - Also called the seed or seed fluid or seminal fluid. This semen is made up of the life-giving male sperm and is ejaculated or spurted through the penis when the male reaches an orgasm.

Sexuality - The state of being a sexual person all over and all the time. One's personality given push and dimension by sex. A person's all-over "posture" in life as a male or female.

Shaft - The long, finger-like part of the male sex organ; that part of the penis as distinct from the tip or head (called the glans).

Sodomy - Inserting the penis into the rectum.

Sperm - The male reproductive cell.

STD (Sexually Transmitted Disease) - See Venereal Disease.

Sterility - The inability to reproduce.

Testicles - Also called testes (slang: "balls," "nuts," etc.). The two male sex glands within the scrotum sac which produce the sperm.

Tubal ligation - Cutting and tying the ends of a woman's fallopian tubes so that the egg can't get through. A form of sterilization.

Transsexual - One who undergoes surgery to obtain the outward appearance of the other sex.

Transvestite - One who has a compulsion to dress up in the clothes of the opposite sex.

Umbilical cord - The tube between the mother's placenta and the baby.

Urine - The liquid waste matter.

Uterus - Also called the womb. The small, pear-shaped organ of the female in which the baby develops.

Vagina - Also called the birth canal. The opening between the female legs, between the uterus and the vulva, which received the male penis and also through which the baby passes at birth.

Vasectomy - The duct that carried the male sperm is cut and tied. A form of male sterilization.

Venereal disease - Any of the variety of contagious sexual diseases. Also referred to as the STDs (Sexually Transmitted Diseases), such as genital herpes, syphilis, gonorrhea, AIDS, etc.

Virgin - One who has never had sexual intercourse.

Vulva - The female outside sexual organs, the two mounds that lead to the vagina and clitoris.

Wet dream - See Nocturnal emission.

Whore - A female who has sex with anyone without money or payment.

Womb - See Uterus.

HEALTH HINTS
SPIRITUAL AND PHYSICAL

At the turn of the century psychologists and psychiatrists used to describe adolescence as the time of great "storm and stress," wild mood swings, inner turmoil, and risky behavior. Well, we know now that they oversold their case. In fact, in making such a general statement, they were wrong. As we saw in the book, the large majority of adolescents (some scientists say 80 percent)—yes, with a few battles here and there—make the transition from child to adult with fairly good grace and with good relationships with their parents.

But one thing, unfortunately, hasn't changed, the one thing you think would: the death rate for teenagers. But what is mind-blowing are the causes. In the old days (back at the turn of the century and earlier and even right up to the 1940s and 1950s) teenagers died for medical reasons, that is, from diseases we have since overcome with immunization and antibiotics. So what are teenagers dying from these days? From "social" diseases: accidents, suicides, homicides, drug and alcohol abuse, and the STDs. The latest statistic is that 77 percent of those deaths for 15- to 24-year-olds are attributed to accident, suicide, and homicide. Moreover, teens' future health is much threatened by the habits they're forming now: smoking, alcohol, drug abuse, lack of exercise, and poor nutrition. Usually these victims are in that 20 percent who don't go through adolescence very well.

Anyway, here's a little health chart that gives you the most common areas that a teenager ought to see a doctor about in a normal routine checkup—and a priest or any adult he trusts for the rest.

AREA OF CONCERN   SUGGESTION

Ears: The loud music you sometimes listen to, especially through headphones, has damaged the hearing of millions.

➡

You should have your hearing tested in early adolescence (maybe 13, 14) and late adolescence (say 18, 19). Plan to take a few days retreat or go on a "Search" weekend. Quiet reflective prayerful times are necessary to grow and learn to listen for God's voice.

Eyes: It is estimated that about one in four teenagers needs some vision correction, especially those who spend a lot of time at computers or TV.

➡

Here you should be screened every year or two. Learn to really see nature which is always healing.

Teeth: Gum disease, tooth decay, and a bad bite are common among teenagers.

➡

To the dentist twice a year!

AREA OF CONCERN	SUGGESTION

Spine, blood, urine: Scoliosis, or curvature of the spine, hit some, as well as anemia.

→ Normal, painless checking here will catch any problems, most of which can be cured (or prevented) if caught early enough.

Sex organs, STD's: The penis and scrotum should be checked as well as the testicles for cancer.

→ We showed you how to check the testicles for cancer in the first "Time Out" in the book. For signs of the STD's, check that chapter. Perfect and guaranteed prevention: chastity.

TV Overdose: Overdosing your body so you lack exercise. Overdosing your head with poor and sexy images so that it distorts reality.

→ How about reading? Try, for example, Norton Juster's *The Phantom Tollbooth* or the lives of the saints. Camping recommended.

AREA OF CONCERN   SUGGESTION

Drugs, alcohol, and smoking: These are current killers. Think of people you know or celebrities and sports figures who are dead from them. To you, these are future killers or disablers and the future seems far off. But the pressures are great.

➡

No hard sell facts or figures, no videotapes of dead bodies or drug war shoot-outs or the role of organized crime , of the teens in mental hospitals damaged from crack is likely to dissuade the teenager who smokes, drinks, or takes drugs. Only a better vision of oneself and the conviction of God's love can do that. Prayer, going to church, faith are called for here.

INDEX

Of Related Interest...

Becoming a Woman
Basic Information, Guidance & Attitudes
on Sex for Girls
Valerie Vance Dillon

Offers a straightforward, Christian version of female
sexuality. Written in simple, conversational style, the
book will assist girls ages 10-15 grow to be loving,
confident, morally upright and sexually integrated
women. Real life situations are used to give facts and
information, accompanied by practical suggestions for
dealing with the problems and joys of growing up
female. Direct, to-the-point discussion questions follow
each chapter.
ISBN: 0-89622-433-3, $7.95

Why Can't We Talk?
Prayers for Parents & Teenagers
Mobby Larson

Provides help to begin a dialogue between parents and
teens. The reflections express the concerns of both, and
serve a threefold purpose: to affirm each person's needs
and worries, to help parents and teens understand each
other better and to help open channels of
communication. Each topic, such as Failure, Life and
Death, Independence, Money, Love, etc., has a prayer
from the parent's point of view and one from the teen's
perspective.
ISBN: 0-89622-449-x, $5.95

Available at religious bookstores or from

TWENTY-THIRD PUBLICATIONS
P.O. Box 180 • Mystic, CT 06355
1-800-321-0411

Toll-Free Hotline Numbers

Counselling and information are available at these national toll-free numbers:

Covenant House 1-800-999-9999
National Problem Pregnancy Hotline 1-800-228-0332
Lifeline Crisis Pregnancy Hotline 1-800-852-LOVE
Birthright 1-800-848-LOVE
Bethany Christian Services 1-800-BET-HANY
The Pearson Foundation Pregnancy Hotline 1-800-392-2121
Child (Physical or Sexual) Abuse Hotline 1-800-422-4453
AIDS Hotline 1-800-342-AIDS
V.D. (or STD) Hotline 1-800-227-8922
National Cocaine Hotline 1-800-COC-AINE
National Runaway Switchboard 1-800-621-4000 or 1-800-231-6946
Suicide Hotline - call INFOLINE
Alcohol Hotline 1-800-NCA-CALL

For free short-term *Volunteers Catalog* for youth interested in the various ministries in the church, either at home or abroad, write to:
The National Federation for Catholic Youth Ministry
3025 Fourth Street, NE
Washington, D.C. 20017